CREATIVE LEGACIES

CREATIVE LEGACIES

Artists' Estates and Foundations

edited by

Kathy Battista and Bryan Faller

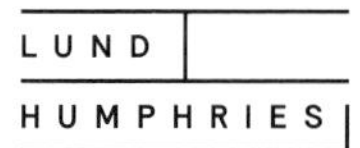

Sotheby's INSTITUTE OF ART

First published in 2020 by Lund Humphries in association with Sotheby's Institute of Art
Lund Humphries
Office 3, Book House
261A City Road
London EC1V 1JX
UK
www.lundhumphries.com

Daniel McClean's essay was first published in: Daniel McClean (ed.), *Artist, Authorship & Legacy: A Reader* (Ridinghouse, 2018)

ISBN: 978-1-84822-352-3

A Cataloguing-in-Publication record for this book is available from the British Library

Copy edited by Abigail Grater
Designed by Oliver Keen
Set in Circular and Whitman
Printed in the United Kingdom
Cover: Detail of Nancy Holt, *Sun Tunnels* (1973-76), Great Basin Desert, Utah; collection Dia Art Foundation with support from Holt/Smithson Foundation

Photography: Tom Martinelli

CONTENTS

PART 2: ARTISTIC LEGACIES IN ACTION

INTRODUCTION

Kathy Battista and Bryan Faller

The genesis of this collected volume of essays is an ongoing discussion about artists' estates and their increasing role in the market, academic, non-profit, and institutional sectors. Both editors work with artists, estates, and foundations on a variety of levels—from research, curatorial, and catalogue raisonné writing to financial planning and long-term stewardship. During recent years working with artists, questions arose regarding several aspects of creating and maintaining their legacies. These include but are not limited to: When is it best to start planning for the eventual transition of artwork and related documents into an estate cared for by a trusted executor? How do financial concerns impact an artist's legacy? How are ephemeral and non-traditional forms of art (video, performance, sound, etc.) maintained for future generations? What should happen to an artist's papers? Who is the best person to entrust a legacy to? All of these and more were repeatedly broached in conversations with artists at various stages of their careers. This led to our idea to publish a book that could provide case studies that show real-life examples of many of these topics.

Through our teaching at Sotheby's Institute of Art in New York as well as our practical experience with artists, we are fortunate to be surrounded by colleagues from an array of backgrounds who work on aspects of estate planning from legal and fiduciary work to appraisal, editorial, curatorial, and conservation issues. Many of the core issues around legacy planning—from steps as simple as naming an executor and writing a will, to more in-depth discussion around back-end solutions to storage, conservation, archiving, and access to the artwork—are discussed in courses offered at the Institutes in New York and London. We include as many of these as possible in this book. We have also invited esteemed professionals from the legacy-planning world to participate in this publication. We are honoured to have authors who are working at or have been employed by the Aspen Institute, the Institute for Artists' Estates, the Holt/Smithson Foundation, the Robert Rauschenberg Foundation, the Fischl/Gornik Foundation, the Glass House Foundation, Sotheby's and Christie's auction houses, and New York University's Bobst and Fales Libraries in this book. While we tried to cast as wide a net as possible, there are always parameters in a single-volume publication, so we conceived this as a starting point and springboard for other scholars and art professionals to dive deeper into these topics to develop a body of knowledge on this nascent field of study. We also acknowledge that the book is skewed to the United States and Western Europe. We hope that specialists from other regions, particularly Latin America, Asia, and Africa, can use this as a model for similar enquiries.

THOUGHT LEADERSHIP

When researching and teaching about artists' estates we have looked at several important sources for models of thought leadership on this topic. Magda Salvesen's prescient book of interviews, one of the first publications on the topic, presented a personal view of how estates and legacies affect family members of artists.[1] Loretta Würtenberger's *The Artist Estate, A Handbook for Artists, Executors, and Heirs* laid the groundwork for artists and their families as well as professionals in the field.[2] This important publication offers practical advice and even outlines how to work with artists' estates, as well as a section of interviews with stewards of some of the world's most prestigious estates. Daniel McClean's *Artist, Authorship & Legacy* is an important new contribution to this field.[3] With a finely argued introduction, the book also includes a range of authors from the legal, curatorial, and academic sectors. The first of its kind to delve deeper into important case studies, it is a valuable piece of scholarship. The Aspen Institute's series of publications has provided important thought leadership in the field; through conferences and open-access publications this organization is helping professionals to establish best practices and to share their experiences and learning among themselves.[4] The Joan Mitchell Foundation has also provided open-access materials on this topic, as well as much-needed grants to help artists plan their legacies.[5]

Synthesizing these publications as well as a plethora of articles from the art press and mass media, we wondered what was needed to reflect both the challenges and opportunities of this area of study and practice. We acknowledge that each estate is both unique and similar to others. Rather than a one-size-fits-all approach, we wanted to reflect the idiosyncratic nature of the business and how each legacy requires a nuanced set of services and expertise. What we aim to do in this book is to provide in-depth discussion into these topics with case studies drawn from the disciplines of art, architecture, jewellery, and fashion. We believe that experts from these tangential fields can provide information and wisdom that can be shared across disciplines. An architectural sketch or an haute-couture pattern is often treated in similar ways to a work of fine art. In this age of obsessive documentation and awareness of conservation issues, lessons from one field can be shared and used by professionals from another.

We also aim to use specific case studies as learning opportunities. While each estate or foundation comes with its own *sui generis* difficulties, we believe that we should not avoid the mistakes that have been made, but rather use these to inform living artists, curators, conservation experts, archivists, and gallerists of best practices in the field. Each estate or foundation needs to consider the unique challenges that present themselves in terms of legacy planning, its maintenance, and perhaps sunsetting. Legislation also is subject to change, and laws are not the same worldwide. Thus, there is no guidebook that can be universal to all estates, but rather a dialogue that can be started and improved upon with each case. The sharing of information and expertise across borders and disciplines will certainly help to develop best practices and avoid common pitfalls.

THE CHANGING LANDSCAPE OF ARTISTS' ESTATES

Artists have always had two estates: the typical leftovers from a life—real estate, antiques, family heirlooms, financial assets, and objects with emotional significance including correspondence—as well as their artistic body of work, which is a very different kind of asset. Picasso, Rothko, Calder, and Warhol come to mind when one thinks of well-known artistic legacies of the 20th century. Increasingly, however, in the 21st century, there has been a tremendous growth in this sector of the art world. There is no singular reason but rather a plurality of issues that have brought this to fruition. The value of individual works of art from artists with robust secondary markets has driven greater attention and demand for professional services assisting artists, and their estates. Larger galleries are able to provide services as a part of their ongoing business relationship with artists who are commercially viable. To keep successful artists happy within the artist–gallery relationship, many gallerists find they are ever more involved in helping to manage artists' studio practices in addition to facilitating critical relationships with influential curators, collectors, and collections affecting the artist's legacy and market, respectively.

The demographics of the world in general, and the art world as a subsection, is part of this phenomenon. In the post-war era the art world was a smaller place, populated predominantly by men and with a market that was primarily dominated by white American or European artists.[6] In the 1980s this was still the case. The increase in higher education in the 1950s and 1960s—including of war veterans assisted by the 1944 GI Bill, and the proliferation and magnification of MFA programmes—resulted in a larger segment of the population choosing artist as a professional option. Whereas in the past the notion of the starving, bohemian artist was the classic paradigm, today some artists act as CEOs running several businesses and managing scores of staff. As the industry has grown, so too has the size of artworks, and thus the corresponding amount of help needed to produce these works. Artists including Damien Hirst, KAWS, Urs Fischer, Takashi Murakami, Jeff Koons, Sterling Ruby, Marilyn Minter and many more are no longer mythological characters isolated in their studios; we have returned to a Renaissance workshop model, where artists often train and employ many others.[7] Noah Horowitz writes about the effects of artists such as Hirst and the extreme level of his financial success, which was unthinkable for past artists, even those as successful as Picasso:

> One of the most immediate is the sheer rise in the number of artists today, also something unprecedented. This is abetted by increasing coverage of the contemporary art scene in vanity and mainstream media, which has thrust the art lifestyle onto a new level of pop cultural fixation. Indeed, if it were not for the bevy of press on the riches and glamorous habitudes of Hirst and some of his contemporaries, and the varied connections with Hollywood celebritydom that extend from this, it is doubtful that so many would aspire to the profession.[8]

At the time of writing of this book Deloitte's most recent estimate for an aggregate value of art and collectibles was US$1.74 trillion (the figure for 2018)—the art world has grown into a place to park money, and for better or for worse art has become an acknowledged asset class in the financial services industry.[9] It is no wonder, then, that artists' estates are occupying an increasingly bigger piece of the pie chart and will continue to do so as artists age and eventually pass.

Aaron Berlow, Vice President, Business Strategy and Operations for Wildenstein & Co., spoke to us about the evolution of artist estates from the traditional model to the present day:

> The role that artist estates play in the current art markets has fundamentally changed compared to the role they played in the past. For one thing, estates and foundations now are, for the most part, carefully planned, well-staffed, and managed. To anecdotally illustrate this point, Gauguin died intestate, for example. His estate was dealt with through an auction in Tahiti. Bonnard's estate was fought after bitterly by the family. That really doesn't happen anymore.
>
> Now estates are their own respective institutions and behave like economic stewards whose job is to protect the artist's legacy. It's tough to know what that means for the future, but if this trajectory continues one can speculate that if values of works of art continue to increase, then the roles that artists' estates play within the art world and art markets will also increase, and competition among commercial interests will follow.

> The significance that artist estates will play in the future depends on what direction they go. Like the artists themselves, every foundation has its quirks, and it's hard to say for sure whether they will add or detract from the long-term value. What is positive about foundations is that they protect an artist's legacy beyond commercial interests. The dichotomy there, and really the crux of their role, is to walk this tightrope between the commercial and academic legacy.[10]

Berlow's comments reflect both the increase in stakes of an artist's work, as well as the incredibly competitive gallery world of today.

The art market has grown exponentially in the past two decades. One need only look at the art fairs and biennials of the time: Cologne, Chicago, and New York were once the mainstays of the art fair world, and Venice and São Paulo were the dominant biennials. The conditions have changed immensely. Wealth created in the last several decades in Brazil, Russia, India, and China has in turn created a fuller demographic to the art world: these and other countries are occupying a larger space in the art market. As Berlow described above, major galleries are looking for new methods to secure their future, with artists' estates bringing much-needed stock as well as prestige.

An additional factor in the exponential expansion of the art market is that art is used as an investment vehicle among high- and ultra-high-net-worth individuals and serves as a form of currency and as an investment vehicle. For this reason, many corporate banks have established an art branch of estate planning for their clients. And the changing demographic of clients is important: remember that in today's industry some artists acquire vast personal wealth. Monica Heslington, Vice President, Goldman Sachs Family Office—Art Advisory, discussed with us the increasing need for corporate, in-house expertise to deal with artists' estates:

> The biggest challenge with this group [artists] is getting them to focus on estate planning when their natural inclination is to creative production. Family dynamics also come into it, so if someone has a complicated family situation, that's another reason to not want to think about planning. And, in general, most people just don't want to talk about their death. There is usually some kind of a catalyst that motivates people to do planning—a health scare, the birth of a grandchild, a divorce. Because artists would rather be doing something creative, they need even more encouragement. Providing them with a basic checklist that is geared towards artists and asks the right questions would be great—even if it's not going to cover every single scenario because everyone has different assets, family dynamics, and tax situations. Estate planning in itself is an art form, not a science.[11]

The one-size-fits-all approach does not work for legacy planning. Like financial planning, each artist has unique financial and practical issues. And each family has a long-established dynamic. An important part of working with artists is the sensitivity to these challenges.

Further to Heslington's warning of a one-size-fits-all approach, Yayoi Shionoiri, Executive Director to the Chris Burden Estate and the Nancy Rubins Studio, also spoke to us about the current landscape of artist foundations. She warns professionals to choose the correct structure for each artist:

> As the ecosystem in the artist estate and foundation community has developed, there seems to have been a tendency, at least in the US, to privilege the creation of 501(c)(3) non-profit foundations, perhaps in an attempt to advance the field. However, in my personal legal and art historical view, the legal structure should not drive the mission, goals, or visions of an artist estate. Certain factors should be analysed and discussed when deciding whether to create a foundation, including, for example, monetary and operating budget concerns (i.e., "Does the estate have enough to sustain the operation of a legal entity long term?"), short-term and long-term goals (i.e., "What would the mission/vision and goals of a potential foundation be, and for what motive?"), and, above all, the artist's intent.[12]

Another important aspect of legacy planning is to create a market for the artist that is both stable and protected from volatility or manipulation. Flooding an artist's work onto the market would not be useful to anyone—the estate, the artist's reputation, the gallery, or the collectors. Gallerist David Nolan spoke with us about the importance of carefully respecting an artist's market value:

> Continuity is essential, because otherwise people want to sell top works that can cause damage (to the value of the estate later) so they go to auction or they want to give it to another dealer who may have little experience or responsibility to the artist. Then the new dealers are competing with the artist's original representative in a way that's not productive towards helping the estate gain greater value, and not just a monetary value but also reputation. What you want is the estate to have greater value and increased exposure, through solo shows as well as significant institutional group exhibitions. And the essential part in all of that is also publications: you have to have publications to educate a new group of curators and collectors.[13]

Nolan's words reflect the competitive nature of the global art market, where artists can have several major galleries in different cities. How does a family or a foundation navigate through those various galleries and decide which work is to be released? For a professional this is challenging; for a family member new to the art world it is incredibly easy to misstep.

NEW DIRECTIONS IN ARTISTS' LEGACIES

A welcome change in the landscape of artists' estates and foundations is the proliferation of wider inclusivity in the art world. Statistically, while women occupy slightly over 60% of art and about 40% of architecture programmes, they are still less represented in positions of power and market prestige.[14] In particular, in the past decade more female artists and artists of colour have been represented in the commercial sector. The estate and foundation world is following suit. As the demographic of the art world changes and time passes, an increasing number of these artists will need legacy work. The Joan Mitchell Foundation and the Helen Frankenthaler Foundation are examples of prestigious organizations dedicated to the legacies of female artists. More recently the Easton Foundation has been established in New York to preserve the legacy of Louise Bourgeois' work, studio, and home. Carolee Schneemann, Jack Whitten, and Lygia Clark are examples of artists who were under-recognized in market value, but whose practices in terms of prestige and art historical importance are huge. These recently deceased artists have been picked up by leading international galleries and their legacies will certainly outperform their living value in terms of market worth. Other ageing artists—Geta Brătescu, Carmen Herrera, Yayoi Kusama, etc.—who have found success much later in life, will need to scramble to organize their legacies; fortunately, each of these artists is represented by major galleries who can assist. What happens to those who are less fortunate and die without major accolades?

Sadly, for queer and trans artists, some of the legacies have been lost due to family negligence, discrimination, and market obscurity. Organizations such as Visual AIDS, the Leslie-Lohman Gay Art Foundation, HOWL!, and several others have helped saved queer artists' work from the dumpster. The work of artists in this era has seen a resurgence in popularity: those such as Martin Wong and David Wojnarowicz have had museum shows dedicated to their practices, and their archives have been acquired by caretakers, both institutional and private. Not only does this mean that their legacies can thrive, it also means that a younger population of artists can benefit from seeing the work, which had been obscured for two decades.

It is in this exciting era that we find ourselves navigating artistic legacies. With the world more turbulent than it has been in decades, and with economic disparity endemic, a big challenge for the industry will be how to serve artists who have not passed with the money to create a foundation. How do we preserve this work? Should we preserve this work? It is our prediction that as the number of artists' foundations grows, these will in turn support the work of lesser-known artists or practices that inherently are difficult to preserve, such as performance, sound, or ephemeral art.

As Aaron Berlow stated in discussion with us:

> Estates function as a buffer for an artist's market and will continue to do so with varying degrees of success. Historically speaking we're standing close to where we were in 1929. We are at the end of a long period of expansion, but find ourselves without the economic levers at our disposal to influence markets (i.e. quantitative easing, interest rates, etc.), so these foundations (those who are well-funded) will likely find themselves having to aggressively buttress these new market forces. We are also at a moment in time where for-profit institutions are consolidating and gathering estates. As the value of art rising makes estates more attractive economically for gallerists, the market, and collectors, it more than ever also necessitates greater stewardship.[15]

This book is a response to the need that Berlow discusses and that we have seen in the preceding years.

STRUCTURE OF THE BOOK

Creative Legacies is organized in two sections, each with seven essays. The first section focuses with a broader lens on building an artist's legacy, presenting universal issues of estate planning including organization of inventory and valuation, estate and foundation structures, as well as best practices. The second half of the book examines specific case studies in an attempt to understand how certain topics in artists' estates are dealt with by professionals and scholars in those fields. We hope that this publication will provide critical analysis and assistance to both artists and their families in estate planning and that it will be of use to researchers and professionals who are contending with this increasingly fast-growing field. Hopefully these examples will provide some cautionary tales and perhaps an equal dose of proven strategy to ameliorate stress and to help guard against legal hiccups in the future.

Notes

1 Magda Salvesen, *Artists' Estates: Reputations in Trust*, New Brunswick, NJ: Rutgers University Press, 2005. See also her "Etched in Memory" symposium webpage: http://waand.rutgers.edu/iwa/etched/site/EiM-video-salveson.html (accessed 25 February 2020).

2 Loretta Würtenberger, *The Artist Estate: A Handbook for Artists, Executors, and Heirs*, Berlin: Hatje Cantz Verlag, 2016.
3 Daniel McClean (ed.), *Artist, Authorship & Legacy: A Reader*, London: Ridinghouse, 2018.
4 See these helpful publications published by Aspen: *The Artist as Philanthropist, Vol.1—Findings: Overview of the Field*, 2010, https://www.aspeninstitute.org/publications/volume-one-artist-philanthropist-strengthening-next-generation-artist-endowed-foundatio/; *The Artist as Philanthropist, Vol.2—Considerations in Practice*, 2010, https://www.aspeninstitute.org/publications/artist-philanthropist-strengthening-next-generation-artist-endowed-foundations/ (both accessed 25 February 2020).
5 https://joanmitchellfoundation.org/artist-programs/call (accessed 22 March 2020).
6 Of course there were many women artists, albeit with less critical and commercial success. For an interesting and accessible discussion of women artists in this era, see Mary Gabriel, *Ninth Street Women: Lee Krasner, Elaine de Kooning, Grace Hartigan, Joan Mitchell, and Helen Frankenthaler*, New York, NY: Little, Brown & Company, 2018. Kathy would like to thank Sarah Jones of Gagosian Gallery for sharing this book.
7 It is worth noting here that many MFA graduates go on to work for artist studios and, increasingly, artists' foundations and estates.
8 Noah Horowitz, *Art of the Deal: Contemporary Art in a Global Financial Market*, Princeton, NJ and Oxford: Princeton University Press, 2011, p.6.
9 *Deloitte Art and Finance Report*, 6th edition, 2019, p.46, https://www2.deloitte.com/lu/en/pages/art-finance/articles/art-finance-report.html (accessed 22 March 2020).
10 Aaron Berlow in discussion with Bryan Faller, 19 September 2019, at Wildenstein & Co., 54th Street, New York City.
11 Monica Heslington in discussion with Bryan Faller and Kathy Battista, 11 July 2018, at Goldman Sachs Global Headquarters, New York.
12 Yayoi Shionoiri email to Kathy Battista, 25 November 2019.
13 David Nolan in discussion with Bryan Faller, 21 October 2018, at David Nolan Gallery, New York.
14 See https://datausa.io/profile/cip/visual-performing-arts for information on gender distribution in arts programmes in the US and https://www.acsa-arch.org/resources/data-resources/where-are-the-women-measuring-progress-on-gender-in-architecture/ for information about gender diversity in architectural programmes (both accessed 22 March 2020).
15 Aaron Berlow in discussion with Bryan Faller, 19 September 2019, at Wildenstein & Co., 54th Street, New York City.

PART ONE

ESTABLISHING ARTISTS' LEGACIES

INTRODUCTION TO PART 1

Establishing Artists' Legacies

Bryan Faller

Each time I start working with an artist I listen. The artist and I quickly introduce ourselves, exchange social niceties, and then dig into the most important part of the conversation, the art. I listen to an artist talk about his or her work. What is the artist's motivation? What are the intentions of the artist? Is the art good? Is there a market for the work? What public and private collections own work by the artist? What is the artist's *story*? There is a litany of questions that we go through in a process of discovery until eventually the information about who, what, where, and when is discussed and understood before we are able to get into the *why* behind the artist's approach and practice. Before one is able to discuss practical matters such as how an artist's work is inventoried or when the artist's last museum show took place I find it essential to understand what constitutes the artist's voice—his or her intentions, motivations, and how he or she hopes the work will affect an audience—i.e. the who, what, where, when, and why questions. Once I understand the artist's voice I am then able to understand how best to advise on any number of issues concerning legacy.

We define and understand legacy in this context as the reputation and place in the art world in which an artist's work is thought of, discussed, and historically represented. This could commercially mean the artist's market. It could critically mean an artist's publication history or how a critic or curator places the art into a narrative. Legacy is a nuanced and sophisticated concept. It means different things to different people, but one is only ever able to discuss legacy after the artist's voice is understood.

I spoke with David Nolan, of the eponymous gallery, who has been working with estates such as Martin Kippenberger's for many years. He emphasized the nuanced aspects of legacy planning and the questions that need to be asked of those left in charge of the artist's legacy:

> So the question is who's in charge of the estate? Is it children? Is it a widow? Because depending on whom you're dealing with, it becomes very complicated. And the most complicated classic one is that there are several children involved, and inheritors who don't agree with each other. That makes it very hard for everyone. Because they usually have no experience whatsoever, they usually need an advisor. And it must be somebody who generally understands the art world and what the dealer is talking about. And then they can work with the dealer because as a dealer, working with an entire family of people you don't know and who don't see things the same way, you try to educate them overnight. The trust is not built up so easily because the inheritors then usually question the dealer: well can I believe that or can I not believe that? Because if you're dealing with an estate, one of the main things is you have to make it known, and you do it through exhibitions, art fairs. You have to have somebody who represents you who is going to make sure that other dealers in other countries, Europe, Asia, and America are all dealing with that—so you've got to have one person, one person must have knowledge that can be trusted.[1]

These specialized fields—of advisor, dealer, etc.—are often unregulated and challenging even for seasoned art world professionals to navigate. So for a descendant of a deceased artist with little experience of the machinations of the industry, Nolan's advice regarding an advisor is particularly apt. This person can

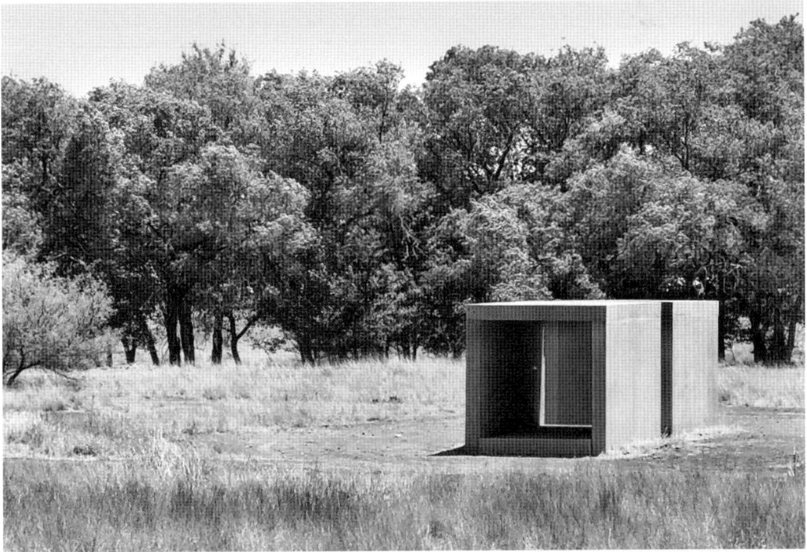

Donald Judd, 15 untitled works in concrete, 1980–84 (detail). © 2020 Judd Foundation / Artists Rights Society (ARS), New York. Photo by Bryan Faller

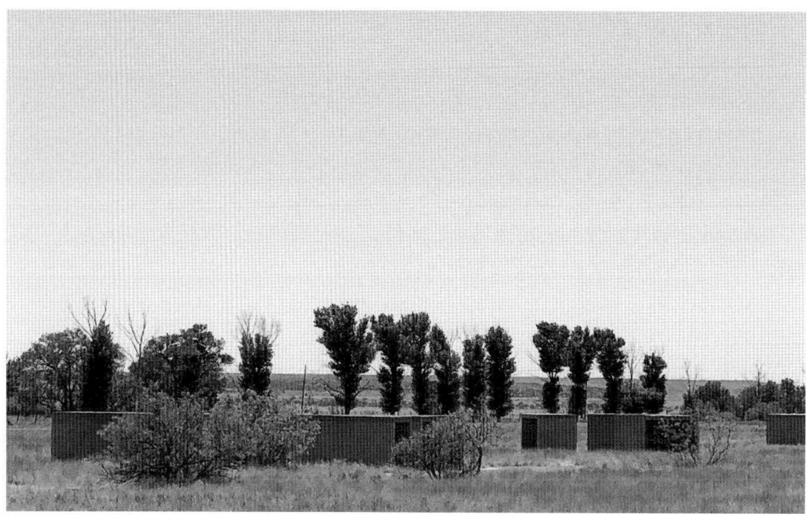

Donald Judd, 15 untitled works in concrete, 1980–84. © 2020 Judd Foundation / Artists Rights Society (ARS), New York. Photo by Bryan Faller

objectively represent the family's interests in many of the specialized negotiations and conversations that will shepherd a creative legacy through time.

Ideally an artist is still alive to have conversations with art professionals and to set a legacy plan in place with a properly executed will and specific instructions. Sometimes, sadly, the artist dies without taking these measures, and those responsible for the artist's estate, or his or her heirs, are the only ones left to discuss the artist's work, life, and the different successes he or she may have enjoyed. Hopefully these individuals were close enough to the artist to have understood his or her voice and art well. Often this is not the case, but we still do our best to understand how the art was intended to be engaged by an audience. There have been many celebrity artists whose estates have garnered significant attention, but not every artist achieves the commercial or critical success of Donald Judd, Robert Rauschenberg, or Andy Warhol. There are many mechanisms to carry out an artist's wishes once he or she has died—that is, if there are sufficient resources. Having enough affluence affords an artist access to influential and competent professionals who can help plan and execute how an artist's legacy can be realized. With careful planning and strategy, the voice of the artist can live on.

Monica Heslington, from the Goldman Sachs Family Office—Art Advisory, spoke with my co-editor and me about working with living artists:

> Thinking about what they're going to do with all of their artwork can be very overwhelming, especially for major artists whose heirs may face a significant estate tax bill. You must present a sale not only as an opportunity to fund the tax bill, but also as an opportunity to curate the sale

> itself. Otherwise, someone else will decide which pieces to sell and which things go to the family. Many artists not only have their own artwork, but they also know other artists and own valuable artwork by them as well. Are those necessarily things that should be sold? How do you decide what to hold on to?
>
> And what about setting up a foundation? Many artists automatically assume that they should set up a foundation, which leads to many other questions. Are your kids really interested in running it? If not, who will run it? A foundation requires certain principles and goals, and if these are not put in place during your lifetime, how can you expect someone else to execute on an unarticulated vision when you are no longer here? When you're already in a cash crunch because you have to pay estate taxes, you're going to have to put some artwork in the foundation in addition to cash. So, which pieces? Will the intention be to sell some of them over time? And if so, which ones? Does the person running the foundation know enough about your market to make wise sale decisions? It is easy to understand why artists would rather avoid the subject.
>
> It doesn't have to be this hard. Often we just need a place to start and to have things broken down into smaller pieces. And this applies to any collector with a very large collection—not just artists. Once the collector has passed away, the heirs may want to divest. They have to start with the pieces that they know they don't want to keep, figure out the best sales venue and when the sales take place, and put together a sales calendar and slowly start selling things off. They can also imagine that if they had half the exhibition (or storage) space, which pieces would they need to keep in order to represent the spirit of the collection and which pieces would they not need. This exercise often helps people psychologically get to the point where they can let things go.[2]

The sobering reality is that many artists never achieve relatively significant critical or commercial success. Their work may be strong, but for any number of reasons they were never able to generate enough commercial or critical momentum or reach a consensus generating enough interest from influential curators, collectors, or dealers. These artists may have made competent work and may only need help marketing or branding their art, or they may only need organization and a curatorial focus to present their work in a way that resonates with other influential art world denizens. It does not just take a village to raise a successful artist; it takes engaging an entire art world for an artist to reach a greater level of commercial or critical success.

I most often find artists in a situation where they are relatively cash poor and asset rich. They may not actually be impoverished, but they do not have enough money to carry out many of their legacy aspirations. They may own a home, have a large body of their own work, a collection of work by other artists and a studio—for example—and in reality it takes a significant amount of capital to manage and care for an artist's estate. Without enough money, artists are not able to properly care for their work or to design and execute strategies to carry out legacy plans. In cash-poor situations an artist's expectations need to be managed. The publication of a monograph is most likely not possible and a foundation likely not feasible. Artists need both capital to organize and care for their work, and enough critical success to justify major museums acquiring and possessing work to be cared for in perpetuity, a situation which is often supported by a robust secondary market for work and an influential gallery and academic consensus supporting an artist's place within the art historical canon. One only needs to consider artists later discussed in this book's essays as evidence for what kind of validation might be necessary for an artist's body of work to justify significant resources for care in perpetuity—Donald Judd, Robert Rauschenberg, Agnes Martin, Leigh Bowery, Maya Lin, etc. These artists have both significant critical acceptance and robust primary, and for the most part robust secondary, markets.

There are certain works from an artist that are stronger than others; taste is indeed relative, and opinions abound, but there is generally consensus around how important an artist's body of work is and which works are significant to understanding an artist's evolution into making mature work. For artists that have not achieved a significant amount of critical success the options for a legacy plan are also less clear even still if there is enough money to support one. Often regional museums and institutions such as universities and hospitals would be eager and very grateful for donations of this kind of artwork. Work can be beautiful and technically well executed even if it has not achieved a critical level of significance. There is always interest and appreciation for work that is conceptually interesting, thought-provoking or just aesthetically beautiful. There are many audiences for art, and it is important to manage an artist's expectations for which audience will have a demand for his or her work. Sometimes it is the Metropolitan Museum, and sometimes a local library. Knowing where an artist's market and audience lies is essential for understanding how his or her work can be engaged in a legacy context after he or she dies.

There is no right or wrong way to make art or be creative, and the variety of artistic approaches or philosophies is one of many reasons why we see so much diversity in contemporary artistic practice. This is also one of the main reasons we decided to write this book. The diversity in how artists create and make work also requires the professionals working with them to have an interdisciplinary and organic approach. The ability to work fluidly and flexibly, and to create bespoke solutions for artists, is essential. This is also why it is important to learn about an artist's history and practice before diving into executing any kind of strategy and trying to provide insight that is valuable. One must understand why an artist makes work, how the work engages the world at large and how the artist's intentions may be understood.

By understanding how rich and diverse contemporary art making has become, art professionals are better equipped to manage, plan for, and execute strategy that supports an artist's voice during and after his or her lifetime. This understanding also prepares art professionals for the reality that a one-size-fits-all approach can never work. Each situation and artist is unique; expectations, resources, and ambitions vary significantly from artist to artist and throughout every artist's career. In order to create valuable legacy plans and strategies it is also important to know what constitutes an artist's creative estate, which generally speaking includes his or her studio contents, archive, and body of work. It is essential for artists to organize their creative estates separate from their general estates; furniture, real estate, and cars should be itemized and distinguished from the studio contents, archive, and body of work unless there is some significance of those items pertaining to the artist's professional practice or creative process.

The essays in this section deal with specific technical, critical, and nuanced aspects of managing an artist's or collection's legacy. They address the mechanics of legacy planning and include insights from practitioners and other thought-leaders in the field to consider when thinking about legacy planning or working with an artist's estate. Christine J. Vincent describes the organizational mechanisms of trusts and foundations. Loretta Würtenberger graciously did an interview with Kathy Battista and me during Art Basel Miami Beach 2018 in which we discussed the origins and evolution of this nascent discipline. The interview also highlights some distinctions between legacy planning in Germany and the United States. Daniel McClean investigates the fine line between how foundations act as either gatekeepers or custodians for artists' legacies. Ann-Marie Richard, the late Tom McNulty,[3] and Eric Wolf—all esteemed colleagues of ours at Sotheby's Institute of Art in New York—respectively navigate insights and complications of valuation practices with estates; how artists' archives are used to propel the artist's voice and legacy; and how specific, large-scale, and public works are used to facilitate an artist's legacy. The interview with Lisa Le Feuvre discussing the Holt/Smithson Foundation provides a broad overview of how an art professional can begin thinking about how to create an organization designed to realize an artist's wishes. The dialogue provides insight into what might be considered when making decisions and establishing goals. Kathy and I organized the essays in the book to first explore generalized concerns about an artist's creative legacy, mechanics, and topical insights, which then leads into case studies exploring more nuanced topics of creative legacies that are both academic and practical. The goal at the end of reading this book is for the reader to hopefully have a better understanding of the diversity and interdisciplinary nature of this nascent discipline, the larger academic and practitioner dialogues that exist in the art world at the time of this text's publication, and how the field and its subsequent scholarship may evolve and affect the legacies of all artists that may broaden the cannon to be more inclusive in the future.

Notes

1 David Nolan in discussion with the author, at David Nolan Gallery in New York, 21 October 2018.

2 Monica Heslington, Goldman Sachs, in discussion with Bryan Faller and Kathy Battista, 11 July 2018.

3 This is the last published work by Tom McNulty before his untimely passing in late 2018. His insight and expertise were essential in maturing the conversations we had into publishable material.

1

ARTIST-ENDOWED FOUNDATIONS

Mapping the Field[1]

Christine J. Vincent

Artist-endowed foundations (AEFs) are increasing in number due to the convergence of three factors—demographic trends in the artist population, the continuing rise in the global art market, and artists' desires to provide for their creative works and philanthropic interests in the long term. Long flying under the radar, the AEF field is becoming more visible as it expands. Being visible, however, does not translate automatically to being understandable, even among professional art circles.

And with lack of understanding comes confusion. Despite important distinctions, AEFs are often mistaken for artists' family collections (usually referred to as artists' estates) or assumed to be similar to art museums, both of which also own artworks and undertake exhibitions and related activities. Even among AEFs themselves, there are wide variations in activities based on artists' intentions, factors associated with the different stages in a foundation's life cycle, and the law regulating tax-exempt charitable organizations, all of which can make it difficult to ascertain precisely what one is actually looking at when viewing an "artist-endowed foundation". The purpose of this chapter is to offer a guide to the AEF field specifically within the United States, providing the general reader with a map that can help locate foundations within the broader realm of actors involved in stewarding artists' creative and philanthropic legacies.[2]

DISTINCTIONS AMONG STEWARDS

For the purposes of research conducted by the Aspen Institute Artist-Endowed Foundations Initiative/AEFI, AEFs are defined as private foundations created by an artist, the artist's family members, or other beneficiaries, to own the artist's creative works, copyrights, and other properties for use in furthering educational and charitable activities serving a public benefit.

Artist-Endowed Foundations Versus Artists' Family Collections/Estates

This term—*public benefit*—is key to our discussion because to qualify for tax exemption under Section 501(c)(3) of the federal tax code, a foundation is required to serve the public benefit exclusively. This is the fundamental difference between an AEF and an artist's family collection or estate, which is a private entity benefiting private individuals, typically the artist's family members.

An artist's family collection/estate may be organized under state law in various forms, for example as a non-charitable trust or a limited liability company (LLC), or may not be organized formally at all, with the collection simply owned outright by the artist's heirs. In any case, the income it generates generally is taxable. In contrast, charitable, tax-exempt organizations are formed under state law as charitable trusts or non-profit corporations, and then seek recognition of their tax-exempt status from the Internal Revenue Service (IRS), based on their charitable purposes serving a public benefit. In general, income generated by a charitable, tax-exempt entity is not taxed and is retained by the organization to support its charitable purposes.[3] Further, donors to charitable, tax-exempt entities enjoy favourable tax treatment for their gifts.

Charitable Tax-Exempt Entities Generally

The recognition of tax-exempt status by the IRS further defines the organization as either one with the tax status of "public charity", which is an entity supported by members of the general public, or one with the tax status of "private foundation", funded by a single individual or family. Most organizations familiar to the public as non-profits, such as museums, universities, hospitals, etc., are public charities and seek grants to support their charitable activities. In contrast, most AEFs are private foundations, drawing on lifetime gifts or bequests from the artist or the artist's family members. Private foundation tax status is determined by the nature of the entity's support, not by whether or not it uses the word "foundation" in its name, which many public charities indeed do.

"Private foundation" is the charitable tax status regulated most strictly under the federal tax code, due to Congress' view that by being closely held, private foundations have been subject to abuse by their insiders. As such, private foundations must comply with numerous rules not applicable to public charities. Among the most important of these are: the prohibition on transactions between a foundation and its insiders and, more broadly, on activities benefiting a foundation's insiders (self-dealing); the annual distribution requirement (payout) by which foundations must expend for charitable purposes an amount based on the fair market value of their investment assets; the excise tax on investment income (including proceeds of sales of assets such as artworks); and the obligation to disclose donors' names and gifts on the annual tax return for private foundations, Form 990-PF, which must be made available to the public and is online at sites such as www.guidestar.org.[4]

Artist-Endowed Foundations Versus Art Museums

While AEFs differ from artists' family collections/estates by virtue of the critical distinction between public benefit and private benefit, foundations and art museums are both charitable tax-exempt entities committed to providing public benefit. Despite this commonality, most art museums hold the tax status of public charity, supported by members of the general public, while most AEFs hold that of private foundation, funded by an individual or family. Beyond this, the most significant distinction between AEFs and art museums is the nature of their art collections, how they deploy the artworks they own, and how these art assets are treated for tax purposes.

Art museums typically hold works by many different artists and are committed to building and maintaining permanent collections for educational use. As such, they procedurally accession works into their permanent art collections and operate according to governance policies, required by the national museum accrediting association, that prohibit de-accessioning of works for sale to generate proceeds for any use other than collection acquisitions and direct care. If they comply with this, art museums are permitted by national accounting standards to exclude the fair market value of their art collections from their audited financial statements and, similarly, do not report that value on the annual federal tax return filed by public charities, Form 990.

AEFs also may utilize their art collections as charitable use assets, deployed in educational and scholarly activities, but they generally do not accession works into their collections. As major distinctions from art museums, AEFs typically hold extensive collections of works solely by a single artist, or a few related artists; and, consistent with the artist's intentions, they may sell these artworks to generate the income needed to support the organization and its programmes. Further, the fair market value of all assets, including art assets, owned by an AEF with private foundation status is reported in the Form 990-PF, although the value of artworks may be adjusted by a blockage discount, a reduction reflecting the difficulty of quickly liquidating a large volume of an asset without depressing its market value.

The private foundation payout requirement, mentioned above, can be a particular concern for AEFs, often created with few liquid assets. However, when an AEF uses its art assets as charitable use assets, or holds them for such use, they are not classified as investment assets, so their value is not subject to the payout calculation—although once consigned to an art dealer for sale, the same art assets become investment assets, with a value subject to this calculation. In some cases, as noted below, AEFs do not conduct direct charitable activities using their art assets, meaning their art collections are considered investment assets at all times and as such, the collection's value is subject to the payout calculation at all times.

Having charted distinctions among AEFs, artists' family collections/estates, and art museums, we can turn now to considering the different types of AEFs, based on their charitable functions.

FUNCTIONAL TAXONOMY

AEFs fulfil their charitable purposes by conducting activities serving a public benefit, for which they have been granted tax exemption. For most AEFs these activities fall into two broad categories: cultural philanthropy and art stewardship. The particular types of charitable activities in which a foundation is involved are determined by several factors, including the artist's intentions for the foundation, how it will steward the artist's artworks and related assets, and what its philanthropic focus should be; the resources available to the foundation; the current stage in the foundation's life cycle; and considerations with respect to interactions with foundation insiders. Speaking generally, there are four functional types of AEFs: grantmaking foundations; study and exhibition foundations; comprehensive foundations; and estate distribution foundations.

Grantmaking Foundations

Grantmaking foundations fulfil their charitable purposes exclusively by providing grants to support non-profit organizations as well as individuals, such as artists and scholars. They do not claim their art assets as charitable use assets, deployed directly in educational and scholarly activities, even though they may lend them for exhibition or even prepare a catalogue raisonné. The Andy Warhol Foundation for the Visual Arts; the Pollock-Krasner Foundation; the Renate, Hans and Maria Hofmann Trust; the Edward Gorey Charitable Trust; and the Charles E. Burchfield Foundation are examples of this type of foundation.

Study and Exhibition Foundations

Study and exhibition foundations fulfil their charitable purposes by engaging in educational and scholarly activities directly deploying their charitable use assets, typically the artist's artworks, archive, and related properties. Activities might include operating a study centre housing the artist's archive; maintaining a collection of the artist's works for exhibition; conducting study programmes focused on these art assets; and facilitating scholarly research and publications, such as a catalogue raisonné. As long as they maintain their status as charitable use assets by being used or held for use in this way, the value of the art collections owned by a study and exhibition foundation are not subject to the payout calculation unless they transform to investment assets by virtue of being consigned for sale. The Roy Lichtenstein Foundation, the Irving Penn Foundation, the Richard Diebenkorn Foundation, the Niki (de Saint Phalle) Charitable Art Foundation, and the Willem de Kooning Foundation exemplify this type of foundation.

Comprehensive Foundations

Comprehensive foundations fulfil their charitable purposes by conducting multiple charitable functions in various combinations. The activities of this type of foundation might include making grants to organizations and individual artists and scholars, as well as using art-related assets in direct charitable activities, such as maintaining a study centre, archive, and/or exhibition collection; or operating an artist residency programme, art education classes, internship programme, or historic property; etc. This is the predominant functional form for AEFs today, exemplified by the Robert Rauschenberg Foundation, the Joan Mitchell Foundation, the Helen Frankenthaler Foundation, the Dedalus Foundation, the Josef & Anni Albers Foundation, and the Mike Kelley Foundation for the Arts.

Estate Distribution Foundations

Estate distribution foundations accomplish the charitable disposition of the artist's assets owned at death. There is no intention to exist in perpetuity. During the distribution period, this type of foundation undertakes some aspect of the various charitable activities described above, often with an emphasis on organizing the artist's archive and producing a catalogue raisonné. Estate distribution foundations are increasing in number, perhaps reflecting artists' recognition that perpetual existence can be costly. Likewise, for some artists or their family members, there may be a preference not to operate beyond the point at which the governing body can include people who knew the artist personally. Examples of the estate distribution foundation include the Georgia O'Keeffe Foundation, the Emilio Sanchez Foundation, the Mark Rothko Foundation, the Judith Rothschild Foundation, the Richard A. Florsheim Art Fund, and the (Beatrice) Mandelman-(Louis) Ribak Foundation.

THE FOUNDATION LIFE CYCLE

This functional taxonomy sets out key distinctions among AEFs by charitable function; however, these functions may change significantly over the course of the foundation's life cycle. An AEF may be established during the artist's lifetime (inter vivos), under the artist's estate plan (testamentary), or by the artist's surviving spouse or other family members or beneficiaries (posthumously). At each of these points, particular considerations having to do with the types of assets owned by the foundation and the roles of its insiders will influence the functions undertaken by a foundation. Thus, AEFs may differ considerably based on their point in the foundation life cycle (see chart, p.30).

Artist's Lifetime Foundation

Artists' lifetime foundations typically focus on grantmaking to support charitable organizations that address issues of concern to the artist. Some conduct direct charitable activities, such as operating community arts centres and residency programmes, or assembling collections of works created by other artists as gifts to

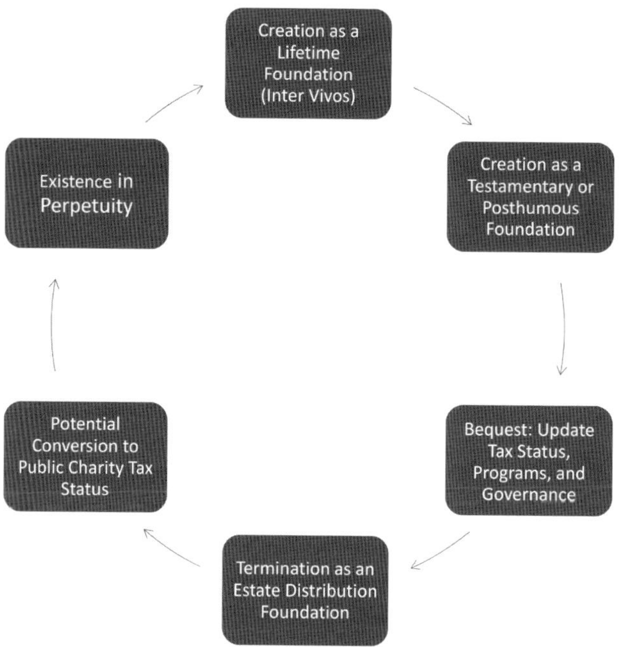

The artist-endowed foundation life cycle, as illustrated by the Aspen Institute Artist-Endowed Foundations Initiative/ AEFI, 2019

museums. Due to the prohibition on activities that benefit a private foundation's insiders, lifetime AEFs do not undertake the activities common to AEFs whose associated artists are deceased. They do not own, exhibit, sell, or make grants of the artist's works; publish about the artist; maintain the artist's archive and studio; or make grants to support efforts focused on the artist's works, such as scholarship, exhibitions, films, or museum acquisitions of works created by the artist.

Artist's Testamentary Foundation

An AEF created under an artist's estate plan might develop in a straightforward way, receiving the artist's bequest and then taking up activities according to one of the four types of foundations described previously. Alternatively, the foundation might enter a period of circumscribed activity as it exists concurrently with the artist's non-charitable beneficiaries—family members or other heirs—who operate the family collection/estate. For example, the foundation might receive no assets and simply exist in expectation of benefiting from the estate plan of the artist's surviving spouse. Or it might receive financial assets and focus on grantmaking while the surviving spouse receives lifetime use of the art assets, which ultimately will go to the foundation upon the spouse's death.

In the most complicated scenario, the provisions of the artist's estate plan may split the artist's assets definitively between the foundation and the artist's family members, meaning that the AEF and family collection/estate operate side by side. There are a variety of reasons this happens but, as a general principle, it is not an optimal arrangement because it puts the family members and the foundation, on whose governing body they likely serve, into a difficult relationship with respect to potential conflicts of interest that can lead to self-dealing risks.

Artist's Posthumous Foundation

An AEF might be created posthumously, for example under the estate plan of the artist's surviving spouse who had inherited the artist's assets. In this case, upon receipt of the spouse's bequest, the foundation would take up its role as one of the four types of foundations discussed above. Alternatively, the surviving spouse or other family members who own the artist's assets might create the foundation during their own lifetimes, perhaps as a grantmaking foundation but more commonly as a study and exhibition foundation with a focused purpose, such as producing a catalogue raisonné or maintaining the artist's archive, activities which require careful consideration as they may in some cases entail potential conflicts of interest leading to self-dealing risks.

Fully Endowed Foundation

Whether an AEF is created as an artist's lifetime foundation, or as a testamentary or posthumous foundation, when it finally receives its full bequest—following the death of the artist or the artist's surviving spouse or other heirs—or has received all of the lifetime gifts intended by the surviving spouse or other heirs, it will take up its role as one of the four types of foundation discussed above. Its board will review the foundation's programmes in light of its assets, resources, and the artist's intentions for art stewardship and philanthropy; update its tax status if necessary; and refine the board's membership to encompass the types of expertise now required to serve its fiduciary role.

Foundation Termination

As noted, an increasing number of AEFs are created as estate distribution foundations with a defined or assumed term limit. This type of foundation, having operated as either a grantmaking, a study and exhibition, or a comprehensive foundation, will complete the charitable distribution of the artist's works to appropriate public collections, place the artist's archive in a suitable institutional repository, transfer the artist's copyrights to a fitting non-profit to steward them for the balance of their term, and distribute any remaining assets to charitable recipients. Alternatively, a foundation may make all of these distributions to a single charitable recipient. In any case, a 20-year term may be just enough time to accomplish all of these complicated tasks with the requisite care.

Foundation in Perpetuity

Although some AEFs that are intended to exist in perpetuity maintain a collection of their artists' works, many engage over a period of decades in the liquidation of all or a major portion of their art holdings. They use the proceeds to build an endowment over the long term while simultaneously supporting the ongoing operation of the foundation and its charitable programmes

Conversion to Public Charity Status

Some AEFs intended to exist in perpetuity find that the artist's bequest is not sufficient in value to support activities the artist had envisioned. This typically is the case for foundations operating facilities open to the general public, such as house museums. At this point, the foundation will convert its tax status from private foundation to public charity, taking advantage of the more appealing income-tax treatment donors enjoy for gifts to public charities as opposed to those to private foundations. To sustain this change, the organization must meet the "public support test" requiring that a good portion of its annual revenue be contributed by members of the general public. If it fails this test, the entity will be required to return to the less advantageous tax status of private foundation. In another scenario, a few artists have been able to create their foundations as public charities from inception, again where operation of a public facility, such as a house museum or botanical garden, is involved and the artist has significant stature in the eyes of donors and members of the general public so that the public support test can be met.

TAX STATUS TAXONOMY

We could leave it at that. For those wishing to grasp the complete map of the AEF field, however, it is necessary to explain that in addition to the functional taxonomy and the foundation life cycle, a third dimension exerts a strong influence to shape the field—a deeper elaboration of tax status.

Non-Operating Versus Operating Tax Status

As noted above, the recognition of tax-exempt status by the IRS further defines an organization as either a private foundation or public charity. Private foundations are then defined additionally as either "non-operating" or "operating" foundations, with those that have non-operating tax status described generally as fulfilling their charitable purposes by making grants to other charitable organizations, and those that have operating foundation tax status described generally as fulfilling their charitable purposes by directly operating programmes themselves, rather than making grants to other charitable organizations to do so.[5]

For quite some time, many believed that with respect to AEFs, the tax status taxonomy and the functional taxonomy were virtually one and the same, i.e. that non-operating foundations would be grantmaking foundations and operating foundations would be study and exhibition foundations. Some even believed that operating foundations were not permitted to make grants. In particular, common wisdom held that foundations endowed with substantial art collections—non-liquid and with high value—should avoid non-operating status because these art assets could pose a liability in that their values would be subject to the charitable distribution requirement, generating a need for liquidity that could potentially require art sales beyond what the market would sustain before depressing the value of the artist's works.

Multiple Modes

It is true that AEFs fulfilling their charitable purposes exclusively by making grants typically utilize the non-operating tax status. But the reality for the rest is more nuanced. Study and exhibition foundations as well as comprehensive foundations can use either the non-operating or operating tax status. If the non-operating status is used, the foundation may choose to deploy its art assets as charitable use assets in educational and scholarly programmes, exclude the value of these from calculating the payout requirement, and attribute the expense of conducting the associated direct charitable activities to the payout requirement. Operating foundations may include the expense of a grantmaking programme in meeting the payout requirement as long as the grant programme is operated as an integral dimension of their direct charitable activities. And beyond that, if their qualifying expenditures have fulfilled the payout requirement, operating foundations can make non-qualifying grants for charitable purposes.

While both non-operating and operating foundations can make grants, non-operating foundations are able to make grants to a broader array of concerns in that they are not constrained as are operating foundations by the requirement that their grants be integral to their direct charitable activities if the associated expenditures are to count toward meeting the payout requirement. This is a key point for foundations that own and deploy art collections in direct charitable activities but fulfil their artists' intentions by making grants to charitable purposes unrelated to their direct charitable activities, such as to support animal welfare, HIV-AIDS research and services, and mental health programmes.

Lifetime Foundations and Tax Status

The matter of tax status intersects directly with the foundation life cycle for artists' lifetime foundations. A few artists' lifetime foundations use operating tax status, for example those that conduct direct charitable activities such as operating community arts centres, conducting residency programmes, or assembling collections of works created by other artists and then granting these to museums. Most lifetime foundations, however, use the non-operating tax status because they are not conducting direct charitable activities, only making grants.

When it becomes time for such a foundation to receive its artist's bequest, its governing body will evaluate the nature of the assets it will own and the charitable activities to be conducted with them in light of the artist's intentions and the available resources, and then make a decision, informed by professional advisors, as to the tax status the foundation should use. The requirement to conduct direct charitable activities cannot be fulfilled by making occasional grants, so a lifetime foundation claiming operating status but not conducting direct charitable activities may risk finding its tax status in question at precisely the moment it needs to receive the artist's bequest.

Supporting Organizations

As a final point, despite being funded solely by an individual or family, it is possible for an AEF to eschew private foundation status entirely and instead utilize a public charity tax status, that of "supporting organization". Supporting organizations are separately formed legal entities with their own charitable tax-exempt status, but exist in relationship to an established public charity, the "supported" organization, such as a museum or university, by virtue of the fact that the supporting organization's activities support or fulfil the charitable purposes of the supported entity. This supporting relationship is noted in the founding documents of the supporting organization, and representatives of the supported organization also serve on the governing body of the supporting organization.

As public charities, artist-endowed supporting organizations are not subject to the private foundation payout requirement, do not pay taxes on net investment income, and comply with more lenient rules on relationships with insiders, although they cannot be controlled by their donors or compensate donors or their relations. Further, because they support a public charity that already complies with the public support test, they do not need to meet that test independently. These benefits make "supporting organization" an appealing tax status in some cases, such as when an entity is created by an artist's heirs for the purpose of holding that artist's archive and producing a catalogue raisonné.

CONCLUSION

This map charts a terrain that is much more dynamic and diverse than might be expected when seeking to understand the emerging AEF field, given that the basic building blocks—artists' creative works, their intentions for long-term art stewardship, and their philanthropic aims—may not vary greatly from case to case. Perhaps the most important point to take away from this discussion is that assumptions about any particular AEF cannot be based on superficial comparisons with other AEFs because there are a host of factors at play, many of which may not be apparent to a casual observer. Looking to the future, as the field continues to mature, no doubt this map will change and evolve, continuing to respond to artists' charitable visions for their creative and philanthropic legacies.

Notes

1 The author is grateful to the editors of the *Brooklyn Rail*, which published the first iteration of this essay online in December 2018.

2 This essay is strictly educational and informational in nature and does not purport to provide legal advice or professional guidance. All references to laws and regulations pertaining to artist-endowed foundations are based on research findings and scholarly briefing papers detailed in *The Artist as Philanthropist: Strengthening the Next Generation of Artist-Endowed Foundations*, Volumes 1 and 2, along with subsequent updates, together comprising the findings of the National Study of Artist-Endowed Foundations, available at www.aspeninstitute.org/aefi.

3 As exceptions with respect to taxes, private foundations pay an excise tax on net-investment income, including income generated by sales of artworks, and any type of charitable, tax-exempt entity pays a tax on business income unrelated to its charitable purposes.

4 Other private foundation rules include: restrictions on holdings in a business enterprise, individually and in combination with insiders; the prohibition on risky investments; the requirement that procedures for grants to individuals be pre-approved by the IRS; and the prohibition on payments to government officials.

5 All private foundations must fulfil a charitable distribution requirement. The non-operating foundation distributes approximately 5% of the value of its investment assets while the operating foundation expends approximately 3⅓% and also meets other requirements pertaining to the sufficiency and relationship of expenditures and assets to charitable purposes.

2

INTERVIEW WITH LORETTA WÜRTENBERGER

Loretta Würtenberger is founder of the Institute for Artists' Estates, based in Berlin. Kathy Battista and Bryan Faller interviewed her during Art Basel Miami Beach on 8 December 2018.

KB: Did your experience with Hans and Sophie Taeuber-Arp help you to understand the nuances of working with artists' legacies?
LW: Working with the estates of Hans Arp and Sophie Taeuber-Arp has been a deep learning experience for the last decade. My husband and I were thrown into this situation through dealing with the archive of his grandfather (Wolfgang Tümpel), which has an art historical value because of his being associated with the Bauhaus. The difficulty was that we had this responsibility as he had art historical acknowledgment, but there was no money. So I reached out to a lot of different estates and asked them, "Can we talk? Can we learn from each other?"—and that's how the whole thing evolved. So it's not only Hans Arp and Sophie Taeuber-Arp, but also all those conversations with other estates.
KB: Does your legal training help?
LW: Absolutely. I'm good at asking lawyers the right questions, but the lawyers must answer them. My legal training helps me to understand the impact, and to guide the family as to the stage when they should get a lawyer, and where they could go without a lawyer. But I can't and will never replace a lawyer.
BF: In the US, it is quite similar: the lawyer is key. He is like the quarterback in this situation.
LW: Traditionally, the lawyers were not only quarterbacks, they were the whole team for estates. But in the end they are not art market or museum specialists, they can't replace insights into the academic world. The counselling came from the legal side, but it's important to open up the field and change perspectives. The conference Christian Scheidemann did, "Body of Work", on 9 April 2018 at SVA in New York, was really interesting, because that again asked new questions. Coming

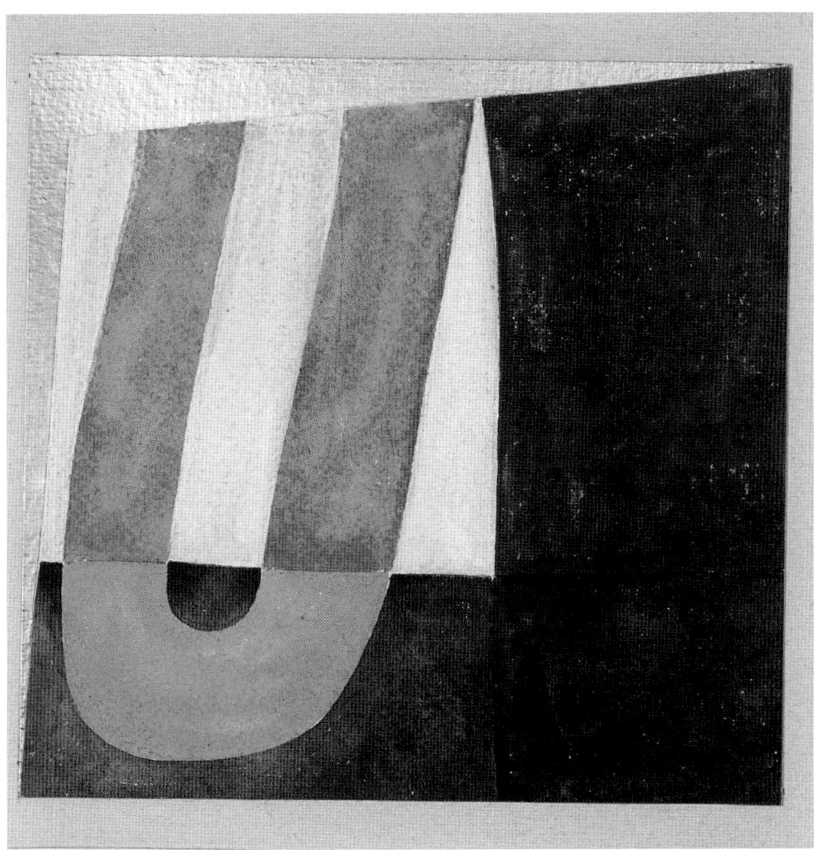

Sophie Taeuber-Arp, *Composition in the Form of a "U"*, 1918

from a conservation background, it had a whole material aspect. That would never have happened ten years ago. I think it illustrates the existing developments of this field.

KB: Because of demographics? There are just more artists passing now . . .

LW: And very wealthy artists. The starting point was the death of Warhol, who was the first really rich artist of his generation. From there it has slowly developed because there were suddenly estates which were worth millions, and it was simply necessary to professionalize the field. That goes parallel to the huge development of the art market. We have more artists because there is a much larger market, so in turn more wealth is distributed to more artists.

BF: Art is used as an asset class now, even if we don't . . .

LW: Want it? It's a fact.

BF: So how does one handle both cultural object and financial instrument?

LW: I think one can learn from estates because they have been dealing with this for a much longer time. Because children inherit art and sell it for cash, we're talking

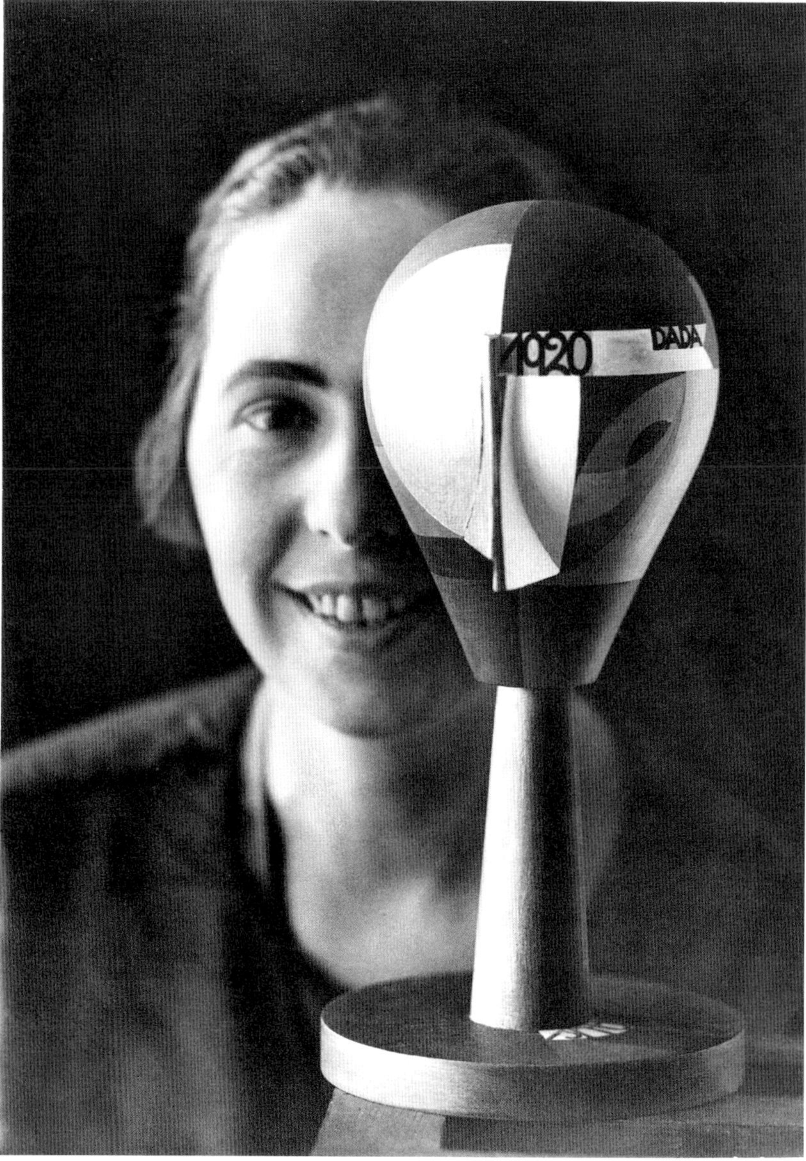

Nic Aluf, *Sophie Taeuber with Dada-Head*, 1920

about two worlds, which are opposites. They must look at it as an asset class because it's their inheritance, but they would treat it differently than if they inherited a car, or bank account, or stocks.

BF: There is this implied moral imperative that seems troubling to some people.

LW: At the same time, it's their inheritance. So they have to balance this. For the past few years, we have worked increasingly with living artists, planning their legacies together with their families. I've been trying to make artists become more aware that they can avoid trouble if they deal with it during their lifetime. I build this bridge by asking them to see it as their last big work of art. I'm working with a wonderful family: the artist is in his mid-80s and has very intelligent children. He had various wives and children, so as often in artists' families, there are many emotional issues. The process kicked off a conversation, and they started talking to each other again. It is really lovely to see that it can bring up negative emotions but it can also bring a positive dynamic. I can express concerns or ask questions, with no own emotional history.

KB: How do you feel about that balance between family and outside professionals on a foundation board?

LW: I find family members often are very valuable resources. They know things that many people don't because they have soaked in details by being raised with the work. We are all aware that estates need marketing, you market the artist posthumously as a personality. And then for very successful estates, they're very good at marketing themselves as an estate body. I find family members most often the best ambassadors and to make a family member the face of a foundation, even if that person may not be the dominant ruling party on the board. It's this emotional bond to the artist and his or her heirs which the family members can transport in a way that none of us can. And that's why I would always try to integrate them.

BF: You were talking about setting up living artists' legacies, and one question we have regards tax implications. In the US, if you set things up before you pass, it can be advantageous. Is it the same in Europe?

LW: The best example for that was Henry Moore: he set it up during his lifetime not because he had a great vision, but for tax issues. And he was then an employee of his company for the last ten years. I think he stated that he hated it. But it was the right thing to do, so it's exactly the same in Europe.

In Germany for example, we have very advantageous rules about inheriting art: if you give it to the public for a certain period of time or show it in public then you can almost inherit without any inheritance taxes at all. If you give it to museum for ten years, after ten years the children will have it for free. It is a tax cut for inherited art, but almost nobody knows about it. The only precondition is it must be accepted by a public institution as worthy of being shown.

KB: Can it be a small or regional museum?

LW: It can be! For example, for a small local museum, the local artists might be very important. I think we are all too concentrated on the same set of artists worldwide. I find these museums, which take up local artistry and combine it with great movements—there are so many fantastic side movements—often much more interesting.

BF: It's tough, however, when people think they have a Picasso . . . It's heartbreaking sometimes, but you're doing them a service.

LW: How hard the ache will be depends on how empathetic you are. Negotiating contracts with galleries is not about law skills, it's about the emotional skills we have to bring into it. That's one thing I often tell them in the very first meeting when they ask me "What legal structure should I have?" I ask the client, "Does the work stand the test? And is it worth investing time into this?"
BF: What's the Plan B if the work is not worth it?
LW: That's so difficult to answer in general because the situations are all unique. It depends on how much is left. Because it might not be worth it to do all the estate work, but it might be interesting for local museums. Or to divide it amongst siblings. There is so much embedded value which might not be monetized, but it's still a value. And it can be very helpful to work with them on finding that value before putting it in the dustbin.
KB: How do you see the future of overlooked artists' legacies, for example feminist artists? Should they be handled differently if they didn't have a commercial success?
LW: The last five years have opened up a lot of opportunities. One can say it's market driven because galleries need new supplies. On the other hand, there is a chance for overlooked artists to enter the sphere. I find it extremely exciting, because it is one thing if you say we are opening the market for women artists, but they must have the quality to compete on an international level first, to then find the recognition. So this simply opened the door, but if an artist walks into the room he or she is defined by the quality of the work. I think it has become much easier for outsider positions to try to enter the room, and I think it can be developed a little further. We've seen it already with South American positions, and there's again a slight correction at the moment, which is also market driven, and has to do with the fact that the South American collectors haven't been as strong in the last few years, because of economic reasons, as they were five, six, seven years ago. Those positions won't be erased from art history just because the market has subsided.
BF: If there's that quality, if the art stands up . . .
LW: That's the fundamental question when working with every estate. It can sometimes be up to the family to answer that question, because maybe the body doesn't stand up, either the mother or the father was the artist of the family, and we all know how that can affect family dynamics. It can be very hard when somebody has passed away, to admit that the art coming out of this very special world didn't stand up.
BF: Do you find yourself in the position of being that voice?
LW: Yes, and guiding families towards finding that answer themselves. It can be more helpful sometimes to express that early enough, before we invest time or effort into it. In the case that I have this information from the beginning, it would not lead to whatever they had hoped for. Also I think it's very interesting to make clear to family members that impartial advice is the most helpful and that I strongly encourage them not only to ask us, but maybe to ask a museum director or other artists, to get the views of various voices, to then also ask themselves "Should I step

up to this responsibility; should I invest my lifetime in working for the estate?" Because we all know estates are carried by children who usually get no remuneration for it. They should have outside feedback that the quality is sufficient to justify such an endeavour. I help them identify four or five people who can give feedback.

BF: And to create a richer canon. That's what you were saying, the art world is experiencing a broader context of work that should be in the canon.

LW: Yes. If the works is important enough, it'll stay in the canon. That's determined by how interesting these works are to academics and curators, and that is beyond the market. And that's why it's always so important as an estate, to invest money and time into working with academics and curators.

BF: What do you tell your clients if they don't have the resources to engage in any personalized services?

LW: Engaging isn't as expensive as one thinks. One can just go through cash-flow calculations and set up a sensible effective protocol for maybe the equivalent of US$30,000 a year. To really create an impact, you don't need hundreds of thousands of dollars. You can create situations of working with art historians in the archive, which costs a couple of thousand dollars. That's always the first thing we work on—what is the true budget—and it's often surprisingly low in comparison to the impact you can create, if you structure these things intelligently.

And also invest a bit in marketing well, because it's about reaching out to the community of young academics, young curators often, and that is a worldwide community. With social media, you can have a deep reach without huge financial resources. If you are Rauschenberg and you can afford a huge budget, it's fantastic. But it's not a precondition to work with an archive in depth. You can also team up with universities, for academic research. For example if you have conservation issues in the body of work you own, and offer students the chance to practise on those works, that can be a great way of saving cash and time, and you're giving something back to the university community. I think there are a lot of creative ways to minimize costs.

I think archives are such powerful instruments. It'll be about authentication in the long run. It will be about having access to secondary market information because in the archives they know everything to work with. If they own the archive, they also know about pitfalls, and weaknesses.

When I had my conversation with Mayen Beckmann, the granddaughter of Max Beckmann, we talked about this because she linked the aspect of archives directly to the duration of copyright. And when we were talking about her working with academics on doing research on Max Beckmann, she said her most powerful instrument is the control of the archive and copyrights, because every publication must come to her to include images. And she said, "I don't want to control the content of publications, I just want to make sure they are thoroughly made and they don't contain false information. And that I can check with the archives, and I have the power to the copyrights." The Beckmann copyright will end in about two years and she will give away the archive. So when we work with archives, even if they sell it, for example to the Getty or somewhere else, I also advise them to negotiate that they get 100% digital access and copies. So even if they sell the physical value of an archive, the estate keeps this control.

KB: I'm interested in the balance between the academic research, and then the practical aspects. Do you think that the practical has caught up with the idealistic academic thinking?

LW: I think the question of legacy planning for living artists should be the most normal thing to do. If you're writing a will, you should hire an art legacy advisor and work with them and it should be something that there's no question about doing once you've reached a certain level of recognition during your lifetime. Working with legacies you must have a very long-term view. For example, we started our work with Arp more than ten years ago, when the estate was in a state of redefining its purpose and strategy. Because the quality of work is so strong, he is one of the masters of 20th-century sculpture. But it took a lot of work: we had to set up the catalogue raisonné, the scholarship programme, organize the conferences, the new gallery presentations. It took almost seven to eight years after the foundation's work became recognized in the public sphere. That's the timeframe you have to deal with when working with estates. And I'm sure in ten years we'll have the situation to plan all those during your lifetime. And the professionalization of existing estates will go on, but we are still in this early phase.

KB: What do you think will happen with estates or foundations of artists that work in performance or the ephemeral?

LW: That's a very interesting field. I'm not a specialist on this. I can just say from my own view I find it often feels awkward to restage performances, but sometimes it feels right. For example I remember the MoMA exhibition of Marina Abramovic in 2010, where you had performances being restaged which originally came from the 1980s or early 1990s. And for me, who didn't see them at the time of their creation, it was great to experience that. I think there is a justification for restaging. I think it makes sense to look at the ballet and dance area, to learn from them more.

The second thing I always ask is: What is the will of the artist? And it's a similar question with the posthumous editing of photography of sculpture. I think there's not just one answer. Did a performance artist say, "I want my piece to end the moment I die", or "just finish certain things we have rehearsed together, you can toy with them but when the artist's gone, it's gone"? When does the artist say "I'm fine with young dancers learning my choreography in 20 years and restaging it"? I think that's the one question we have to answer in the very first sense.

KB: I think these legacies are even more important because there are few or no objects.

LW: Just think of Tino Sehgal: he even says he doesn't want recording.

BF: But it creates problems for us . . . though intellectually it's fun.
LW: It also builds upon the integrity of the parties involved. I think that's the most interesting aspect of the oral contract.
KB: Do you think there needs to be an academic programme set up in estate planning?
LW: Absolutely. I think there should be a masters programme for future leaders in the field, where you could maybe do it in parallel with your work life, like the Getty Leadership Institute (GLI) at Claremont Graduate University.
BF: Our last question is in three parts. What are the major differences between the US and Germany, or the EU, if there are any? Where do you see the field going? And what was the biggest thing that you've learned working in this field?
LW: There is a cultural difference which is to your benefit, which is the Americans are much more used to having advisors. If you want to open up a new field of advising, this is great. It is not that common in Germany or in continental Europe. Britain is in the middle.

The second difference is because of the course of art history in the 20th century. It was the post-war generation which was the most important one in America, who passed away and left a lot of wealth at a time when European artists weren't that important and didn't have any wealth. I think you have developed a sense of professionalization in the field that is beyond what has been developed in Germany or Central Europe in the last 20 years. That will change in the next 20 years because of people like Gerhard Richter, Anselm Kiefer, etc. passing away at some stage. Their art historical development in the 1980s and beyond balanced the importance between Europe and the States, and will be reflected in the way the field develops.

The third difference is your development has also benefitted from your tax and legal environment, because people were forced, more or less, if they didn't want to pay millions, to set up these structures. And the whole non-profit sector is so strongly regulated—they have to have advisors, a board, etc. In Europe the legal situation was more beneficial to private institutions. In the States, if you didn't go into a non-profit situation, you almost killed yourself in a sense. In Europe we have more alternatives or forms to do it, which I find very positive. Because a non-profit structure is not the right answer for every estate. I'm happy that we have these choices regarding the right structure for each family situation, for the size of the estate, for the financial resources in it.

Almost weekly I am delighted and surprised at how diverse this field is. It is extremely fulfilling work. At the beginning it was mainly about the legal and tax aspects. Now, it's about a 360 degree view on the whole field of estate planning and estate management. We talked about the emotional aspects, the museum, the academic. It's about balancing, negotiating with galleries, secondary or primary market. It's also about diving into an oeuvre, which you sometimes need years to grasp. And then you suddenly find something new in the archive, or find a new way of looking at the early work, the late work, whatever. And that constant learning I very much enjoy. The third aspect is more from the business side, how it's really a field in the making. We all need patience to see it come to the fore, which I think is desperately necessary.

If you don't have that intellectual curiosity, you don't belong in the field, because you need that to relate to artists and estates. You need this intellectual dialogue in order to keep the legacies alive. And then you develop this enthusiasm for details in the archive, in the work, and that has to be conveyed to every new generation, collectors, academics, museum people interested to really look at the work—that's what estate work is really all about. You have to get them that enthusiastic to look back at it again, and again, and again. Otherwise the oeuvre dies a second death.

3

ARTISTS' ESTATES AS GUARDIANS OF ARTISTIC LEGACY

Custodians or Gatekeepers?

Daniel McClean

As with many important reflections on artistic authorship, one turns to a work by Marcel Duchamp: the artist's remarkable tableau *Étant donnés: 1. La chute d'eau, 2. Le gaz d'éclairage* (1946–66), permanently installed inside the Philadelphia Museum of Art. Duchamp's enigmatic and erotic final work—which stages and allegorizes the act of looking (through a peep hole in a wooden door onto a landscape with a reclining female nude holding a gas lamp)—was planned secretly by the artist for over 20 years. However, it only came into being upon Duchamp's death, when it was posthumously installed in 1969 inside the museum in accordance with his "Manual of Instructions". With *Étant donnés*, Duchamp paradoxically created the truly "original" posthumous work, thereby symbolically cheating his own death. Duchamp's work presciently opens two lines of enquiry germane to our understanding of artistic authorship and legacy today. First, what is the status of the posthumous iteration of the work, and might a work executed by others posthumously have the same or even greater value than an (identical) work made by the artist during the artist's lifetime? And second, who are the guardians of the artist's work and authorship when the artist is no longer around—and in particular, who has the final say?

For Duchamp, as *Étant donnés* reflects, the long-term guardian of the artwork was the museum: his artwork exists in situ so long as the museum remains. However, although the Philadelphia Museum of Art was the recipient of his final work, the task of executing it was entrusted by Duchamp not only to its curators but to his heirs—his widow and son.[1] Unintentionally, perhaps, Duchamp's final work reveals the ongoing role of the artist's estate as a guardian of an artist's legacy alongside the museum.

ARTISTS' ESTATES AS GUARDIANS

Artists' estates are essentially all the assets bequeathed by the artist on death, including artworks. They are typically privately owned and run by the artist's heirs.[2] However, they may also take varied institutional forms or may be directly transferred to galleries or to museums. In some instances, as seen with wealthy artists' endowed private foundations or public charities (particularly in the United States), they are structured as not-for-profit legal entities with tax-exempt status run as trusts by boards of independent trustees, or in some cases as corporations. (In contrast to private estates, private foundations and public charities are state regulated and transparent to differing degrees.) Artists' foundations may have broad legacy aims beyond promoting the deceased artist's work; for example, the Robert Rauschenberg Foundation works to advance the visual arts through grants and artist residencies, and some, like the Robert Mapplethorpe Foundation, even have social goals, in their case to help find a cure for AIDS. I use the terms "artists' estates" collectively, to refer to all of the configurations referred to above.

In today's art world, artists' estates have come to assume increasing significance as guardians of artistic authorship and legacy, mediating between the art market (blue-chip contemporary art galleries compete aggressively to represent the estates of high-calibre artists), museums, and the domain of art-historical research and scholarship. Artists' estates have unique authority as guardians, often underscored by their mandate from the artist, as expressed in the artist's will, or through the creation of a foundation or charity while the artist was alive. An artist's estate owns not only the artworks and archival materials left by the artist but also the deceased artist's intellectual-property rights, which enables the estate to control in many ways how the artwork is exhibited; reproduced; and even, in some European civil-law countries, authenticated.[3] In addition, artists' estates often have an unrivalled expertise in the deceased artists' work, making them the de facto authority for authentication.

Accordingly, artists' estates sometimes even have the authority to intervene inside the museum to determine whether the artist's work may be exhibited, as revealed in the legal dispute between the Joseph Beuys estate and the Museum Schloss Moyland, in Bedburg-Hau, Germany.[4] At issue was the museum's display, in 2009, of a series of black-and-white photographs by Wolfgang Tischer—which the museum owned—documenting *The Silence of Marcel Duchamp Is Overrated* (1964), a live performance by Joseph Beuys that had been broadcast live on German television. The Beuys estate (run by Joseph Beuys' widow, Eva Beuys), which is the owner of the copyright of all of Beuys' works, objected through the German copyright-collecting society (VG Bild-Kunst) to the museum's display, complaining that Tischer's photographs infringed the artistic copyright subsisting in Beuys' performance by presenting an unauthorized "adaptation". In 2013, after protracted litigation, the case was settled in the museum's favour in the German Federal Supreme Court (the lower German courts had ruled in the estate's favour). The court held that though Beuys' performance was protected under German law as an "artistic work", it was unable to determine whether Tischer's photographs were infringing copies because there was no existing independent recording of Beuys' performance to compare to Tischer's photographs.

CUSTODIANS OR GATEKEEPERS?

The litigation between the Beuys estate and the Museum Schloss Moyland reveals the problems that can arise when different legacy guardians (the estate and the museum) come into conflict. It also reveals two contentious issues: What should be the scope of estates' responsibilities as guardians? And by what standards should estates operate?

Artists' estates perform a wide range of invaluable tasks, often under severe economic constraints—from conservation to archiving; from cataloguing to authentication; from working with galleries, museums, and collectors that are exhibiting the artist's work to instigating art historical research and scholarship about the artist's oeuvre. Yet despite the valuable work that artists' estates do, there are some situations in which they overreach their authority as guardians. These instances of overreach are underscored, perhaps, by the lack of clear normative and professional shared standards among artists' estates, in contrast, for example, to those adopted by public museums (through documents such as the *ICOM Code of Ethics for Museums*, published by the International Council of Museums).[5]

Although guarding legacy can be a complex and difficult task, artists' estates work effectively as guardians of artistic authorship when they act as *custodians*, protecting the work yet encouraging dissemination, rather than as *gatekeepers*, restricting access to and use of the artist's work. The notion of custodianship, like stewardship, implies entrustment rather than mere ownership and suggests that legacy is something greater than the exercise of property rights. Interestingly, the definition of "legacy" as a noun connotes both bequeathed personal property and "something left or handed down", including having an immaterial impact on others.[6] Legacy requires being responsible not just to the intentions of the deceased artist but also to other members of the artistic community, including artists, curators, and scholars, as well as to the wider public and to society and culture at large. The issues of guardianship can be analysed in relation to three crucial areas where artists' estates frequently act as guardians: (1) ownership of the artist's archive, (2) reproduction of the artwork, and (3) the authentication of artworks.

THE ARCHIVE

An artist's archive is critical to his or her legacy. It is an essential resource for scholars, curators, and artists who may wish to research the artist's biography, artworks, or exhibitions, and it enables scholars to write histories of the artist or any associated art movements, galleries, or museums. An artist's archive may also contain records that trace the ownership of the artist's work and enable its authentication. Artists including Lawrence Weiner and Carl Andre operate archival systems that register ownership and transfers in ownership of their works and thus facilitate their authentication. It is perhaps because the archive is so central to the mediation of artistic authorship that many contemporary artists, from Marcel Broodthaers onwards, have a self-reflexive fascination with it—what the art theorist Hal Foster terms the "archival impulse". Artists have imitated the archive's visual forms (vitrines) and typological arrangements (indexes) for ordering documents, records, and materials, as well as questioned its very structures of ownership and control.[7]

If an artist's legacy is to be sustained, the artist's archive should be open to the public (free of charge, where possible) to allow for research and critical interpretation, so that new perspectives can be formed on the artist over time, and his or her place in art history can be consolidated. There are many positive examples in which artists' estates and foundations have opened artists' archives for access to the public—thereby acting as custodians rather than as gatekeepers. Consider the archives of Donald Judd, run by the Judd Foundation, located in Marfa, Texas, along with Judd's permanently installed collection of artwork dispersed across different locations in the town; or the Andy Warhol archive, comprising thousands of artefacts, housed at the Andy Warhol Museum, in Pittsburgh. Yet there are also negative instances, in which artists' estates and foundations (as well as museums) have provided restrictive access to artists' archives or charged exorbitant fees for reproducing the documents contained in them.

In her ongoing project *The Barragán Archives*, the American artist Jill Magid interrogates the Barragan Foundation's control over the authorial legacy of the legendary Mexican modernist architect Luis Barragán.[8] Barragán's professional archive comprises thousands of original drawings by the architect, as well as his architectural models, photographs, and professional letters (Barragán created a separate personal archive of intimate letters and photographs). The archive controversially left Mexico in the early 1990s after Barragán's death. It was bizarrely inherited by the widow of Barragán's studio assistant, Raul Ferrera, to whom Barragán had bequeathed it and who committed suicide in 1993. It was then consigned by Ferrara's widow to a New York art dealer, and it was reportedly purchased for US$3 million by Rolf Fehlbaum, the chairman and board director of Vitra, a Swiss corporation famous for manufacturing products of contemporary design. The archive was then allegedly gifted by Fehlbaum to his wife, the architecture critic Federica

Zanco, as a wedding gift in 1995. The eponymous Barragan Foundation (a foundation not established by Barragán but by Zanco and closely aligned to the Vitra corporation) now controls the archive. The Barragan Foundation also acquired the copyright to Barragán's architectural works and models at some point during the late 1990s.

Magid initiated the project in 2013, when she made an official request to access Barragán's archive at the foundation's premises. She sent the request through the organizers of *Parcours*, a public-art project run by Art Basel, and the request was surprisingly declined. The foundation's refusal to allow Magid (and other scholars, as well as the public) access to the Barragán Archives and reproduction of photographic images of Barragán's architecture inspired Magid to embark upon a series of exhibitions reflecting on the physical and legal restrictions imposed by the foundation, and on what she describes as "the ownership of an artist's legacy by a corporation". While the acquisition of Barragán's archive by Fehlbaum and Zanco may well have prevented it from being dispersed (which is laudable), the foundation's control over access to the archive and wider dissemination is, as Magid's project illuminates, problematic.

Throughout Magid's nuanced project, she has consciously worked within the legal limitations imposed by the foundation, displaying in exhibitions the limited range of images and texts whose distribution has been authorized by the foundation, and framing them as readymades. She uses these displays—which often include previously published books on the architect, including *Luis Barragán: The Quiet Revolution* by Federica Zanco (published by the Vitra Design Museum, 2001)—to mark the archive's very absence, and the absence of images of Barragán's architecture save for those images officially sanctioned by the foundation.

Magid's project has culminated in her spectacular and provocative *Proposal* (2016). The artist, with the consent and assistance of Barragán's relatives, disinterred Barragán's cremated ashes from a public crematorium in Mexico and sent them to a Swiss specialist diamond company to be compressed into a diamond, which was set into an engagement ring. Magid then sent the ring to Federica Zanco. Mirroring the alleged wedding gift of Barragán's archive from Rolf Fehlbaum to Federica Zanco in the mid-1990s, *Proposal* stages the potential negotiated return of the archive to Mexico (in exchange for the ring). The literal legacy of Barragán (the body of the artist) is metamorphosed into a diamond ring—a "tool for negotiation", in the artist's words—to facilitate dialogue between the foundation and the State of Mexico, and to encourage the "return" of the archive, in a form to be determined, to Mexico, and with it the possibility of wider public access.

REPRODUCTION

An artist's estate is usually the beneficiary of the deceased artist's intellectual-property rights, which include copyright, moral rights of authorship, and in some countries (for example, within the European Union) the artist's resale royalty rights. In rare instances, the estate is also responsible for other intellectual-property rights, including trademarks (most artists and estates do not trademark their names), which can control the use of the artist's name and signature. The Picasso family famously licensed the artist's trademarked name and signature to the car manufacturer Citroën—a decision that reportedly divided the family heirs.[9]

Copyright—which controls the copying, distribution of copies, public performance, and public communication of protected "works" (including artistic works)—can be licensed and commercially exploited as a property right by the artist's estate. It typically lasts, in many jurisdictions (including in the European Union and the United States), for the lifetime of the author plus 70 years. Accordingly, copyright is a valuable instrument for an artist's estate in controlling the public dissemination of the deceased artist's work, as well as a potentially valuable income stream, particularly for estates that may otherwise lack a substantial inventory of the artist's artworks to sell in the art market.

Used positively, artistic copyright can help to maintain the integrity of the artist's work and to prevent its misuse through unauthorized commercial reproduction. Copyright can, for example, stop the merchandising of an artist's work on products and in advertising that the artist might have found highly offensive and damaging to the work's meaning. In 2016 the estate of the Los Angeles graffiti artist Dash Snow sued the US corporation McDonald's for copyright infringement, alleging that McDonald's had recreated Snow's graffiti in over 100 of its global locations, thereby wrongfully associating Snow with corporate culture and consumerism, which the artist had strenuously avoided when alive.[10]

Used negatively, however, copyright can restrict the circulation of images of the artist's work by museums, educational institutions, and publishers. It can also prevent other artists from building on the deceased artist's work through being copied, cited, and even contested, thus preventing the work from entering an "artistic commonwealth" of shared images and forms, and conflicting with how the artist would have exercised this copyright as an author when alive.[11] Generally speaking, fine artists do not sue one another for copyright infringement—a notable exception being the litigation in 2014 between the artists Bridget Riley and Tobias Rehberger regarding the alleged infringement by Rehberger of the copyright subsisting in a Riley painting.[12]

The litigation between the Giacometti Foundation and John Baldessari/The Prada Foundation (2010–11) in the Milan courts illustrates how misguided an artist's estate can be when it seeks to use copyright law to prevent the copying by other artists of a deceased artist's work—particularly when that copied work is itself of

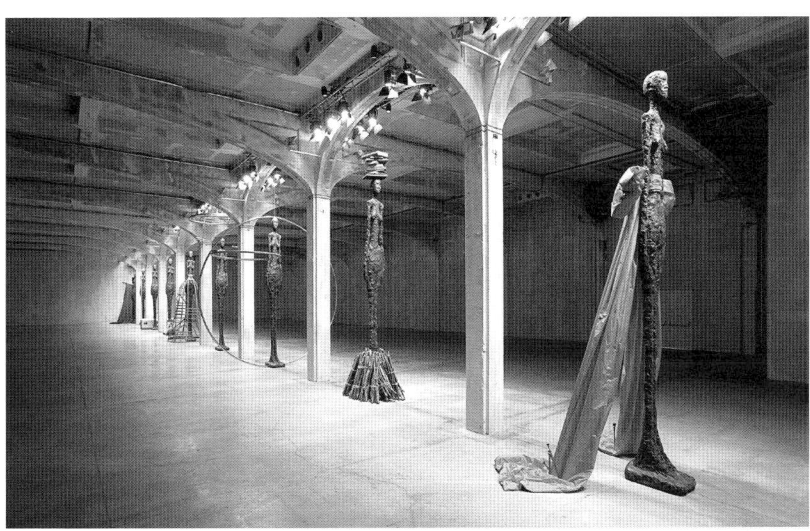

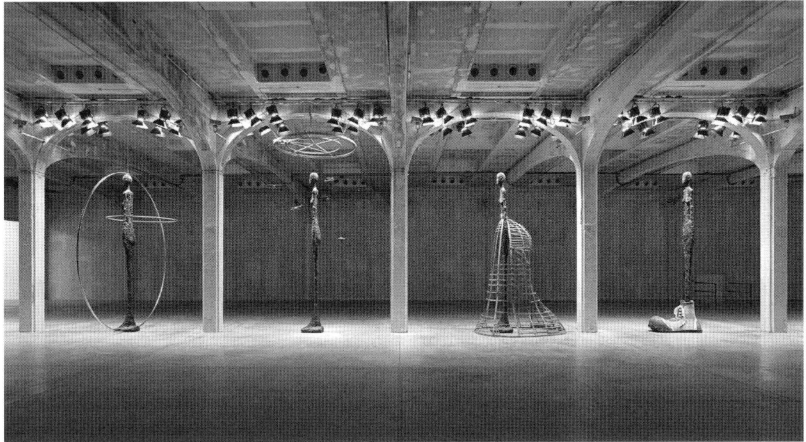

John Baldessari, *The Giacometti Variations*, 2010, installation views at the Prada Foundation, Milan

iconic artistic and cultural significance and hence an invaluable reference point for other artists and culture at large.[13] In this case, the Giacometti Foundation sought a permanent injunction from the Italian court to prevent the exhibition of Baldessari's *The Giacometti Variations* (2010), commissioned by the Prada Foundation, Milan. John Baldessari created without authorization nine enlarged figurines by Alberto Giacometti, each 4.5 metres (14.8 feet) tall and draped in garments and objects designed by Baldessari. The artist did this to comment ironically on the mutation of representations of the human figure within Western culture from the time of Giacometti (his figurines symbolizing post-Second World War humanist notions of existential anxiety) to the present day (the age of postmodern consumerism and fashion). Ultimately, Baldessari and the Prada Foundation were able to successfully contest the injunction under the fair-use/parody exception provided under Italian copyright law, and the court allowed the exhibition to be reopened and to proceed.

By contrast, many artists' estates appreciate the importance for an artist's legacy of the work being copied, transformed, and even contested by other artists (though not used in commercial merchandising or in advertising). The Rauschenberg Foundation allows museums and educational institutions to reproduce images of work by Robert Rauschenberg without paying fees or royalties, and they have given artists wide access to recycle and use Rauschenberg's works, not only appreciating the deceased artist's own reproduction and mixing of images borrowed from high and low culture but also mindful of the importance of such practices for the sustaining of Rauschenberg's legacy. In 2015, for example, the foundation gave the artist Rachel Harrison unfettered access to Rauschenberg's work to use as the basis of her exhibition at the Cleveland Museum of Art, *Gloria: Robert Rauschenberg and Rachel Harrison*, allowing Harrison to juxtapose her own works with Rauschenberg's.[14] The approach of the Rauschenberg Foundation should be applauded as a positive example of custodianship exercised by an artist's estate.

Other artists' estates have also enabled productive dialogues around the deceased artist's work. For example, the Henry Moore Foundation—dedicated to the legacy of British sculptor Henry Moore, but also to the support of sculpture and the visual arts in the United Kingdom—allowed the British artist Simon Starling to reproduce Henry Moore's sculpture in several projects, including in Starling's memorable sculpture *Infestation Piece (Musseled Moore)* (2008).[15] Starling's sculpture is a slightly less-than-to-scale reproduction of Moore's sculpture *Warrior with Shield* (1953–4)—a version of which is owned by the Henry Moore Sculpture Centre at the Art Gallery of Ontario, in Toronto. Referring to this work and to Moore's historical connection with the city of Toronto, Starling submerged his reproduction in the icy waters of Lake Ontario for over a year before exhibiting it encrusted with mussels and shellfish in 2008 at the Power Plant, in Toronto.

AUTHENTICATION

Authentication is fundamental to protecting the integrity of an artist's work and to protecting its market over time. The forgery scandal engulfing the leading Korean minimalist painter Lee Ufan in 2016 is a spectacular example of how doubts about the authenticity of an artist's work can undermine its integrity. In this case, the artist was alleged to have wrongly verified faked paintings as his own work to prop up his market, which led to numerous arrests in South Korea, including of a prominent art dealer.[16] It is not clear what impact the scandal will have on Lee Ufan's market, but it is likely to be negative.

Central to the concept of authenticity are the notions of "original" expressive authorship and the auratic "uniqueness" of the object, as described by the German philosopher Walter Benjamin in his essay "The Work of Art in the Age of Mechanical Reproduction" (1935).[17] Authenticity also refers to an array of characteristics linked to the artwork's aesthetic "quality"—such as the work's age, condition, period, school, and style— that can be used to prove or certify authorship. Without these ascriptions of authorship and unique objecthood, the artwork loses its symbolic and monetary value. The two historical enemies of authenticity are the fake (the fraudulent copy) and the misattribution (the innocent copy), as they undermine the regime of original authorship. Authenticity is also undermined when a work is restored too many times, or restored in a way that changes the object substantially. With contemporary artworks, which are often executed in multiple form, and often fabricated by third parties on behalf of the artist and not by the artist, the question of authenticity has become even more elastic and challenging.

Artists' estates often play a critical role as guardians in the authentication of artworks, by family members and by foundations deciding whether artworks are original or not. This is done through the authentication of individual artworks via certification and the preparation of the artist's catalogue raisonné—a comprehensive catalogue of works by an artist, compiled by experts and usually arranged chronologically with date, medium, provenance, and exhibition history for each work. When an artwork is omitted from the catalogue raisonné, its exclusion undermines the status of its authorship among scholars and in the marketplace. If an individual artwork is specifically denied authenticity in the form of certification, then the result can be arguably even more damaging as it is likely to be very difficult for the owner to sell the artwork (or at least for a sum close to its true market value) without the issued certificate.

Yet if artists' estates are the de facto singular source of authority (and in some countries, the legal source of authority) for authenticating artworks, by what procedures and standards should they do this? The litigation between the art collector Joe Simon-Whelan and the Andy Warhol Foundation for the Visual Arts and its authentication body, the Andy Warhol Art Authentication Board (2007–09), reveals both the control that artists' estates can have in this arena and the legal risks that artists' estates run of being sued over questions of authentication by disgruntled owners.[18] It also reveals the problems caused when boards do not follow transparent and coherent criteria and board members are perceived to have conflicts of interest (principally as dealers in the artist's work they are authenticating).

Simon-Whelan owned a work allegedly by Andy Warhol. *Red Self-Portrait* (1965), one of an edition of ten works produced by Warhol's silkscreen factory, had once been sold by Christie's at auction in 1987 and authenticated prior to this sale as being a Warhol both by the foundation (Vincent Froment, a trustee, stamped the work with Warhol's signature!) and by Fred Hughes, the executor of Warhol's estate. Simon-Whelan purchased the work for US$195,000 in 1989. In 2001 he submitted it to the authentication board. He had been encouraged to do so by Vincent Froment, the Warhol Foundation's exclusive sales agent and a member of the authentication board, who had formerly positively authenticated Simon-Whelan's work. Following Simon-Whelan's application, the board twice rejected the authenticity of the silkscreen, finally stamping "DENIED" in large uppercase letters on its back so as to permanently damage it. The board gave no initial explanation for its rejection, but subsequently, in 2004, explained its decision on the basis that Warhol had not been involved in any stage in overseeing the production of this series of works—a decision that, as Richard Dorment argued in a notable article in the *New York Review of Books*, would appear to be fundamentally flawed in terms of how Warhol worked as an artist and, importantly, perceived the authenticity of his *Red Self-Portrait* series.[19]

Angered by the board's rejection in 2007, Simon-Whelan spearheaded a class action against the board, the foundation, and other parties in New York Federal District Court on the basis of antitrust, fraud, and unjust-enrichment claims, also requesting a court declaration that the waiver of his rights to sue the board and foundation when signing up to the board's Submission Agreement was unenforceable. Simon-Whelan accused, inter alia, the foundation and board under sections 1 and 2 of the Sherman Antitrust Act of conspiring in restraint of trade to artificially restrict the supply of Warhol's work, thereby inflating the value of each work held by the foundation, and colluding to monopolize trade in Warhol's works. (The foundation funds its charitable activities by selling Warhol works, of which it owned a significant market share.) The accused parties achieved all this, Simon-Whelan claimed, through the board wrongfully denying the authenticity of genuine Warhol works, including his own *Red Self-Portrait*. In 2009 a US federal court rejected a motion brought by the foundation and board to dismiss Simon-Whelan's claim, allowing it to proceed on the fraud and unjust-enrichment claims, and in part on the antitrust claims. In particular, the court found that there was a plausible basis for Simon-Whelan to claim antitrust injury because the board prevented him from operating as a competitor in the market by denying the work's authenticity, although Simon-Whelan was not found to suffer injury through the alleged price-inflationary aspects of the conspiracy. Following the court's decision in 2009, the litigation was eventually settled when Simon-Whelan voluntarily abandoned his claim. By then, however, the foundation had incurred over $7 million in legal fees (which it then sought to recover from its insurance company, Philadelphia Indemnity Insurance Company, leading to further litigation), and a dangerous precedent had been set. If Simon-Whelan could bring antitrust claims this far (anticompetitive claims, in this instance), so could other potential claimants.

In 2012 the Warhol Foundation closed the authentication board, ceasing its certification activities (though the foundation continues its comprehensive Warhol catalogue raisonné project to document and authenticate the artist's works). Since then other artists' estates have also voluntarily ceased their authentication activities, including the respective authentication boards of the Alexander Calder, Keith Haring, and Roy Lichtenstein foundations and the heirs of Jean-Michel Basquiat. The voluntary dissolution of the Warhol Art Authentication Board and other artists' authentication boards has arguably caused an authentication crisis in the blue-chip contemporary art market, particularly in the United States, where, unlike in Europe, artists' estates face heavy litigation costs that are generally non-recoverable, even when claims are successfully defended by estates or foundations. Unfortunate owners who lack requisite certificates find it much harder to sell their works and to obtain a fair market value, even when they have strong evidence of the work's provenance and can even point to its inclusion in the artist's catalogue raisonné or other important publications on the artist. Conversely, and paradoxically, the absence of certificates makes it easier for forgeries to enter the art market, as there are fewer barriers to scrutiny. The risks of relying on individual experts' opinions and the seller's representations as opposed to a certificate issued by an artist's sanctified authentication board is dramatically illustrated by the closure of New York's Knoedler Gallery in the wake of its forgery scandal in 2011.[20]

As Simon-Whelan's dispute with the Warhol Foundation and authentication board illustrates, some of these problems could seemingly have been overcome if there had been different standards of governance—that is, if artists' estates acted less as gatekeepers and more as true custodians. The US Federal Court found sufficiently "plausible" alleged facts that the Warhol authentication board lacked the required independence from the foundation (and contained members who were not even experts), and that the board's "policies" were arbitrary and inconsistent. For example, the board sometimes reversed its own prior authentication determinations and even occasionally refused to authenticate works that it had previously attempted to purchase. Compounding this was the board's lack of transparency: it refused to provide clear reasons or explanations for its decisions.

Some of these litigation risks might be mitigated if artists' authentication boards were run in the future by experts independent of the estate or the foundation. These experts could be appointed on a temporary and revolving basis to lessen the development of self-interested attachments. Above all, decision-making should be transparent and consistent. It is noteworthy that the art dealer Richard Polsky has recently created a substitute service for authenticating Andy Warhol's artwork and those of other artists.[21] Polsky proclaims to follow "transparent" and "fair" criteria and to explain how decisions are reached when reviewing works, though it remains open as to whether his authentications will be followed by the market in practice.

To date, the authentication crisis shows no imminent signs of abating in the United States. There have, for example, been various aborted attempts to promote a New York state law that would protect art experts from litigation when offering authenticity opinions, though there is still hope the law might eventually pass.[22] The lawsuit brought in late 2016 in the New York State Court by the Mayor Gallery, London, against the compilers of the Agnes Martin catalogue raisonné and other parties for refusing to positively authenticate 13 "Agnes Martin" paintings formerly sold by the Mayor Gallery illustrates once again the litigation risks assumed by authentication boards when offering opinions.[23] In this case, the gallery alleges that by wrongfully refusing to include these paintings in the catalogue raisonné, the defendants have rendered them valueless, subjecting the gallery to multiple refund claims from disaffected buyers. In doing so, the Mayor Gallery alleges the board committed various torts, including the tort of wrongful interference with prospective business relations. To succeed in its claim, the Mayor Gallery will need to establish "malice" on the part of the defendants, which is a difficult hurdle to surmount. However, as the Warhol litigation illustrates, just defending this type of litigation in the New York courts is likely to be expensive.

For this situation to change, there needs to be legislative reform, offering greater protection to experts, coupled with reform in the governance of some authentication boards, who effectively have a monopoly on determining authenticity in the art market. Whether this can be achieved remains to be seen.

FOLLOWING THE ARTIST'S INTENTIONS AFTER DEATH

The purpose of this essay is to open critical discussion about the role of artists' estates as guardians of artistic legacy—a task that is too often little addressed. Generally, as discussed, artists' estates provide an invaluable role as custodians, as opposed to gatekeepers, of artistic legacy. Nor should we assume simplistically that museums by contrast automatically act as custodians of artistic legacy (a discussion that is beyond the scope of this text). However, there are situations in which the authority of artists' estates is overreached—an overreach perhaps rooted, in part, in the tension between artistic authorship as a bundle of property rights, exercised by third parties when the artist has died, and authorship as the deceased artist's immaterial, creative influence on the language of art and the culture at large. Authorship as property and authorship as legacy can come into conflict because property rights and intellectual-property rights may be exercised in ways that are incommensurate (as discussed above) with the dissemination and use of the artist's work and ideas within public culture.

Yet it should be recalled just how complex and difficult it can be for artists' estates to follow the intentions of the deceased artist and protect the integrity of the work. An artist's authorial legacy can assume myriad forms both material and immaterial; ultimately, it requires an understanding of the artist's intentions behind the work. When artists do not leave specific instructions on how their estates are to be handled, as is often the case, artists' estates must grapple with a bewildering range of questions: Did the artist intend this artefact to be an artwork or not? How did the artist intend the work to be conserved? How did the artist intend the artwork to be remade? And how did the artist intend for it to be viewed? Inherently demanding, these questions are further complicated by the nature of much contemporary artistic production, in which the artwork is often defined not by its "permanent" material form but by its concept (for example, as written instructions that can be re-enacted, as in Conceptual art and beyond); in which production or performance of the artwork is delegated by the artist to others (as in much post-minimalist and Conceptual art, and so-called performative art); and in which the boundaries between the artwork and its environment (installation/relational aesthetics) and the artwork and its documentation (performance art) are often blurred.

Another controversy, interestingly also involving the legacy of Joseph Beuys, illuminates some of these difficulties. The Hessisches Landesmuseum Darmstadt, in Germany, houses Beuys's iconic seven-room installation *Block Beuys* (1970–86), which comprises over 250 objects. In 2009 the museum decided controversially to renovate the rooms housing Beuys's "total work" by removing the decaying beige jute wallpaper and grey carpet that had been in the room since the 1970s.[24] Beuys had been unclear as to whether the environmental "frame" surrounding his installation was intended to be part of the work or not; yet for many scholars and connoisseurs of Beuys, the museum's discoloured walls and fading carpet were an integral and authentic part of Beuys's "entropic" installation, and their removal by the museum violated the work's integrity. This example highlights the difficult decisions artists' estates and museums both face when acting as guardians. On this occasion, the Beuys estate tacitly supported the museum's actions, though some commentators urged it to legally intervene to prevent it. But who is to say—given Beuys's own lack of guidance on this matter—who was right or not?

Notes

1 See Philadelphia Museum of Art, *Marcel Duchamp: "Étant donnés"*, 15 August – 29 November 2009, http://www.philamuseum.org/exhibitions/324.html [accessed 27 February 2020].

2 For a full account on the legal structure of artists' estates, see Loretta Würtenberger, *The Artist Estate: A Handbook for Artists, Executors, and Heirs*, Berlin: Hatje Cantz, 2016. See especially chapter 3, "Types of estate administration: between attics, museum plans, and other desires for perpetuity".

3 In France, for example, the *droit moral* holder has the right to authenticate works by that artist (which is often bequeathed by the artist to his or her heirs). See Judith Prowda, "Expert Opinions", in *Visual Arts and the Law: A Handbook for Professionals*, Farnham, UK: Lund Humphries, 2013, pp.203–19.

4 See "Beuys-Witwe unterlieght vor BGH", *Handelsblatt*, 16 May 2013, http://www.handelsblatt.com/panorama/kultur-kunstmarkt/streit-um-fotoserie-beuys-witwe-unterliegt-vor- bgh/8220192.html [accessed 27 February 2020].

5 See, for example, Principle 2, "Museums that maintain collections hold them in trust for the benefit of society and its development." *ICOM Code of Ethics for Museums*, International Council of Museums, 2017, https://icom.museum/wp-content/uploads/2018/07/ICOM-code-En-web.pdf [accessed 27 February 2020].

6 *Oxford Dictionaries*, s.v. "legacy", https://en.oxforddictionaries.com/definition/legacy (accessed 20 July 2017).

7 See Hal Foster, "An Archival Impulse", *October*, no.110 (Fall 2004), pp.3–22.

8 The author of this essay has been the legal advisor to the artist Jill Magid for this project and has discussed it in Daniel McClean, "Jill Magid and Luis Barragán's legacy", in Nikolaus Hirsch et al. (eds), *The Proposal: Jill Magid*, Critical Spatial Practice, no.8, Berlin: Sternberg Press, 2016. [The removal of the accent from Barragán's name in the title of the Barragan Foundation is a symptom of the archive's deracination—as discussed in Kathy Battista's introduction to Part 2 of this volume (see pp.97–8).]

9 See Alan Riding, "A family feud over a Picasso (on wheels): a new car's logo divides the heirs of a lucrative name", *New York Times*, 19 April 1999, http://www.nytimes.com/1999/04/19/arts/family-feud-over-picasso-wheels-new-car-s-logo-divides-heirs-lucrative-name.html [accessed 27 February 2020].

10 See Alyssa Buffenstein, "Dash Snow's family sues McDonald's for copyright infringement", *Artnet News*, 5 October 2016, https://news.artnet.com/art-world/dash-snows-family-sues-mcdonalds-copyright-infringement-685901 [accessed 27 February 2020].

11 See Daniel McClean, "Piracy and authorship in contemporary art and the artistic commonwealth", in Lionel Bently, Jennifer Davis, and Jane C. Ginsburg (eds), *Copyright and Piracy: An Interdisciplinary Critique*, Cambridge: Cambridge University Press, 2010, pp.311–39.

12 See "Riley v. Rehberger copyright lawsuit settled", *Clanco*, 22 January 2014, http://clancco.com/wp/2014/01/painting-installation-checkerboard-art-law/ [accessed 27 February 2020].

13 Civil Court of Milan, no.79957/2010, judgment of 14 July 2011.

14. See Cleveland Museum of Art, *Gloria: Robert Rauschenberg and Rachel Harrison*, 1 July – 25 October 2015, https://www.clevelandart.org/events/exhibitions/gloria-robert-rauschenberg-rachel-harrison [accessed 27 February 2020].

15 See The Power Plant, *Simon Starling: Cuttings (Supplement)*, 1 March – 11 May 2008, http://www.thepowerplant.org/Exhibitions/2008/2008_Spring/Cuttings-(Supplement).aspx [accessed 27 February 2020].

16 See Victoria Stapley-Brown and Nathalie Eggs, "Forgery scandal surrounding Lee Ufan's work grows in Korea with three arrests", *Art Newspaper*, 21 November 2016, https://theartnewspaper.com/news/forgery-scandal-surrounding-lee-ufan-s-work-grows-in-korea-with-three-arrests/ [accessed 27 February 2020].

17 See Walter Benjamin, "The Work of Art in the Age of Mechanical Reproduction" (1935), translated by Harry Zohn, in Hannah Arendt (ed.), *Illuminations*, New York: Schocken Books, 1968, pp.217–51.

18 See Simon-Whelan v. The Andy Warhol Foundation for the Visual Arts, Inc., et al., no.07 Civ.6423 (LTS) (S.D.N.Y. 26 May 2009).

19 Richard Dorment, "What is an Andy Warhol?", *New York Review of Books*, 22 October 2009, http://www.nybooks.com/articles/2009/10/22/what-is-an-andy-warhol/ [accessed 27 February 2020].

20 See M.H. Miller, "The Big Fake: behind the scenes of Knoedler Gallery's downfall", *Artnews*, 25 April 2016, http://www.artnews.com/2016/04/25/the-big-fake-behind-the-scenes-of-knoedler-gallerys-downfall/ [accessed 27 February 2020].

21 See Richard Polsky Art Authentication, http://richardpolskyart.com [accessed 27 February 2020].

22 Since early 2015, the New York State Legislature has considered legislation limiting the legal liability of authenticators offering opinions. Though passed by the Senate, this legislation has not been passed by the Assembly. See Assembly Bill A1018, relating to the authenticity, attribution, and authorship of fine works of art, https://www.nysenate.gov/legislation/bills/2015/a1018/amendment/original [accessed 27 February 2020].

23 Mayor Gallery Ltd. v. Agnes Martin Catalogue Raisonné LLC, et al., no.655489 (Sup. Ct. N.Y. 17 October 2016).

24 See Tacita Dean, *Darmstädter Werkblock*, Göttingen, Germany: Steidl, 2008.

4
ARTISTS' ESTATES

Tiers of Valuation and Complications

Ann-Marie Richard

FOREWORD

There are many excellent publications on the subject of managing an artist's financial assets; this chapter is by no means a comprehensive study on this topic, but rather an introduction to tiers of estate valuation and ensuing complications.

Standards of tax authorities, laws, and approaches to valuation differ from one country to the next, and within the United States from one state to the other. This chapter illustrates recollections of challenges encountered from the experience of appraising artists' estates during a period of 20 years in New York City. It should be mentioned that the enterprise of managing and valuing an estate are two separate matters that relate to one another. Rarely are these endeavours settled by a single practitioner. Rather, resolutions are most satisfactorily obtained through the collaborative efforts of several entities with experience, professional credentials, and trade expertise. Practical exposure will uncover multiple approached to administering and valuing an estate. The only stable qualifier is that a common goal be the unifier. It is the administrator's fiduciary duty to keep the artist's work relevant in the present and for the future. With the intention of accessibility to the art and related archives, an administrator protects the legacy of the artist and his or her heirs. The same rule applies to estate valuation. Impactful administrative decisions can shape the economic sustainability, growth, or withering of an artist's market.

INTRODUCTION

Artists' estates present intricate issues of planning, collection management, and market valuation. An in-depth knowledge of an artist's oeuvre and the place it holds within the broader canon of art history is fundamentally necessary but not sufficient to embark on the task of sorting the good, better, and best of creative output. Outside of this realm numerous factors impact on the resolution of an estate. In this chapter, through redacted case studies, the author will expose selected categories of discussion, managerial points, and conflicts of interest.

Measure the level of an artist's success—whether commercial or critical—is an objective process. Market data, bibliographic databases, and other information resources provide many answers. However, because no two artists are alike, there is no undertaking that is homogenous. Establishing a strategy in the initial steps is key. Within the chain-link of this bridge between executors and heirs are aspects that require clarity. The articulation of a methodology, a narrative of justification, a comprehensive market analysis, and a summarized end goal are essential chapters to be fleshed out in an academic appraisal study.

The solvency success of managing the assets of an artist estate is driven or drained by the amount of funds available. Based on the location of the artist's residence and/or properties different laws may apply and varying degrees of provisions may ensue.

MANY ENTITIES

In a perfect world artist estates are handled with the aid of a consortium of professionals, including those with intimate knowledge of the artist's practice and philosophy. This group of trusted individuals may include the artist's primary dealer (if still alive), a studio manager and/or assistant, a family member, or a friend. On the periphery of the artist circle, legal counsel may be necessary to set up trusts, an accountant is indispensable to avoid unnecessary tax penalties, and an experienced and qualified appraiser required to conduct a sound assessment of the estate's value. Should the valuation aspect be misunderstood or misconstrued it may lead to fiscal audits and years of litigation, potentially debilitating the estate.

In reality, rarely is the triad of art, finance, and legal advisors prepared for the unexpected "surprises" an artist's legacy might present. No two artists' bodies of work are created equal, and not all artists sustain steady commercial or academic success throughout their careers.

CONFLICTS OF INTEREST

With the emergence of the Internet came the democratization of art market information, traditionally a category of knowledge controlled by a small segment of the art-centric population. The rising development of extraordinary and aberrational auction sales results had the consequence of making art a high-asset category that could no longer be ignored by the financial industry. In this vein, upscale auction houses have been positioning themselves as primarily multi-prong art businesses. No longer limited to selling and liquidating high-end personal property culled from a tapestry of collectors, dealers, debtors, estates, charities, and foundations, the auction house now seeks the role of artist-estate manager. This represents a conflict of interest, as an auction house may have an economic incentive to underestimate fair market values in order to obtain exclusive selling rights and profit from their commission structure.[1] Artists' values and corresponding markets are subject to manipulation through intimate knowledge of trade players and marketing practices. Whether the conduit of sales is private or public, the distribution of stock is not necessarily conducted objectively. Sales have to benefit the trading agent. An appointed independent estate administrator working in tandem with a non-aligned appraiser and a brokerage advisor would be clear of these conflicts.

RECORD KEEPING

Few are the artists that leave a complete inventory or descriptive ledger of their life's work and possessions. Rare are the artists that are as talented as their record-keeping skills. Without the privilege of funding to employ a registrar it is unusual to find in an artist's studio a document that meticulously lists individual works. An ideal catalogue would record each work's title, date of execution, medium, exact dimensions, exhibition history, and citations in publications, as well as qualifying editions and processes; identifying authorized fabricators/publishers/printers; offering a general description and a condition report and detailing commissions, gifts, donations, and inclusion in public or private collections. In the event of gallery representation and with the benefit of the primary dealer being alive, an inventory of works and sales records might be located. At the minimum, interviews with individuals close to the artist and cognizant of his or her practice may be helpful. In the event of an artist self-representing, records may or may not exist. In each case, detective work, to determine the amount of works created, will have to be initiated. Only with an exact accounting of works can the valuation process begin.

INVENTORY

In the United States the legal definition of an artist estate is . . . everything. There is no differentiation between what encompasses art, process and source material, kitchenalia, and the remnants of a small appliance closet. A comprehensive stock inventory by category of art, and archival and studio material (sales stock as opposed to non-sales stock) as well as personal property should be the first step in organizing an estate. The next step should entail making individual condition reports to further weed out the good from the better and the finest. Lastly, locating where the art is placed—whether with a gallerist, in a museum, or in a private collection—is necessary. A compendium or full-list inventory is an essential tool for compiling an artist's catalogue raisonné. A document aimed at guiding an accurate assessment of quality can ultimately be used as one measure for authentication. A close analysis of the inventory will posit the oeuvre's historical significance and can be used as a reference to determine tiers of market value for the various categories of artworks.

Within the process of inventorying for valuation purposes, in an ideal world, it is assumed that the artist did not share studio space, or did not store his or her archives/work with that of other family members who are/were also artists in their own right. In the reality of jumbled professional multi-generational familial ties, the depth of research to identify who created what and what belongs to whom introduces a new set of complications. Prior to undertaking a valuation assignment, it is necessary to clearly define the scope of work. In extraordinary cases a reassessment might be necessary. This to illustrate the magnitude of the project and underline foreseeable problems of valuation.

METHODOLOGY

A valuation methodology that can be usefully applied to one artist's assets may not fit another's. It is a field that is fraught with questions. What is the correct market to investigate in order to obtain value data for the artist's work? What is the geographical limitation of the artist's market? Is the primary market a reliable source of information? Are the gallery's records accessible (if any exist)? Where does the paper trail of invoices lead? What is the most common market for the artist's work? How far back should one investigate auction records? How does one value artist collaborations, editions, outliers, unique works, or works created outside of the artist's known area of excellence? What is the value of works with related associations—those dedicated to, modified by, or owned by a specific person of interest? How does one assess the positive or negative value of such an association? How does one quantify an insider's association to an artist's signature accessory? For example, what is the value of a hair wig (one of many—but of how many? and perhaps not in pristine condition) presumably worn by a leading 20th-century visual artist, later mounted in a shadow box, which was signed and inscribed by the artist and gifted to another equally celebrated and sought-after artist? How does one value a miniature sculpture made to complement an established author's Lilliputian-size replica of an unpublished manuscript? Or signed and unsigned works by a noted artist dedicated to individuals outside of the art world cognoscenti (family, friends, doctors)? Or unsigned works by master artists legitimately gifted to individuals within their close professional circle (fabricators, studio managers, assistants)? Or works known to have been denied, disavowed, or repudiated by the artist? Or unsigned works immediately recognizable as being by a master artist, known to have been made specifically for a special project of unprecedented dimensions? Or works marked by the artist as "Not For Sale"? Or works that were meant to be destroyed? These questions illustrate that each artist estate has its own set of complications. There are no prefabricated answers.

VALUES

The date of the individual's death is the effective valuation date to be applied on the estate appraisal report.[2] There are several tiers of price points within the inexact science of art valuation; for estate purposes the fair market value of works of art is the monetary measure accepted by the United States Internal Revenue Service (IRS).

The IRS defines fair market value as: "the price at which the property would change hands between a willing buyer and a willing seller, neither being under any compulsion to buy or to sell and both having reasonable knowledge of relevant facts. The fair market value of a particular item of property includible in the decedent's gross estate is not to be determined by a forced sale price. Nor is the fair market value of an item of property to be determined by the sale price of the item in a market other than that in which such item is most commonly sold to the public, taking into account the location of the item wherever appropriate."[3]

Blockage discount is a business concept that takes into consideration the depression of a market if a large amount of works by the same artist were to be offered for sale at the same time. For the purpose of tax liabilities, in order to reflect the commerce of the actual market, appraisers apply a blockage discount that must take into consideration the assumption of a bulk sale and future risk premiums.[4] Several legal cases involving master artists illustrate the misapplication of discount blockage by appraisers and IRS art panel committees. Because there are no uniform standards in calculating a percentage discount within an artist estate, opinions as to what a correct economic measure is may greatly differ from one art expert to the next.[5]

ARTISTS WITHOUT WILLS AND ARTISTS WITHOUT HEIRS

Pablo Picasso and Prince Rogers Nelson (the performing artist known as Prince) are prominent examples of artists who died intestate, i.e. without a will, leaving no control over their own assets at death. Holdings are then distributed according to the degree of familial relationship. In such circumstances, the estate will be vulnerable to lawsuits. To address and settle lawsuits in an expeditious manner, executors will be compelled to monetize the artist's estate. Before it can be monetized, the estate will require a large pool of specialists to inventory, assess, and value the tiers of item categories. The difficulty in this lies in aligning market values proposed by consultants from various tiers of expertise. Fine art and design, popular memorabilia, costume, music gear, and musical instruments specialists do not share the same databases of publicly recorded prices. Copyright and future earnings are valued according to different standards. Each of these categories has specific markets and limitations, and requires a sound justification of value methodology.

Artists who die without heirs, without a will, or with a will which names an executor who does not want to serve, have their estate handled by a public administrator. It is this official who chooses the professional services, appraiser, and/or auction house to liquidate the estate. The public administrator's compensation is commission-based. In this instance there is very little control over the artist's legacy.

TIERS OF ARTISTS

Artist estate complications may result from disorganized and dispersed volumes of work and personal property. Archival, bibliographical, and photographic documentation may help to untangle chaos. Primary research, including interviews with heirs and individuals within the artist's close circle so as to obtain recollections and contextualization, is essential.

THE ARTIST RECOGNIZED AS MASTER

Not every artist will have the privilege of a well-managed estate. Unresolved questions about estate and market legacies endure today and are an inevitable part of the contemporary art market conversation—as in the case of Robert Indiana's estate, which is being disputed and legally challenged with no clear end in sight.[6] The estate's executor, Indiana's former caretaker, is accused of neglecting the artist in his late years. Many aspects of this relationship are being tested: the competence of the caretaker, chosen to manage the artist's legacy, who has no expertise in the matter of estate administration; the legitimacy of generous gifts from the artist to the caretaker; and, perhaps most troublingly, the alleged authorization by the artist, at an advanced age, to engage in a business of commercial works which are void of his underlying creative philosophy and far from his traditional practice in terms of subject matter, colour, and scale.

The phenomenon of taking artistic liberties to profitable ends or visually altering works in the name of the artist posthumously is not new and takes many forms. Degas' heirs removing unique wax, clay, and plastiline sculptures from the artist's studio and subsequently casting these models in limited bronze editions—and this without regard as to the artist's intention to exhibit these works publicly—is one example.[7] The art critic Clement Greenberg, in his role as estate executor, authorizing sandblasting of a selection of David Smith's sculptures is another.[8] In one extraordinary case, the master photographer O. Winston Link, in his advanced age, produced prints from the vintage negatives of his most recognizable work. This in itself is not an unusual course of action: many artists and artist estates have been accused of diluting market value by reissuing editions in limited editions at a later date.[9] What is unusual in the Link case is that the late prints were apparently produced under psychological duress.[10] The discovery of the photographic oeuvre of Vivian Maier, an artist whose talent was not recognized during her lifetime, is another well-documented case.[11] The question of estate market value is multilayered: has it been diminished or enhanced by historical facts, unauthorized initiatives, or anecdotal episodes?

In the event of a sudden death, who will decide what is art? Theoretically, an artist's studio could be broom-swept and every item left on the floor, stored on shelves, or discarded in bins could be subsequently labelled art. This is especially dangerous in the case of an artist with a large following and limited easel-painting production (traditionally a high-asset category). If the artist's work is known to be a market performer, i.e. recognized to be in high demand and with the potential to exceed expectations in the trade, there might be legitimate concerns to be had. Without written intentions, there is no control as to the designation of art outside of the traditional canons of paintings, sculpture, and works on paper.[12] Analogously, without contractual signatory authorization, the sorting of vintage and posthumous editions can present another tier of complications.[13] Estates and foundations may exercise the right to reject early or unfinished works by an artist as well as works conserved or restored without their stamp of approval.[14] Loans and gifts to friends donated before the artist's death and subsequently offered for sale on the public market platform may also be subject to an executor's endorsement.

The estate of a master artist may also present difficulties in the valuing of works that are atypical and/or unique from his or her known creative practice—for example, the discovery of an unusual suite of furniture made by a conceptual artist for his or her own family, or of a previously unknown collaboration. In this case, a sound methodology of value would be to research artists of comparable ilk that have engaged in this design category and then extrapolate from an achieved compendium of sales records.

THE PERFORMANCE/INTERDISCIPLINARY ARTIST

In the race to monetize an entertainer's estate so as to settle legal expenses, respond to lawsuits, and pay ancillary fees, operation managers and entrepreneurs may be appointed to commercialize the studio/residence of the deceased. From a historical-house preservation perspective, the risk lies in having an interior space that is staged to meet fans' expectations. How the public perceives the life of an artist may not mirror the reality of the artist's life. The experience of lifestyle conceived with commercial ends as a priority, selling tickets and merchandise, is diametrically opposed to the mission of a house museum, which in most instances is to teach social history. This is not unlike the phenomenon of historical homes where the interior is a composite of donations accrued through the years. The veracity of the period house/studio interior is manufactured to please patrons, not to conform to accuracy. Individual value, in this instance, is not only subject to provenance but is also related to the frequency and exposure of usage by the deceased.

THE ARTIST NO LONGER RECOGNIZED AS A MASTER

An artist once lauded as a 20th-century talent in the rank of a Renaissance master, with a prestigious exhibition track record, a presence in significant museum collections, and favourable reviews in respected trade newspapers, may at the time of his or her death have lost art historical relevance. A lack of sales records, or a weak sales presence on either the primary or secondary market, makes the valuation aspect a sensitive task. An artist may have died without fulfilling a satisfying sales record potential.

Without art market tenure, and as it falls into oblivion due to the changing ideologies of art criticism and cultural trends, such an artist's oeuvre presents a case of anaemic monetary value. As a result, in these instances, the uncomfortable reality is that the cost of assessing the economical worth of the estate far exceeds its aggregate fair market value, taking into consideration the blockage factor.

THE PROLIFIC SUNDAY ARTIST

Whether their activity is designated as craft or recreational habit, many artists have no presence on the upscale and international fine art and design market. In this instance, research for comparable artworks on e-commerce platforms is acceptable. Fair market values are calculated by extrapolating from sold works of art of comparable medium, date, process, dimensions, and quality.

CREATIVE SOURCE MATERIAL AND UNREALIZED PROJECTS

Undeveloped rolls of film, unpublished audio tapes and music recordings, props, and symbols associated with an artist's creative process are all problematic categories. Without strict instructions and guidelines left by the artist, these questions require handling on a case-by-case basis. Unpublished work, editions, merchandise, residuals from reproduction rights, licensing, and art copyright have to be accounted for, for estate tax purposes.[15] Both retrospective and potential market research is necessary to calculate future earnings.

Archival material, ephemera, early works, and works disowned by the artist[16] address additional tiers of value complication.

In summary, the outcome of a successful artist estate resolution and corresponding valuation report resides in the structure of numerous anchored factors. The depth of art historical investigation, selected methodology, and cohesive market data analysis initiated by the individual appraiser with the assistance of a collaborative research committee is key to clarifying the complicated tiers of valuation.

Notes

1 Jeffrey Marks and Amelia Brankov, "Appraisal relied on by estate undervalued paintings by $1.77 million", 31 March 2017, https://www.wealthmanagement.com/estate-planning/appraisal-relied-estate-undervalued-paintings-177-million; Robin Pogrebin, "As top-tier artists age, the art world hopes to cash in", 30 January 2017, https://www.nytimes.com/2017/01/30/arts/design/decision-time-for-aging-artists.html (both accessed 25 February 2020).

2 As fluctuating market conditions may negatively impact an estate, an executor may elect an alternative valuation date i.e. six months after the date of death. This option is irrevocable and must be made within a year of the estate tax filing date.

3 Regulation §20.2031-1: "Frequently asked questions on estate taxes," https://www.irs.gov/businesses/small-businesses-self-employed/frequently-asked-questions-on-estate-taxes (accessed 30 July 2018).

4 Ronald D. Spencer, "Blockage discounts for valuing art collections . . .", *Spencer's Art Law Journal*, vol.6, no.1, Winter 2015/2016, pp.2–8, http://www.clm.com/docs/7740959_1.pdf (accessed 8 August 2018).

5 See Emily M. Lanza, "Blockage discounts and artists' estates: the De Kooning post-mortem", 28 March 2018, https://itsartlaw.com/2018/03/28/blockage-discounts-and-artists-estates-the-de-kooning-post-mortem/ (accessed 30 July 2018); "Estate of David Smith, deceased, et al. . . .", US Court of Appeals for the Second Circuit—510 F.2d 479 (2d Cir. 1975), https://law.justia.com/cases/federal/appellate-courts/F2/510/479/194840/. Other notable benchmark blockage dispute cases include the estates of Georgia O'Keeffe and Alexander Calder.

6 Graham Bowley and Murray Carpenter, "How Robert Indiana's caretaker came to control his artistic legacy", 1 August 2018, https://www.nytimes.com/2018/08/01/arts/design/robert-indiana-legacy-jamie-thomas.html (accessed 25 February 2020).

7 Clare Vincent, "Edgar Degas (1834–1917): bronze sculpture", October 2004, https://www.metmuseum.org/toah/hd/dgsb/hd_dgsb.htm (accessed 25 February 2020).

8 Hilton Kramer, "Altering of Smith work stirs dispute", 13 September 1974, https://www.nytimes.com/1974/09/13/archives/altering-of-smith-work-stirs-dispute-stripped-of-paint.html (accessed 25 February 2020).

9 "In Sobel v. Eggleston limited edition is NO limit to subsequent editions", 15 April 2013, https://itsartlaw.com/2013/04/15/in-sobel-v-eggleston-limited-edition-is-no-limit-to-subsequent-editions/ (accessed 25 February 2020).

10 There are many articles and a documentary relating the abuse Link suffered in his advanced age at the hand of his much younger wife.

11 Jillian Steinhauer, "A Vivian Maier collector opens up about posthumous printing, Maier's only heir, and her legacy", 11 August 2014, https://hyperallergic.com/142822/a-vivian-maier-collector-opens-up-about-posthumous-printing-

maiers-only-heir-and-her-legacy/ (accessed 25 February 2020).

12 Michael Paulson, "Edward Albee's final wish: destroy my unfinished work", 4 July 2017, https://www.nytimes.com/2017/07/04/theater/edward-albees-final-wish-destroy-my-unfinished-work.html (accessed 25 February 2020).

13 The estates of Edgar Degas, Salvador Dalí, Pablo Picasso, Marc Chagall, Constantin Brancusi, and Alexander Archipenko are but a selection of problematic cases.

14 "Executed by Lucio Fontana: the story of one painting", 24 October 2014, https://www.wright20.com/auctions/2014/10/design/186 (accessed 25 February 2020).

15 The case of the estate of Vivian Maier is multifaceted and may never be settled: Jillian Steinhauer, "Settlement draws near in Vivian Maier copyright fight", 11 May 2016, https://hyperallergic.com/298101/settlement-draws-near-in-vivian-maier-copyright-fight/ (accessed 25 February 2020).

16 Henri Neuendorf, "Collectors alarmed as Gerhard Richter disowns early works from West German period", 21 July 2015, https://news.artnet.com/art-world/gerhard-richter-omits-art-from-catalogue-318665 (accessed 25 February 2020).

5

ARCHIVES AND PERSONAL LIBRARIES

Maintaining the Artist's Legacy through Scholarship, Exhibition, and Publication

Tom McNulty

How does an artist garner attention during his or her lifetime, and secure his or her place in the canon of art history? Working artists' careers are validated (or not) through sales, public exposure, and the quantity (and perhaps more importantly, the quality) of critical and scholarly reception. How can these metrics be secured and maintained, or—even better—expanded posthumously? Artists' archives and libraries present a unique opportunity in this arena. This essay will explore the evolution and current state of artists' documentation, and present an overview of best practices for the strategic placement and management of artists' libraries, personal papers, memorabilia, and digital legacy. Before we explore issues related to contemporary artists' archives and libraries, however, it behoves us to take a retrospective look at the evolution of archives and libraries in general terms, highlighting along the way the unique issues that confront artists and their estates.

BACKGROUND

Archives and libraries, along with museums, represent the three primary establishments that are increasingly referred to collectively as "memory institutions". While each has a distinctive history, with features that differentiate it from the others, all three share some overarching characteristics and objectives—the most obvious being that each represents an organized collection of physical and, increasingly, "virtual" items (texts, artworks, and the like) whose caretakers are charged with organizing, preserving, and, to varying degrees, allowing or facilitating access and use. Of the three institutional types, perhaps the most amorphous is the archive, whose very definition can vary from situation to situation. With this in mind, we will begin with an overview of archives, including the various definitional challenges of the word.

ARCHIVES

Librarians regularly encounter readers who ask simple questions like: "Do you have an archive of the *New York Times*?" Typically, the vast majority of library patrons who have asked this question really want to determine if the library owns a collection of the major national newspaper dating back to its first issue, through to the present (or some similarly large time period). They do not really want the *New York Times*'s own (institutional) archive, which would either be in the possession of the newspaper, or deposited (in its entirety, or in parts) in one or more larger "memory institutions".[1]

The term "archive" is sometimes applied to any collection of related objects, whether large or small. In an episode of the popular television series *Antiques Roadshow*, for example, a guest appraiser applies the term to a group of fewer than ten items (including ticket stubs, some photographs, and a baseball or two) related to a certain World Series baseball game.[2] Here, each item's importance, measured in monetary value, is enhanced by its relationship to the whole collection; in order to ensure the maximum value to the collection, appraisers advised its owner not to break up this important "archive". This alternative use of the term is offered to support the fact that archives are not necessarily large collections. Indeed, they can be quite small, as evidenced here.

For our purposes, archives will be considered in the traditional sense as collections of research material—whether physical or digital—assembled or produced by its creator/owner. We will explore issues that should be considered by foundations and estate planners from the perspective of various stakeholders, including the artist, his or her heirs, and institutional repositories (including general and specialized libraries, museums, and other institutions large and small).

Traditional archives feature a wide range of materials, including correspondence, business records, clipping files and the like. These might be focused on a particular person (e.g. an artist) or an organization, association, or collective (e.g. White Columns—the not-for-profit alternative exhibition space in New York City). Larger institutions (like museums) frequently maintain their institutional records internally, collecting materials from their various departments and arranging them for ease of use within the organization.

Because we are focused here on estates and foundations of individual artists that are charged with, among other functions, the maintenance and expansion of their subject's legacy, only individual artists' archives are explored. For the reader who is unfamiliar with the theory and practice of archival processing and description, I will next provide a brief overview of this all-important aspect of archival administration. There is, after all, quite a bit of pre-processing that can be accomplished before the collection is offered for donation or sale to a larger archive. But before embarking upon a plan to organize any collection, be sure that you are following the currently recognized processing standards, which will also be explored here.

ARCHIVAL COLLECTIONS: APPRAISAL AND ARRANGEMENT

Official record-keeping systems have a long history that predates the era of the modern archive. In the United States, the professionalization of archival work has its roots in the late 19th century, with the founding of the American Historical Association. It was not until the 20th century, as a result of various government-funded initiatives including the Works Progress Administration (WPA), that the archival studies field began to professionalize. Note that libraries and librarianship had been making significant progress in this direction since the middle of the 19th century. Numerous factors account for this discrepancy in the two professions' maturation, but one comes to the fore: that is, the rapid advances in printing and other technologies that resulted in a cavalcade of books, magazines, and other printed resources for which an information- and entertainment-hungry citizenry clamoured, making the public library a very heavily used community-based institution in cities and towns. During this same time period, collections of records, or archives, by contrast, continued to grow like weeds, but the actual need or desire for access to any particular archive by the public, or by the community of scholars, for that matter, continued to pale in relation to those for the offerings of its far more popular counterpart, the library. The metrics of use of libraries' holdings (published texts, for the most part) and archival collections have changed significantly over the years. Given their mass production and hence ubiquity, published works will certainly continue to attract far greater numbers of consumers, but it is those very special archival collections that make the production of a good portion of the world's books, journals, and other media even possible.

Institutional and individuals' archives are distinguishable from libraries by one important characteristic: for the most part, their contents are either unique or otherwise distinguished by the fact that they have been selected individually, and the individual pieces gain meaning from their relation to the collection as a whole. Unique works—including, for example, handwritten letters, drafts of poems, or sketches in the margins of books—are obvious candidates for preservation, as these will be cherished by scholars for the light they shed on the process of creation. Additional mass-produced items, like the exhibition announcements (in the form of flyers or postcards) amassed by an artist, for example, give us a clue as to the possible influences on the artist who thought enough of these pieces of ephemera to save and, perhaps, arrange and preserve them for future personal use, if not posterity.

The arrangement of items in a collection is probably one of the academic institution's most important defining principles of the archive, and certainly the one that differentiates the archive from the library. Generally, library materials are arranged by subject matter or by author (particularly collections of fiction), or a combination of both.[3] Archivists, by contrast, adhere to the concept of *respect des fonds*—that is, provenance, here defined as the person, persons, institution, or organization responsible for the collection's creation. Individual items relate to each other internally, even as certain of them may have counterparts in other archival or bibliographic collections. A simple illustrative example of the latter phenomenon would be correspondence received in response to a letter sent by an artist to his or her dealer. If the dealer keeps the artist's letter, it might become part of his or her archive. The response to the letter (again, assuming it is kept) would find itself within the archive of the artist. Even if both the dealer's and the artist's collections are owned by the same institution, the principle of *respect des fonds* dictates that each letter remain within the collection of its ultimate owner (i.e. its recipient), rather than that of its author/creator.

Libraries and archives both have collection development responsibilities. "Development" connotes "building", which in turn evokes images of acquiring, by whatever means, increasing amounts of material. More broadly speaking, collection development or management is the umbrella term for a variety of stewardship functions, beginning with acquisition but persisting in a variety of ways through the life cycle of the collection. That includes, at a bare minimum, arranging (i.e. classifying), housing, and preserving; archivists—particularly those employed by large repositories—usually have to justify their existence not only by the size, comprehensiveness, or other metrics of collection quality, but also by their impact on the research community. This might require regular reporting on specific activities ranging from individual consultations with researchers to responding to requests for information received via e- or snail mail, teaching classes, or mounting exhibitions (both physical and virtual), among others. That said, let us start at the beginning, with the appraisal process.

In the art world, the term "appraisal" brings to mind the process of assigning monetary values to works of fine art and other types of collectible objects. Archivists who are engaged in appraising a collection are generally trying to establish its *research* value rather than its monetary value.[4] In its Glossary, the Society of American Archivists (SAA) defines appraisal as:

> n. ~ 1. The process of identifying materials offered to an archive that have sufficient value to be accessioned. - 2. The process of determining the length of time records should be retained, based on legal requirements and on their current and potential usefulness. - 3. The process of determining the market value of an item; monetary appraisal.[5]

While librarians are sometimes called upon to provide similar appraisals of large collections,[6] their acquisitions are typically selected item by item, and acquired either by traditional sale or by gift. See below for more discussion of the issues surrounding artists' libraries and their disposition.

CLASSIFICATION

Systems of classification are based upon standards that have been developed or have been adopted by the professionals charged with implementing them. Libraries in the United States generally use one of two systems of classification: the numerical Dewey Decimal System or the alphanumeric Library of Congress System. The latter is favoured by large research libraries while the former is widely applied in school and public libraries. Note the role of the Library of Congress here. As the national library of the United States, it serves as the nation's repository of works for copyright deposit. In fact, most domestic presses submit copies of forthcoming books to it for pre-publication cataloguing. Prior to the digital era, the Library of Congress served an even more urgent need: the creation of various "Union Catalogs". These were used to locate which libraries (in addition to the Library of Congress itself) owned copies of individual published works. By the middle of the 20th century, the need for a central record of archival collections gained traction among librarians and archivists alike. The resulting product—based upon card-catalogue "technology" of the day—was the *National Union Catalog of Manuscript Collections* (NUCMC). All of these massive printed sources were digitized over the last quarter of the 20th century, affording the contemporary researcher immediate access to the riches of the world's primary-source collections.

As noted earlier, individual collections within an archive are maintained with a strict adherence to provenance. Perhaps the greatest distinction between the archive and the traditional library is the mechanism constructed to enable researchers' access to the institution's contents. The library employs the well-known catalogue; formerly composed of interfiled cards leading readers to works based upon their titles, authors, and subjects, catalogues in almost all libraries have by now migrated to a digital version of the same intellectual content. Individual collections in archives, by contrast, are rendered usable through "finding aids". These highly structured documents might represent the collection's contents in varying degrees of detail, but most US archivists adhere to the strict standards set forth by the Society of American Archivists.[7] Estates or foundations that are investigating archival institutions as potential recipients of their subject artist's collection are well advised to investigate each institution's experience with the construction of standardized finding aids; this, and additional considerations, are detailed at the end of this essay.

BORN-DIGITAL CONTENT

Since the advent of the Internet in the 1990s, tremendous human and capital resources have been expended upon the creation of digital facsimiles of both traditional library materials (largely, books and journals) as well as individual items within archival collections. Some archives digitize materials based upon use; that is, they create digital surrogates for use upon request, keeping the original under lock and key. Others digitize highlights, offering online "exhibitions" based upon selected works in their institutions.

This book is geared toward estates and foundations that are either already in existence or are in the planning stages. Most contemporary artists with active careers and markets are probably not committing a great deal of time to worrying about the future of their digital footprint, but this is where a treasure trove of archival materials of the present and near-future are being constructed and maintained. The archival folders of most of our own correspondence would likely include relatively few items handwritten, typewritten, or printed on paper over the past few decades. Rather, it is the collected emails, tweets, and perhaps Instagram or Facebook accounts that will dominate the artist's archive of the future. With this in mind, it behoves living artists and their estate planners to investigate the future of these digital resources. As an immediate measure, it might even make sense to print out, on acid-free paper, emails that are particularly important to the artist's life and career. It might come as a surprise to executors that while they are in control of the physical and monetary assets of the estate for which they are charged, individual state laws differ as to the future of any person's digital assets; in many cases, ownership of, and even access to sources like Google email might require specific language in the artist's last will and testament. This might be one of the most important discussions to have in the estate planning of any artist who is at all concerned with his or her legacy. Perhaps even more importantly, if the artist's estate or foundation ultimately decides to place the archival collection (whether by donation or sale) in a repository (i.e. institutional archive or library), the receiving institution's experience with born-digital content might be an important issue to investigate in the negotiation process.

Contrary to popular belief, digital media are not eternal; indeed, some early computerized information resources were rendered unreadable. As the *New York Times* columnist Stephen Manes has observed, "The archival problems begin with the furtive nature of digital data storage itself. Paper may crumble, but its condition is usually obvious based on its appearance. But for a typical disk or tape, short of running it in a proper computer, there is no easy way to determine whether it holds data or whether the information is deteriorating."[8] Archival institutions' expertise with, and infrastructure for dealing with issues relating to long-term preservation represent just one of several factors that donor estates and foundations should consider in their selection of a final repository; additional factors are identified at the end of this essay.

ARTISTS' PERSONAL LIBRARIES

Personal libraries can tell us a great deal about their owners. Those of fictional works' authors are particularly prized, as these often shed very direct light on their owners' influences. Indeed, entire books have been devoted to the libraries and reading habits of literary authors. While visual artists' influences are often (or usually) more visual than verbal, like practitioners in other fields their libraries can give us an insight into their intellectual interests and development. As such, their libraries' placement within a larger institutional collection might accompany the estate or foundation's sale or donation of their subject artist's archive. The value of maintaining the library as a collection will vary greatly from artist to artist. For example, if an artist's library includes books whose illustrations or other content correspond directly to his or her subject matter, these items should be maintained—preferably in tandem with the artist's archival collection.

Very often, libraries are offered collections of books of varying degrees of value or quality. Some, for example, include a great many inexpensive paperbacks in less than pristine condition; at the other end of the spectrum, some libraries include a great many rare, valuable books. If a university, museum, or other large archival institution accepts an artist's papers, they will consider accepting even a mediocre collection of books. In a large library with a circulating collection, items that are not terribly valuable and have no personal annotations or inscriptions might be relegated to the regular stacks. Works that are in some way "special"—for example, a book that has been used directly in some way by the artist in the production of his or her work—would be given special treatment; this title would probably be added to the non-circulating, rare books room collection. Note that very large collections of books are often a problem for libraries; physical space is a major issue in an ever-increasing number of "memory institutions", but especially so in libraries. If a library is reluctant to accept an artist's library, there is a reason. It is very expensive to process and house book collections, and most large libraries will probably already own a large percentage of the published titles in any artist's collection.

POINTS TO CONSIDER IN THE DONATION OF ARCHIVAL AND LIBRARY COLLECTIONS

Very few foundations have the resources required to process, house, and provide access in perpetuity to their subject artist's archives and library. Most will, at some point in time, consider donating or selling their collections to a larger institution. The following represent two of the key points to consider in the selection of the most appropriate repository:

- Consider placing the collection with an institution in which related artists' archives are housed.
- Related to the above, consider donation rather than sale. If the collection languishes for years in a very large institution, unprocessed and unavailable to the community of researchers, the resulting lack of research and, by extension, of publication and exhibition, might negate the financial gains of the sale.

Notes

1 A search of the database Archives Grid conducted on 19 June 2018 reveals that the *New York Times* has donated various historical components of its institutional archive to the New York Public Library. Examples include discrete sections, including "New York Times Company records, 1838–2006" and "New York Times Company Records. Pamphlets 1851–2006".

2 *Antiques Roadshow*, Public Broadcasting Service (PBS), June 2014, https://www.pbs.org/wgbh/roadshow/season/19/birmingham-al/appraisals/henry-elmore-archive-ca-1960--201403T05/ [accessed 22 March 2020].

3 In rare instances, libraries have adopted alternative arrangement schemes, including physical size of individual volumes—a method that is intended to make maximum use of shelving space.

4 Note, however, that research value would be an important factor to be considered in the establishment of the collection's monetary value by a professional appraiser, if this process is undertaken prior or post-acquisition.

5 https://www2.archivists.org/glossary/terms/a/appraisal [accessed 25 February 2020].

6 Frequently, libraries are offered gifts of books, magazines, and other items. Before accepting a donation, the library will survey the collection on site before deciding whether or not to accept the entire collection for integration into the library.

7 *Describing Archives: A Content Standard*, second edition, Chicago: Society of American Archivists, 2013.

8 Stephen Manes, "Time and technology threaten digital archives . . .", *New York Times*, 7 April 1998, https://www.nytimes.com/1998/04/07/science/time-and-technology-threaten-digital-archives.html [accessed 8 April 2020].

6
SPECIFIC LEGACIES

Eric M. Wolf

> It takes a great deal of time and thought to install work carefully. This should not always be thrown away. Most art is fragile and some should be placed and never moved again. Some work is too large, complex and expensive to move. Somewhere a portion of contemporary art has to exist as an example of what the art and its context were meant to be. Somewhere, just as the platinum-iridium meter guarantees the tape measure, a strict measure must exist for art of this time and place. Otherwise art is only show and monkey business.
>
> *Donald Judd,* The Chinati Foundation/La Fundación Chinati, *1987*[1]

Ultimately (and obviously), an artist's principal and greatest legacy is the work that survives him or her, and its subsequent reception. The importance of controlling the fate and reception of works from beyond the grave varies greatly among artists; indeed, there is not even consensus among artists concerning conservation of works of art when they leave the studio. None the less, most art is sold to collectors and institutions who will exhibit, store, and care for these works as they please. Such work may be sold by a collector, deaccessioned by a museum or institution, and acquired by others; this is the typical life of art objects, be they paintings, drawings, prints, photographs, or even most sculpture and installation art. There are, however, specific types of works that do not and cannot follow this typical path. Some examples of such work would include public art projects, truly site-specific works, artist-installed and sanctioned hangings of their own work, or, broadly, any work with aspirations towards permanence regarding its context and installation. While such works often present the most difficulty for later stewardship, they are usually the most important works for establishing and preserving an artist's historical, intellectual, and artistic legacy (should an artist be fortunate enough to have had the opportunity in his or her lifetime to realize such a work).

The works that will be explored below are objects that are regarded as major works and works of record both by the artists who created them and due to the circumstances of their commissions or acquisitions and installations. These examples highlight various problems that accompany the work that should be the capstone of the legacy of an artist. This essay considers successes, failures, and compromises that have preserved, destroyed, or altered these specific works, and in so doing, altered the artistic legacies of their creators.

PUBLIC ART, PUBLIC TRUST, AND ITS LIMITS

Among the oldest forms of opportunities afforded artists for large, permanent installations of works are those offered by large government commissions. Yet these are also among the most fraught. Throughout the history of art these commissions are threatened by regime changes (consider the history of the movement of Michelangelo's *David*, whose meaning either supported or challenged the various regimes of Renaissance Florence until it became merely an iconic image of the place of this city, its patrons, and the great Michelangelo himself and was once again relocated, this time to a museum).[2] In a nation that purports to be a democracy, the notion of such public art is further complicated, as it naturally depends on the consent of "the people", though the metrics for determining the will of the citizenry in such matters are often vague. As recent debates in the United States regarding monuments to Confederate soldiers and politicians reveal, artistic merit or its lack do not necessarily enter into the discussion, nor should they, as the discourse is rightly concerned with whether or not such works are acts of state oppression against parts of the very people over whom the state exerts power.

Among the most successful and beloved of such public sculpture must be numbered Maya Lin's *Vietnam Veterans Memorial* (1982), just off the National Mall in Washington D.C.[3] This competition-winning work not only elevated the then-obscure architecture student Lin to prominence in the art world, it also was a major milestone in healing a divided nation regarding the horrible scars caused by the divisive and fraught war in Vietnam fought in the previous two decades. Yet even this work, which was immediately embraced by veterans, their families, and the general public was initially opposed by conservative politicians and their constituents, to the point that a more conventional, representational sculptural group of monumental soldiers was placed at Lin's memorial's site, altering the powerful simplicity of her granite wall of names which left interpretation to the viewer.[4] The overwhelming success of Lin's work has outlived the political controversy around its creation, but the statuary group remains, though largely ignored, at the site.

If Maya Lin's *Vietnam Veterans Memorial* can be considered the greatest success of such federally funded public commissions, the highest-profile failure would no doubt be Richard Serra's *Tilted Arc*, commissioned in 1979 by the United States

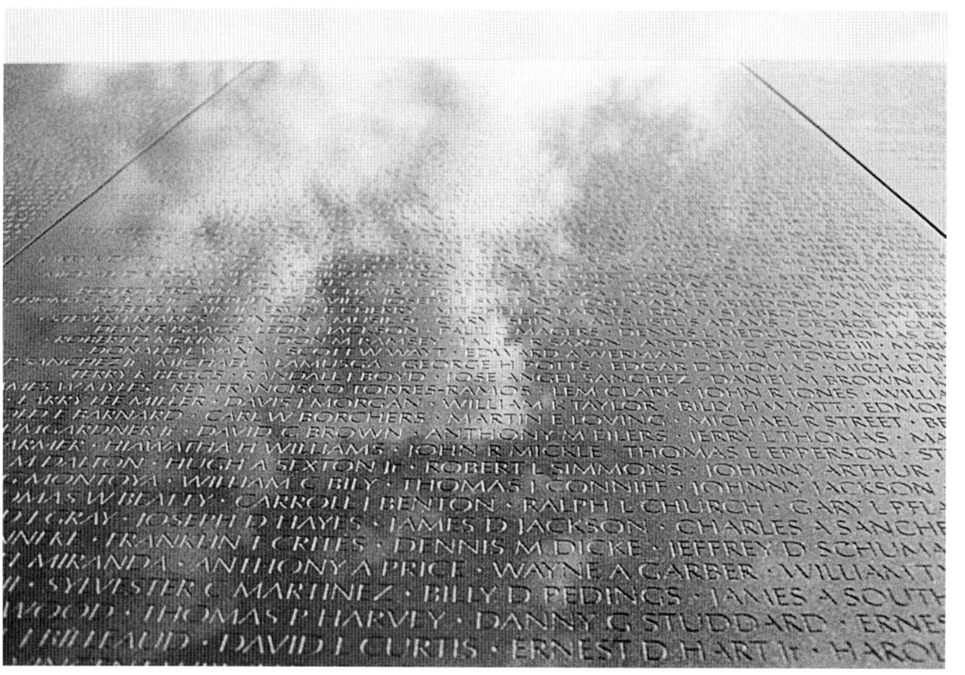
GEORGE H POTTS · EDGAR D THOMAS
RANDALL J BOYD · JOSE ANGEL SANCHEZ · DANIEL M BROWN
REY FRANCISCO TORRES-RAMOS · LEM CLARK · JOHN R JONES
LARRY LEE MILLER · DAVIS J MORGAN · WILLIAM K TAYLOR · BILLY H WYATT
CARL W BORCHERS · MARTIN E LOVING · MICHAEL R STREET
DAVID C BROWN · ANTHONY M EILERS · JERRY L THOMAS
HIAWATHA H WILLIAMS · JOHN R MICKLE · THOMAS E EPPERSON
HUGH A SEXTON Jr · ROBERT L SIMMONS · JOHNNY ARTHUR
WILLIAM C BILY · THOMAS J CONNIFF · JOHNNY JACKSON
CARROLL J BENTON · RALPH L CHURCH
JOSEPH D HAYES · JAMES D JACKSON · CHARLES A SANCHEZ
FRANKLIN T CRITES · DENNIS M DICKE
ANTHONY A PRICE · WAYNE A GARBER
SYLVESTER C MARTINEZ · BILLY D PEDINGS
THOMAS P HARVEY · DANNY G STUDDARD
DAVID L CURTIS · ERNEST D HART Jr

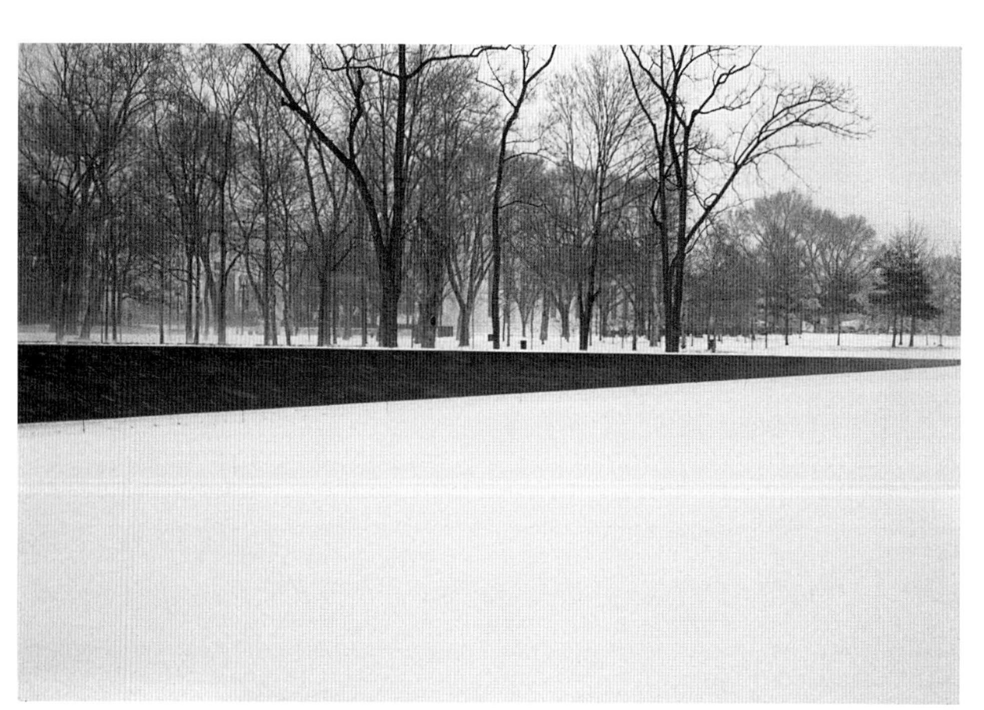

General Services Administration for Foley Federal Plaza in New York City and completed in 1981.[5] Unlike the then-unknown Lin who won a competition for her memorial, Serra was a leading artist of his generation and was selected for the commission. The colossal work he designed for the space was consistent with his oeuvre, a solid sheet of his preferred medium of COR-TEN steel, 37 metres (120 feet) long and 3.7 metres (12 feet) tall, creating a giant arc across the centre of the public plaza. Workers in the vicinity of the piece claimed to be inconvenienced by its presence, blocking direct passage across the square, and high-ranking federal employees filed suit for its removal. After much litigation and controversy, the work was dismantled in 1989 and placed in storage. Serra stood by his intention that the work was site-specific and therefore intended only for its original site and could not be installed elsewhere; thus the removal of the work from its intended site equalled its destruction. While it is hard to argue against the fact that the philistines won, in a society that purports to be democratic, such work in a public sphere must be amenable to the people; the instruments of said society, in this case the courts, here ruled against the artist, and the work, irrespective of its importance and merits, was erased from the physical legacy of the artist, though it did, perhaps, enhance his mythic legacy in the history of art.

LARGE, PERMANENT INSTITUTIONAL COMMISSIONS

Some very fortunate artists are granted the rare chance of creating large, permanent works for private institutions and patrons: museum, religious, or other corporate clients. Freed from the ebb and flow of politics and the vagaries of questions of "public trust", such works are among the greatest opportunities to create lasting visual legacies. They typically come only late in the careers of the most prominent artists, but afford such artists the ability to make works that serve as summations of their ideas, practices, and oeuvres. Of course, for such works to succeed, the institutional patrons must be as committed to the project as the artist and must back up the artist's vision completely.

Emblematic of such a shared commitment between artist and patron is the commission that would become the Rothko Chapel in Houston, Texas. It was initially intended to be the university chapel of the Roman Catholic University of St Thomas, and a chapel was part of architect Philip Johnson's master plan for the campus as early as 1957.[6] In 1964, Houston philanthropists and patrons of the University John and Dominique de Menil commissioned Mark Rothko to paint a cycle of 14 paintings to decorate the chapel. After a series of well-documented disputes, first between Rothko and Johnson, and later between the de Menils and the Basilian Fathers who ran the university, Johnson was fired as architect, the chapel was re-sited to land owned by the patrons, and it became the non-sectarian institution dedicated to art, spirituality, and human rights that we know today. The chapel is defined by Rothko's 14 dark

Maya Lin, *Vietnam Veterans Memorial*, Washington D.C., 1982

Maya Lin, Vietnam Veterans Memorial, Washington D.C., 1982 (detail)

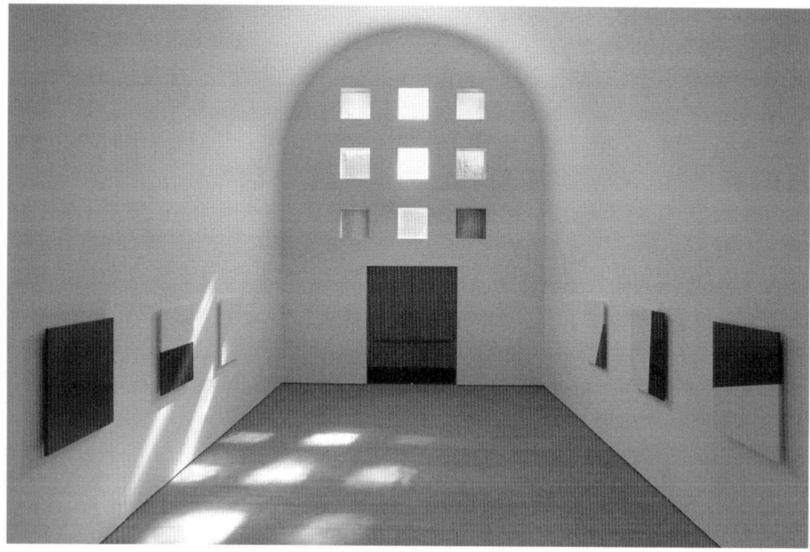

Ellsworth Kelly, *Austin*, Blanton Museum of Art, University of Texas at Austin, 2015

canvases, still following the initial Catholic programme of the stations of the cross, with three triptychs, though devoid of an altar or any liturgical devices. Here the patrons clearly advanced the vision of the artist, protecting it from outside threats. Unfortunately, Rothko died before the opening of the chapel in 1971.

More recently, the realization of Ellsworth Kelly's *Austin* at the Blanton Museum of Art at the University of Texas at Austin, which opened to the public in February 2018, reflects the importance of committed patrons. Initially conceived as a private chapel on a vineyard in Santa Barbara, California in the 1980s, the project would sit dormant for close to 30 years before being brought to life through the tenacity of Ellsworth Kelly, the Houston dealer Hiram Butler, officials of the University of Texas, and Blanton director Simone Wicha. While Kelly lived to see ground broken on the site in Austin, he too passed before the completion of the work.[7]

Yet even solid backing and firm commitments on behalf of institutions do not ensure the survival of large site-specific works. *Tending Blue*, a "Skyspace" created by artist James Turrell at the Nasher Sculpture Center in Dallas, Texas, completed in 2003, was intended to be just such a permanent installation. Like all of Turrell's skyspaces, *Tending Blue* revolves around a central opening in its ceiling that requires an unimpaired view of the sky. When real-estate developers erected a large high-rise building adjacent to the sculpture garden housing the work, there was little the museum could do to protect the work. When litigation failed, the artist demanded the work be closed, though he proposed alterations that would allow for it to be reopened. The museum has not been able to enact these proposals and the work remains closed.[8]

DONALD JUDD'S "PERMANENCE"

Perhaps the only way to ensure that a work exists permanently (or as close to permanently as is possible in a world that exists in time and space) is to place it in a remote environment and make sure that the artist has absolute control over its positioning and stewardship. This was certainly the aspiration of Donald Judd in his placement of his own work and that of other artists he selected in Marfa, Texas at his own properties and in the collection of the Chinati Foundation. Of course, such practices are only possible when an artist has incredible financial resources behind him or her, or the support of similarly wealthy patrons. In the latter situation, those patrons will have some control of both the execution and later stewardship of the works, unless complete legal control and ownership is included or obtained as part of the commission or after the completion of the work.

Despite having enjoyed an extremely successful career, Judd felt that too much of his intent had been violated by collectors, and that works had even been recreated outside of his authorization. He thus felt the need to set up his own foundation and wrest control of other foundations that had been tasked with stewardship of his work, to make certain that his artistic legacy was properly preserved.[9] Unfortunately, most artists will not have the wherewithal to undertake such colossal projects; further such works become accessible to a very small group of people with the time and means to visit them. On the other hand, they exist exactly how the artist envisioned them and do indeed create an ideal metric for understanding other works in the artist's oeuvre that do not have the ideal siting, installation, and stewardship.

CREATED AND RECREATED LEGACIES

All of the examples of "specific legacies" cited above are firmly rooted in the notion of the primacy of the artist's intent and vision, whether they were public commissions, institutional commissions, private commissions, or works executed, owned, and placed by the artist on his or her own property. Their veracity as the artist's true measure of his or her own intent and desired legacy is clearly recorded, even when the works themselves do not survive or have been altered. Yet other classes of work exist that are often perceived in a similar light.

There are art objects that become works of record of artists that were never intended to be permanent installations, but are acquired by institutions and so installed. A prime example of this would be Judy Chicago's iconic work of feminist installation art *The Dinner Party* of 1974–9, which was acquired by the Brooklyn Museum in 2002 and is now permanently installed and forms the centrepiece of the museum's Elizabeth A. Sackler Center for Feminist Art.[10] While such a permanent installation may not have been the initial intent of the artist, her approval of it is not in question.

Progressively more ambiguous are two beautiful installations of works by Agnes Martin. The first, in the Harwood Museum of Art in Taos, New Mexico, is an installation of seven paintings by Martin in an octagonal gallery. The museum's website states:

> This gallery was built specifically for these paintings. Martin, who never conceived of her work as a series, or as being exhibited in this fashion, was thrilled by the display – even going so far as to suggest the four yellow Donald Judd benches which are arranged under the Gallery's oculus. During her life Martin visited this gallery frequently, and would sit quietly on the benches experiencing its unique setting. Scholars have compared the Harwood Museum of Art's Agnes Martin Gallery to the Matisse Chapel in Vence, Corbusier's Ronchamp Chapel, and the Rothko Chapel in Houston.[11]

While thus not intended by the artist, the seven works were created by her in the same year (1993) and she was aware and approved of their installation in this manner. However, the comparison with such works as Matisse's Vence Chapel, the Rothko Chapel, or Le Corbusier's Ronchamp become problematic as those three examples were all clearly intended to be site-specific, permanent installations, and all their parts were designed in relation with each other and with the whole installation, which was conceived as a work in and of itself. More complex still is the Agnes Martin installation at the San Francisco Museum of Modern Art. As at Taos, the SFMOMA installation places seven paintings by Martin in a bespoke gallery in the form of an octagon. Unlike the Harwood installation, the paintings in the SFMOMA gallery (all part of the Fisher Collection) were painted over the course of three decades, acquired at different times, and installed together without the knowledge of the artist, many years after her passing. In both cases there exists no clear statement of the artist regarding the installation in an octagonal gallery, which has art historical associations with sacred space, particularly the sacred spaces of Roman Catholicism—this being the very reason Mark Rothko employed it at his eponymous chapel in Houston, which was originally intended as a Roman Catholic chapel for the University of St Thomas. This link with sacred form is not lost on viewers. In an early review of the installation of the Fisher Collection, *San Francisco Chronicle* art critic Charles Desmarais observed, "The SFMOMA gallery devoted to Martin's work has rapidly acquired an informal nickname 'the Chapel,' which seems perfectly appropriate to works that evoke a sense of the spiritual."[12] Given that the spirituality which Martin is known to have been interested in derived chiefly from East Asian religion, and not the Roman Catholic tradition that Rothko embraced in his chapel, the appropriateness of such installation for Martin cannot be interpreted as deriving from her artistic intent. This begs the question of whether this installation can be seen as reflecting her artistic legacy or the vision of curators, collectors, and exhibition designers.

Yet there are also cases when it is none other than curators and exhibition designers who alone allow an audience to understand the actual intent of artists who were never able to realize their goals of creating such specific legacies in their own lifetimes. Though not permanently installed, the Solomon R. Guggenheim Museum's recent exhibition "Hilma af Klint: Paintings for the Future" exhibited works of an artist who intentionally repressed the display of her work until after her death. Her fascinating oeuvre was rooted in esoteric spiritual practices of her times, including Theosophy, Anthroposophy, and Rosicrucianism, as well as channelling the dead. A very important series of her work, *Paintings for the Temple* (1906–15), was executed for a round temple she was never able to realize. So the Guggenheim's Frank Lloyd Wright-designed rotunda, with its round, colossal, temple-like form, becomes the closest proxy to the artist's desired experience that could possibly exist.[13]

CONCLUSION

While there are many ways in which artists can attempt to control their legacies, ultimately, it is the survival, stewardship, and accessibility of their work that will determine how and if they are remembered. Other tools, such as archives, single-artist museums, catalogues raisonnés, and important retrospective exhibitions will always be available to those interested in learning more of an artist and of his or her oeuvre or intent. Yet all of these are curated and mediated by other minds and hands. A very blessed and fortunate group of artists are afforded the rare opportunity of creating large, seemingly permanent, installations of their work. These works not only epitomize their careers but also offer what Donald Judd has termed a "meter" for understanding the rest of their respective oeuvres. When evaluating such works, it is important to consider what went into their creation, and to understand the various circumstances of their survival, to properly evaluate whether indeed these works do form "specific legacies". When they do, we as viewers get to enjoy a rare opportunity of appreciating an artist's intent on a grand scale, and with little mediation.

Notes

1 Judd quoted in Marianne Stockebrand, *Chinati: The Vision of Donald Judd*, New Haven, CT: Yale University Press, 2010, p.281.

2 See section "David" in Mark Stocker, "Public monument", 2003, *Grove Art Online*, https://doi.org/10.1093/gao/9781884446054.article.T059390 (accessed 22 April 2019).

3 "Lin, Maya", 2003, Grove Art Online, https://doi.org/10.1093/gao/9781884446054.article.T051132 (accessed 22 April 2019.

4 The controversy surrounding the memorial and the political decision to add a figurative sculpture by Frederick Hart is recorded in countless contemporaneous newspaper articles, such as Isabel Wilkerson, "'Art War' erupts over Vietnam veterans memorial", *Washington Post*, 8 July 1982, Thursday, Final Edition.

5 For documents of the proceedings around *Tilted Arc*, see Clara Weyergraf-Serra and Martha Buskirk, *The Destruction of Tilted Arc: Documents* (October Books), Cambridge, MA: MIT Press, 1991.

6 Sheldon Nodelman, *The Rothko Chapel Paintings: Origins, Structure, Meaning*, Austin, TX: University of Texas Press, 1997. See also Susan J. Barnes, *The Rothko Chapel: An Act of Faith*, Houston, TX: Menil Foundation, 1989.

7 Eric M. Wolf, 'Austin', *CAA.Reviews*, New York, NY: College Art Association, 2018.

8 Michael Granberry, "'Destroyed!' The Nasher posts bold new sign in front of (what used to be) James Turrell's 'Tending, (Blue)'", *Dallas Morning News*, 9 August 2012.

9 For an explanation of Judd's strong feelings on the misuse of his work and violations of his artistic intent, see Donald Judd, "Una stanza per Panza" (1990), reprinted in Donald Judd, Judd Foundation, and David Zwirner (Gallery), *Donald Judd: Writings*, edited by Flavin Judd and Caitlin Murray, New York, NY: Judd Foundation, 2016, pp.630–99.

10 "The Dinner Party by Judy Chicago", https://www.brooklynmuseum.org/exhibitions/dinner_party (accessed 22 April 2019).

11 "Agnes Martin Gallery", http://www.harwoodmuseum.org/exhibitions/view/59 (accessed 22 April 2019).

12 Charles Desmarais, "SFMOMA: our 2-hour tour", *San Francisco Chronicle*, 13 May 2016.

13 Tracey R. Bashkoff (ed.), *Hilma Af Klint: Paintings for the Future*, New York, NY: Guggenheim Museum Publications, 2018.

7

INTERVIEW WITH LISA LE FEUVRE

Lisa Le Feuvre is the inaugural Executive Director of an artist-endowed foundation dedicated to furthering the creative legacies of Nancy Holt and Robert Smithson. Kathy Battista interviewed her at Sotheby's Institutue of Art in New York on 11 July 2018.

KB: What do you think are the biggest challenges to be the first Executive Director of the Holt/Smithson Foundation?

LLF: It is, without question, such an honour to be there right at the start of a foundation, to think about a beginning, and the potential of an end. We are growing this foundation into being by thinking through what we want our impact and legacy to be.

The biggest challenge in being the first director is ensuring the structure is right for not just now, but also for my successors. An organization is a living body and, like all bodies, it needs a strong skeleton and it needs to be healthy. We are talking today at the start of building this foundation—in fact, if we were a building, what we are doing now is setting the foundations. We are spending a lot of time getting all of our policies ready—and this is such an interesting and important process. Policies are led by values and, in the case of an artist-endowed foundation, these values come from the artist, or artists, whose name you bear. And we are being incredibly thorough, simply so it doesn't have to be done again and to enable us to go forward spending time on our programmes.

I have learned from experience that if you know what your mission is you can find all of the answers to questions that come your way—even super-difficult ones. Our mission is to continue the creative and investigative spirit of Nancy Holt and Robert Smithson. Both artists were born in 1938; Smithson passed away in 1973 and Holt in 2014. These are two artists that developed innovative ways of exploring our relationship with the planet, and who expanded the limits of artistic practice. Our job is to formulate programmes developing their creative legacies, continuing the transformation they brought to the world of art and ideas. It's a big responsibility to do this—and I am so fortunate to be a part of the team initiating this project.

Creative legacies are central to us, and creative legacies are different from legacies. There is this amazing thing the critic and curator Lawrence Alloway once wrote about legacies. He noted that the best way an artist keeps their legacy is by having different generations of artists take their ideas and run with them to places he or she would never think to go. And in explaining his point, he looked to Robert Smithson. I think for all artist-endowed foundations your mission is to get people talking about the artists you are named after, and to keep the conversation going. You can only do that if you work with artists, writers, curators, and thinkers, and it's got to be about developing new ideas. Holt and Smithson recalibrated the possibilities of art. So that means their foundation has to recalibrate the possibilities of art. It's a massive task we've got, and everything comes down to the values of the artists.

KB: How does their position relate to today's issues with the planet?

LLF: I think this term that is so familiar to us, "environmentalist", wasn't so familiar to them. And of course, Smithson was as interested in pumping derricks and freeways as he was in nature. Their work was, and is, concerned with human beings and their place in the world. And in 2018, we know that human beings and their place in the world is all about the environment: Holt's and Smithson's work today is more urgent and relevant than ever. There's this great 1972 text by Smithson called *Cultural Confinement*—originally published in the catalogue for documenta 5—where he asks (and I am paraphrasing now) why nobody ever wants to go on vacation to a garbage dump. Why not? We create them. And if you think about Nancy Holt's work—it is all about perception. She makes us look harder, and it was so forward-thinking that she worked on land reclamation projects—there is *Up and Under* in Finland, and the unfinished *Sky Mound* in New Jersey. Our task at Holt's and Smithson's foundation is to investigate and demonstrate how these artists' works are necessary and relevant for our times, past times, and future times.

KB: How familiar were you with Nancy's and Robert's work before this?

LLF: I knew their work really well. In fact, their work is the reason why I became interested in art in the first place. I remember being introduced to them both (along with artists such Gego [Gertrud Goldschmidt] and Gordon Matta-Clark) by an inspirational tutor while I was studying architecture—and at this time I had never even stepped into an art gallery. It was like a bolt of lightning—I realized that art really did matter, there was something at stake with it. I read everything I could on them both, and that was it: I was hooked on the power of art.

KB: Did you have a model for setting up the Foundation?

LLF: There are three specific foundations we spent a lot of time thinking about.

The Rauschenberg Foundation is one—they absolutely think about making a difference in the world. I love the way they are bold: this is a foundation committed to testing ideas—if something works it continues, if it does not work there are details to develop and learn from.

Another foundation model we looked at is the foundation of the Patricia Phelps de Cisneros and Gustavo Cisneros Collection, based in Caracas and New York. What is so innovative, and brilliant, is that this foundation works in the United

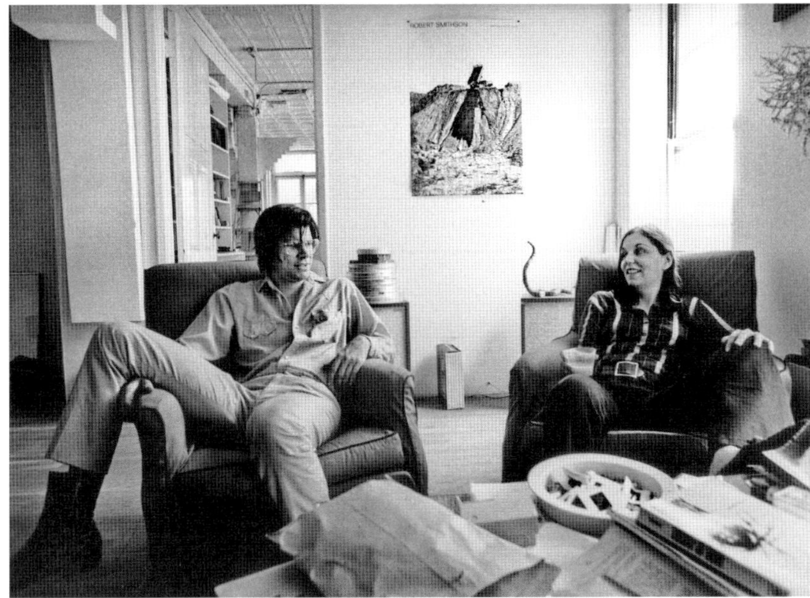

Robert Smithson and Nancy Holt in their West Village loft, New York City, 1970. © Holt/Smithson Foundation, Licensed by VAGA at ARS, New York. Photograph by Gianfranco Gorgoni.

States without a building: it is partnerships that matter. And, both the mission and vision are clear: the ambition is to change the way museums in America collect, and to ensure Latin American artists are embedded in that discourse. This has been achieved by enabling people to be in museums doing this work, and with this there has been change in the culture of collecting. I spent a lot of time thinking about this model, and it helped us decide we would not have a building. Partnerships are what matter to us too—and you can just see how effective Patricia Cisneros has been by not constructing the Cisneros Centre for Latin American Arts. Every time you have a building, whether it's a home or a museum, almost two thirds of your budget goes into looking after it. And we want to do something else than be real-estate managers.

I also learned so much from my last position. Until 2017 I led the Henry Moore Institute, a fundamental part of the Henry Moore Foundation in Great Britain. Moore did this amazing thing when he set up his foundation in 1977: he knew that for his work to be necessary and relevant, sculpture had to exist, and he knew his own work would go in and out of fashion. It is from this imperative that the Henry Moore Institute came to exist—a centre for the study of sculpture that keeps the context of Moore alive.

More broadly, we continue to learn from the growing sector of artist-endowed foundations—such as the Dedalus Foundation, Helen Frankenthaler Foundation, Willem de Kooning Foundation, Mike Kelley Foundation—and from the Aspen Institute Artist-Endowed Foundations Initiative. All prioritize the importance of good governance and good financial management—this is key.

KB: It's interesting because we become enslaved to the real estate.
LLF: Right. And we need to bear in mind that artist-endowed foundations are different from any other institutions in the art ecology. They are different because they're independent. Every museum will always be dependent on its donors. A commercial gallery will always be dependent on the market. But an artist-endowed foundation is independent, and it starts with art. Not having a building enables you to keep independence to an even greater extent.
KB: Will part of your plan will be to engage younger artists or artists from other parts of the world?
LLF: The first thing we have to do is get our own house in order, and make sure that everything works. Down the line we absolutely want to commission artists—it is integral to this idea of creative legacies.

One of the things I'm thinking through at the moment with my board and with the team is about how to commission artists. We are thinking about what's needed, thinking about what museums need, and what artists need. We own some land in fairly remote places, and one of my dreams is that we will commission artists in partnership with museums. The model we are debating (and remember I am just in dream mode still!) is to invite an artist to respond to these specific plots of land, and for the resultant work to be donated to a museum. Smithson talked often about the site/non-site dialectic. Taking inspiration from this, the invitation will be that the artist works with the land and makes a work that can operate in a museum context.

Thinking about the Rauschenberg Foundation model of testing, the Holt/Smithson Foundation Artist Commissions will start with a series of projects on an island in Maine in 2020. We will make sure we learn from our experience of *The Island Project*, as we are calling this, then apply these lessons to our second plot two years later with *The Inland Project*, a land parcel in Utah. Then (okay I am really dreaming here), two years later again we will work with this knowledge in other sites that are not part of our ownership, and beyond the US. Being time-bound is part of this commissioning vision—perhaps each of these three phases last five years, working with one artist per year. We are thinking about in the programme addressing ideas of near and elsewhere, of remote and local . . . and most importantly we're thinking about the spirit of Nancy Holt and Robert Smithson.
KB: Will there be access to the archive, the sketchbooks, for scholars and for the public? Without a building, how are you going to cope with that?
LLF: Smithson's papers are already held at the Archives of American Art, and Holt willed her papers there too. Developing scholarship is key to our mission and we are working on creating an expansive website that will be the hub of all things Holt and Smithson. Our website will be the equivalent of a building. Integral will be images, critical essays, exhibition histories, artist writings, sketches . . . all the things a researcher needs. We will commission a mix of emerging and established scholars, artists, and curators to write on Holt and Smithson too—each will be short texts

opening up scholarship in new directions. If we do sunset, we will need to think about what we will do after our life with this resource, and will find the right home where it can live beyond our foundation. Very importantly, this resource will be free to everyone—this a value high on our list.

KB: Did Holt and Smithson leave instructions for this foundation? Or was it created posthumously?

LLF: Smithson died unexpectedly in 1973, and he was a young man, in his thirties. You don't think about that kind of thing when you're 35. His estate and legacy was looked after by Holt—Nancy Holt and Robert Smithson met in 1958 and married in 1963. We know Smithson's work so well because of all the work she did. Holt literally willed the foundation into being—and she wanted there to be a foundation that would look after legacies and encourage scholarship.

KB: Did she select the board members?

LLF: She chose people to be on the board whom she trusted. As we gradually expand the board, we are bearing in mind people whom Holt wanted to be involved, and bringing skills in governance and charitable foundations onto the board. You have to get the governance right—foundations are the most tightly regulated organizational structures in the US.

KB: Smithson is the better-known artist. Are you going to try to recalibrate that and promote Holt's work more?

LLF: You are right—and we are prioritizing Holt. 2018 was our first year of activity—we had formed two years previously, and I was appointed at the end of 2017. We were so happy that this year we could enable Dia Art Foundation to acquire her earthwork *Sun Tunnels* and the room-sized installation *Holes of Light*. It would have been a dream come true for Nancy, having Dia as the home for these works. And Dia also worked on a wonderful exhibition of her work at Dia:Chelsea. This immediately addresses exactly what you said.

In the near future we want to look at publishing Holt's writings, get people reading them. We want to make sure that her extant work is cared for really well. We're working with the amazing museum Bildmuseet in northern Sweden to develop in 2023 a solo exhibition of Holt's work that will travel. We are going to focus on Holt, but also will not forget Smithson—he has wonderful drawings included in a forthcoming group exhibition at the Centre Pompidou, we want to publish a new edition of his writings, and we are thinking through a few long-term exhibition projects.

KB: Does the foundation have instructions about the right to recreate works that were destroyed or temporary? Holt's *Missoula Ranch Locators: Vision Encompassed* from 1972, for example—can they be recreated?

LLF: In all truth: we really don't know yet. Every time we come across a question we don't know the answer to, we will make a conference about it. More minds on a matter are always best. Should works be reconstructed? Maybe, maybe not. And then it depends on the stage that the work was at. And why it no longer exists.

There is one work, though, that we know can be brought to realization as Holt literally put a spike in the ground on its site and worked-up complete plans and installation instructions. Located in Santa Monica, it is called *Solar Web*. Everything was planned, it just missed getting through planning permission by one vote. That is so close to being completed by the artist that, probably (and the "probably" word is really important), it should be realized. But, if there's another work that was just a sketch, maybe it shouldn't be realized. I think we need to just think about it on a case-by-case basis.

KB: For Smithson I guess it was so sudden, but for Holt it sounds like she had time to make plans.

LLF: Well, she had short notice that she was going to disappear from the world. There's not much detail that she left us, but the values and the principles are there.

KB: Is part of the foundation's remit to conserve and look after works by Smithson and Holt? Because that seems like a huge task.

LLF: It is, and it is something Holt specifically said in her will she wanted us to do. Conservation with Holt and Smithson's work is a really interesting question, and a complicated one. Entropy and the passage of time were important to both. To conserve a work like Smithson's *Amarillo Ramp*, for example, is so fascinating. It is in this glorious state of ruin, and perhaps that's how it should stay.

By the end of this year, I am determined to physically see with my own eyes every single outdoor work by the artists—I am on the road a lot, and am nearly there with seeing them all . . . Talking to the people looking after these works is really important—and there are great people involved in this care. We want to make sure all the stewards know how special what they have is. Part of stewarding an artwork is making sure that people know about it. *Sun Tunnels* and *Spiral Jetty* are both looked after by Dia, and provide perfect examples of how things should be done. We want people to know about the works, and we want people to respect the artwork, to not leave a trace, to not take anything from the sites too. At the same time, you don't want a roadblock of people going to see the works. So, it's about getting the balance right. And that's why working in partnership is the best way forward for us.

One of my ambitions for our online presence is to have a map of all the works and show that by seeing them all you can understand the US.

KB: And what about your team?

LLF: We are a tiny team. There is me. And our Head of Operations & Finance, a brilliant person who knows all the organizational systems inside out and back to front, and who also knows how to think laterally. One of the many things she enables us to do is to look at how we can make our money work as hard as it can. Having trained as an accountant, an artist, and a cultural anthropologist she is perfect for keeping us on track. And our Archive & Digital Resources Manager, who worked with Holt for 13 years, is a crucial part of the team—he is brilliant, and has so much knowledge.

That's it at the moment—although, having said that, we bring into our fold expert registrars, archivists, database and website developers, legal advisors, financial advisors, copyright agencies, film and video distributors, gallerists . . . And we have a great board.

Our plans are next to appoint an assistant for the three of us, so we can slowly start to delegate. Our plan is to make a perfect job that each of the three of us would have liked to have done when we first graduated, where one can learn about finance systems, image management, making books and exhibitions, collections care, research—in short, everything involved with how to run a foundation. If I tell the truth, this is strategic. We want to work with someone who's really smart, who'll work with us for three years, and will then go off to be Chief Curator of MoMA, and then become Director of Tate. We want that person to remember our artists, so when they're directing the most influential museum in the world, they'll go, "I began with Holt and Smithson, now I want to make sure that other people know about their work." Sustainability is central to our planning.

KB: Is the team in New York or Santa Fe?

LLF: At the moment, we're all in Santa Fe as our base, but we are moving the whole time around the US and internationally. I tend to have two weeks at our home base, and then have two weeks on the road.

KB: Are there conservationists or scholars that the foundation will seek to work with?

LLF: Yes, absolutely. There needs to be new thinking about Holt's and Smithson's work, and we are committed to encouraging this. As one example: this year we hope to launch the Holt/Smithson Foundation Lecture Program—an annual series hosted by a different museum every year that brings together thinkers to break new ground.

KB: Will there be a commercial relationship with galleries?

LLF: Yes—and I feel one must never shy away from the importance of the market in the ecology of art. Neither Holt nor Smithson did that. If you are doing the best for an artist's work, you need to ensure they have position in the market. Holt, in fact, did not want to gift work even when a piece was site-specific because she knew value is economic as well as intellectual. If you're an artist-endowed foundation, perhaps the best thing to do is to work with the market to ensure the artworks do not disappear. When you generate revenue from selling work, you put that money back into the foundation, to develop research programmes, to give grants to other artists, to students—all so that you fulfil public benefit. The artist Andrea Fraser famously said there is no outside the institution. You have to work within the institution and maybe you can address the market by working with it and then thinking about what you do with those funds. Much more pragmatically, as a charitable foundation, you have a fiscal responsibility to be wise with your assets.

KB: We all know Holt's *Sun Tunnels*, we all know Smithson's *Spiral Jetty*. Are there things that you are trying to bring out into the light?

LLF: The earthworks by Holt and Smithson are really important, and they also made films, sculptures, drawings, works on paper, photographs, collages, process-based works, language pieces . . . Holt made concrete poetry, which we especially want to share with the world. We want to get the breadth of their efforts out in the realm of ideas. I so want to get Holt's writings published.

There is an amazing body of work based on tours and trips that has so much potential—Smithson's 1967 *Tour of the Monuments of Passaic* is well known, but there are more. There is a wonderful *Stone Ruin Tour* made by Holt in that same year, and a series of audio works where she describes overlooked details in, for example, her studio, or the John Weber Gallery. So, if Nancy made a tour of this office, she would describe the people in the bar on the balcony we can see outside of this window, she would describe the tower block I can see to my left, she would point out a cracked window across the street, and a break in the pavement down below. She was really interested in the perceptual realm. And then she made systems works—and these are so fantastic. In one she used the hot-water system in a gallery to form a sculpture, in another the ventilation system, and in another the electrical system. These are palpable, tangible works. We want to get those artworks out—just talking about this makes me impatient to do so.

KB: And they're extant?

LLF: Yes—they are just waiting, in fact we recently moved the components out of Holt's former garage. And then with Smithson, there are brilliant drawings and collages. He's not just *Spiral Jetty*.

KB: There are a hundred shows here, it's quite exciting . . .

LLF: And artists of course don't work in a void, they work with their peers, and in context, so we are as interested in bringing Holt and Smithson works into the company of other artists. What happens if you put Smithson collages in conversation with an artist who is at the forefront of thinking about collage today? Or what happens when you put Smithson drawings that look to natural history around the dinosaurs at the Natural History Museum? Smithson loved that museum.

Maybe the hardest thing, though, is that we can't do that quite yet. We've got to get our house in order. We've got to build a database, we've got to build a numbering system for works in our collection. We've got to work out the insurance values, we've got to condition-check the works, we've got to measure the works, we've got to barcode the works. So, we've got to keep our patience and build the skeleton to this body and set policies—whether it's an investment policy, a loan policy, or any other kind of policy. Then we can do all the crazy stuff. This might be an apocryphal story, but I will tell it anyway. Apparently Frank Zappa used to keep a quote by Flaubert posted above his desk that said, "Be regular and orderly in your life, so that you may be violent and original in your work." If we are regular and orderly as we set up the Holt/Smithson Foundation, we can do things that break the mould and make a difference.

PART TWO

ARTISTIC LEGACIES IN ACTION

INTRODUCTION TO PART 2

Artistic Legacies in Action

Kathy Battista

In the first section of this book the reader has access to critical information regarding the establishment, management, and sustainability of artists' estates and foundations. As noted in the main introduction, while each artist's legacy has its particular demands, concerns, and opportunities, there are some issues that are relevant to all. These universal concerns were addressed in the essays that you have read thus far. We aimed to present texts that can be used across a variety of legacy structures. In this second section of the book our focus is to provide more detailed, granular investigations of case studies that illustrate topics related to a range of creative legacies. Hopefully it will be a welcome addition to learn more about specific cases that highlight the pitfalls as well as the unique aspects of certain artistic legacies. Bringing an interdisciplinary approach will likewise add to the excellent and foundational body of knowledge begun by our peers. Like visual artists, fashion designers, architects, performance artists, jewellers, and other creatives have bodies of work as well as archives to preserve and maintain. Many of these professionals use conservation safe-storage facilities for the preservation of their body of work or papers. Thus, it is for this reason that we spread our remit into a broader realm. In my own practice as a writer, curator, and educator, I have found that issues of legacy that we consider for artists are also being questioned in the worlds of fashion, architecture, jewellery, and other disciplines including performance and dance. For this reason we invited scholars and practitioners from these respective fields to bring their experiences into view so that others may learn from them and build on their research.

Another inspiration for creating this anthology, in addition to it being useful to older artists, their heirs, and estate professionals, is a younger generation of artists whose work engages with and challenges the accepted practice of artistic legacies. New York-based Eddie Martinez is already taking control of his own legacy and its future interpretations by utilizing catalogue raisonné software (panOpticon) to inventory his work, thus ensuring the accuracy and authenticity of his oeuvre while he is still considered a young artist. Instead of leaving this work for a future archivist or historian, who typically is piecing clues together to form a complete history, he is writing his own story as it unfolds. Using new digital catalogue raisonné tools is a recent development that will make legacy planning become more common, perhaps even widespread practice during an artist's life. panOpticon and Artifex are the leading developers of these tools, and between them host a selection of major artists: David Smith, Jack Tworkov, Agnes Martin, Jim Dine, and many more.[1] Roger Shepherd, CEO and Creative Director of panOpticon, speaks about the virtues of using catalogue raisonné software as opposed to or in conjunction with actual printed books:

> Researchers who use panOpticon are raising the bar for their teams and for their communities. For the first time curators, writers, historians, teachers, students, appraisers, wealth managers, galleries, museums, libraries, archives, auction houses, collectors, insurers, educational institutions, estates, foundations, artists, and all the others invested in this vast territory are able to share credible information and give feedback to one another.
>
> The results of their efforts are no longer static collections of records and documents to be occasionally referenced by a few, but are instead, organic *processes* that play a dynamic and public role in both the appreciation and the business of art.[2]

Other artists, such as Tino Sehgal, are resisting accepted institutional and market norms. Sehgal does not issue any written certification with the sale of his performances. Photographic and video reproduction of his work is forbidden and the records of the works are passed to museum registrars and curators through an oral process. It will be fascinating to see how his work is preserved and interpreted by future generations and how institutions will face this challenge to the accepted administrative channels of acquiring works. Sehgal's practice, which is now integrated into international biennials and major museum shows, is one example of the burgeoning forms of practice that challenge typical archival and conservation procedures. How will a catalogue raisonné of this work be compiled? Who will guide the preservation of the work after Sehgal's lifetime?

Michael Asher is an example of an artist whose work was always site-specific and can never be recreated. It also cannot be bought or sold. In this instance then, how does his archive, trusted to the care of his foundation, protect his conceptual work and its legacy when ownership changes hands?

Jill Magid's work, discussed by art lawyer Daniel McClean in Part 1 of this book (see pp.48–59), also challenges conventional notions of artistic legacy by working within and around the estates of deceased artists. In an ongoing project on the estate of Mexican architect Luis Barragán, Magid created a body of work that has used the legal, financial, and cultural parameters around Barragán's legacy to inform her own practice. For example, she has altered books and photographs related to Barragán to create artworks that are just distinguishable enough to escape copyright infringement. More recently, she convinced the remaining relatives of Barragán to exhume his ashes, a portion of which she had transformed into a diamond ring through carbon processing. This ring was then proposed as a swap to Federica Zanco, the owner of Barragán's archive, which is now housed at the Vitra headquarters, in exchange for the return of his papers to his native Mexico; while Barragán lived and worked mostly in Mexico City, and indeed his home is now a museum there, the archive was taken to Europe and essentially deracinated with the removal of the accent from his name. Magid's proposal has not yet been accepted; however, an extraordinary dialogue on the role of the architect's legacy has begun. I am particularly interested in this notion of an artist's legacy being mutable or unfixed; rather than set in stone (pun intended), an artist's legacy might be altered by future generations. Magid has stated, "Artistic legacy, in that sense, is inevitably open-textured and susceptible to intervention, regardless of how hard someone might try to protect and control an archive."[3] Further into the same interview Magid indicates how issues around Barragán's legacy affect her thinking on her own legacy:

> I am inspired to consider the future of my own artistic legacy, and how I would feel for a corporation to own my name, my work, and the rights to it while strongly limiting access to it for more than twenty years. Who would be permitted to write about or critically engage with my work? More importantly, who wouldn't? How as a society can we participate in an author's creative practice? Does our participation threaten the integrity of the original? I don't see art or an archive as a fixed (dead) body but as something alive and that continues to give. . . . The worst thing anyone can do for an artist, or an architect, is overprotect him or her.[4]

This delicate balance between guardianship and overprotection has been discussed by McClean in Part 1 of this book. Writing elsewhere on the fluidity of artistic authorship, he says, "Despite the enormous symbolic and monetary value attached to it, artistic authorship is not constant and stable. Instead . . . artistic authorship is fluid, iterated by different protagonists (including the artist) through different structures and practices over time."[5] Indeed, artistic legacies, once considered suspended in time like a still photograph, might be considered in a more adaptable and intersubjective way. How can one engage with an artist's legacy and perhaps add to or refine it within their practice, be it artistic, curatorial, or scholarly? It will be enlightening to understand how performance art will be maintained and re-enacted (or not) in the future. Marina Abramović is one artist who comes to mind who is already ensuring her legacy through her eponymous institute (MAI) as well as her New York gallerist Sean Kelly, who helped to build a market around her practice. In addition to these examples, we also have found that there are cases of artists whose work challenges traditional notions of conservation, preservation, and the art market.

There are so many fascinating examples that could be included in this book. It would be interesting to understand how the estate of Dash Snow, an artist whose work often utilized ephemeral materials and who died unexpectedly at the age of 27, will be guided. Likewise, how will scholars, writers, curators, and advocates of untrained (sometimes referred to as "outsider") artists work with their legacies? As there are organizations dedicated to cultivating the careers of untrained artists—including the Creative Growth Art Center in Oakland, California, the Fountain House Gallery in New York, and Creativity Explored in San Francisco—this interest group will certainly have legacies for the future. How will the legacy of choreographers who have collaborated with artists, such as Merce Cunningham, be understood in succeeding generations? How will born-digital art be conserved and sustained for future generations? These topics will hopefully be addressed by scholars in the future; professionals in the form of gallerists, artists, curators, and archivists are already grappling with these challenges.

Three of the essays in this section deal with artists who are household names: Robert Rauschenberg, Eric Fischl, and Franz West are discussed as well as the architect Philip Johnson. I am particularly grateful to Christy MacLear and Judith Prowda for their contributions to this book, which allow us to hear how these prestigious artists' legacies are being carefully managed and maintained. While there are many specifics in these texts, there are also lessons that can be used by any practitioner managing an estate or planning an artist-endowed foundation. Alexandra Bowes-Lyon's essay about an English aristocratic estate discusses larger concerns of tax planning and deaccessioning work. As wealth distribution changes across generations, will important homes and collections transition from private to public, as has been seen in the past?

As Bryan writes in the Introduction to Part 1, not all artists are household names. Many toil for decades without market success or have periods of success that wax and wane. Others choose to remain in the more marginal areas of the art world, which may be more appropriate to their practice. This is especially relevant for figures such as Leigh Bowery, whose design and performance practice straddled the worlds of fashion, art, and nightlife in London. His work has impacted on many young designers, artists, and choreographers, and yet he is not a canonical artist. How, then, does one deal with his legacy? Fashion historian and theorist Nathalie Khan has written an essay that examines Bowery's legacy from the custodial as well as collector's points of view.

Robin Wright, in her chapter, looks at jewellery's unique aspects and corresponding emotional engagement. Like art, jewellery passes hands at both retail and auction venues. Like art, its value system has less to do with its inherent value and much to do with its historical or emotional significance. A fake pearl necklace worn by First Lady Jacqueline Kennedy holds a value far beyond its intrinsic worth. Likewise, Mark Morris presents a case for the value of architectural models, particulary in regard to professional education. While these objects may not have a high monetary worth, they are vital for the training of generations of architects and architectural historians. I am grateful to these authors who have extended the legacy dialogue beyond the parameters of the art world, into tangential disciplines of common interest: architecture, fashion, and jewellery estates have similar challenges to those of artists. Perhaps more cross-disciplinary voices can help move the discussion of artist estates and foundations into new territories.

Notes

1 See https://www.artifexpress.com and https://panopticondesign.net/design/ for more information on these projects (both accessed 25 February 2020).

2 Email from Roger Shepherd to the author, 18 November 2019.

3 "Locating legacy: Jill Magid in conversation with Nikolaus Hirsch and Hesse McGraw", in Nikolaus Hirsch, Carin Kuoni, Hesse McGraw, and Markus Miessen (eds), *The Proposal: Jill Magid*, Berlin: Sternberg Press, 2016, p.7.

4 ibid., p.19.

5 "Introduction", in Daniel McClean (ed.), *Artist, Authorship & Legacy: A Reader*, London: Ridinghouse, 2018, p.25.

8
DEFINING LEGACY

Fischl/Gornik, Rauschenberg, Noyes, and the Philip Johnson Glass House

Christy MacLear

For an artist foundation, the artist's legacy can be considered in two fundamental ways—what you physically leave behind upon your death (artwork, archives, real estate); and how your work and ideas need to be described as a set of guiding values for others. These constitute the artistic legacy's two basic ingredients.

Although the first is simple (almost a matter of accounting and can be captured in lists), the latter is more difficult. The idea of defining your legacy as an artist, when you are still alive, is daunting. It is too final to describe your own life when you may not have created your final or greatest artistic acts yet. This is one of the major contributing barriers for artists to overcome during their lifetime. Another barrier for the living artist is that describing one's own self is riddled with issues—clarity of context, self-esteem, or humility, to name a few. I want to focus on this more personal aspect of legacy first, and we will move to the more basic elements—which take physical form—after. I am going to use examples from my own work with artists or estates, so this is less of a manual and more of a narrative.

DEFINING YOUR LEGACY WHEN YOU ARE LIVING

Having the honour to work with Eric Fischl and April Gornik has taught me a lot about defining one's legacy while one is living. The summary of my story is that it requires observation from a close ally to craft a description of one's life and one's work. It is a rare artist who will do that for him- or herself. What is important is that legacy can simply focus on the work—but is better when it captures a complete understanding of the artist's life and values.

When I asked Eric, "What describes your work within the larger art historical continuum?"—he simply laughed. The question is too scholarly and requires artists (who speak through their artwork) to somehow step outside of themselves to become exactly who they are not—critics or pontificating observers. Actually

Eric gave a flip answer, self-deprecating at best. His response was telling. He is an artist who deals with the tensions of people and society. The angst of adolescence, the angst of politics and complacency, the angst of the laissez-faire of the art fair or any other tribal tradition. For me the lesson was to listen, to watch and capture that which described best his work, philosophy, realizations, intentions and, most importantly, his actions.

When I met with April I did not ask that same question. We went to her studio where she described her practice and what inspired her. Nature, observation, conservation, a rootedness to the earth, animals, empathy, preservation of what we were given and what binds us together, humanity, community, and history. These are the words which I heard while listening to her and watching her actions and intentions. What I gleaned from that time is that April is a master artist but on the early arc of females getting their due, and the lacklustre interest in landscape puts her into a historic moment of transition and consideration. Her values captured her legacy best, describing the aspects which made her a humanist and creator, beyond an appreciator, of beauty. April's legacy in the immediate would be recognized for her humanistic values and, over time, with the evolution of artistic taste, for her masterful art.

For Eric and April, their legacy became a bit more layered when you took inventory of their contribution to their home town, Sag Harbor. Repeatedly they would aid the purchase and transfer of native lands to the conservation society.

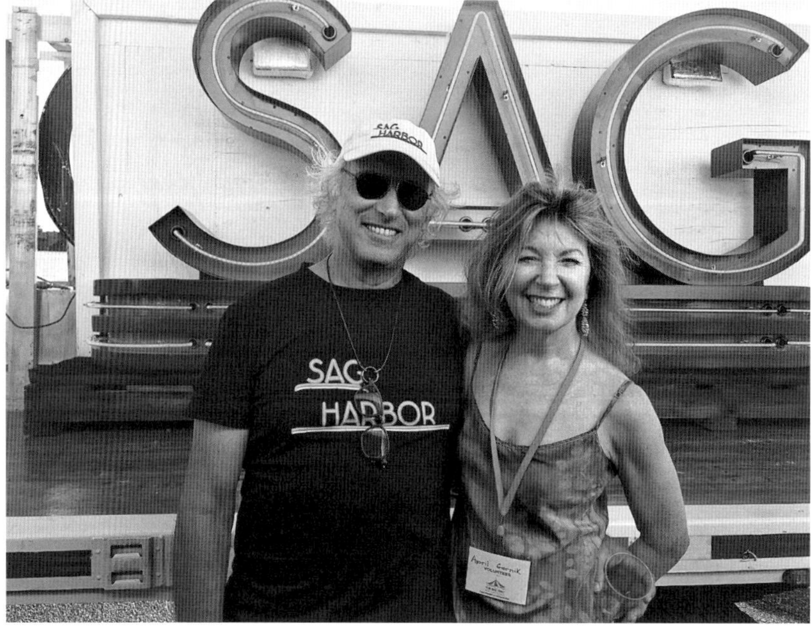

Eric Fischl and April Gornik in Sag Harbor, Long Island, New York, 2017

They are active participants in Long Island cultural and historical organizations. This stepped up when the Sag Harbor Cinema burned down, putting April in a leadership position among other community leaders to raise money and rebuild the theatre. Time and time again they have led the preservation of their historical, ecological, and cultural community.

In dialogue with Eric and April, we decided to centre the foundation's mission statement beyond what defined them as artists and to focus the mission around the love of their town, the preservation of its historic core, investment in the town's creative culture, and the involvement of all people in its vibrancy. In the process of defining this mission, a historic church came on the market and they decided to buy it to renovate as an arts incubator for the town. The mission crystallized in their minds and helped further direct this major investment by honing in on the efforts and investments they had been making steadily for years. Eric and April will each have independent artistic legacies, but by working with them we determined that the legacy they hoped to leave was really about community impact. This is the benefit of working on the direction of your estate or foundation while you are at your most vibrant.

DEFINING THE ARTIST'S LEGACY POSTHUMOUSLY

Creating a clear articulation of an artist's legacy after his or her death obviously lacks direct input from the artist and relies instead on aggregated input from those who knew the person best. I would say that one of the greatest dangers for foundations started after an artist's death is a generic mission statement. An example of this might be: "The mission of the XX Foundation is to hold, conserve, expand, and promote the legacy of the artist XX." This leads to generic activities and the total effect is not supportive of what is most distinctive. I have two stories to share in this respect—one from the Philip Johnson Glass House and one from the early days at the Robert Rauschenberg Foundation.

At the Glass House—the home Philip Johnson designed for himself in 1948–9 in New Canaan, Connecticut—we were faced with comparable organizations who used a historic home to recreate and celebrate the life of its owner. This is the fairly generic mission of most historic homes and is part of the downfall of the single-visit business model. I share this as many artists have homes which convert into centres for their archive, historic homes, or even locations for artist residencies—so the use of a home is a central tactic for real-estate assets. It is a challenge to expand beyond the simple focus on "celebrating the life (or work) of the artist"—but that approach is not descriptive enough to provide a guide for future generations. At the Glass House we discussed how the focus of celebrating the architecture of Philip Johnson might in fact be polarizing. It brought to bear that what Philip Johnson contributed was not consistently remarkable architecture—that was not his main

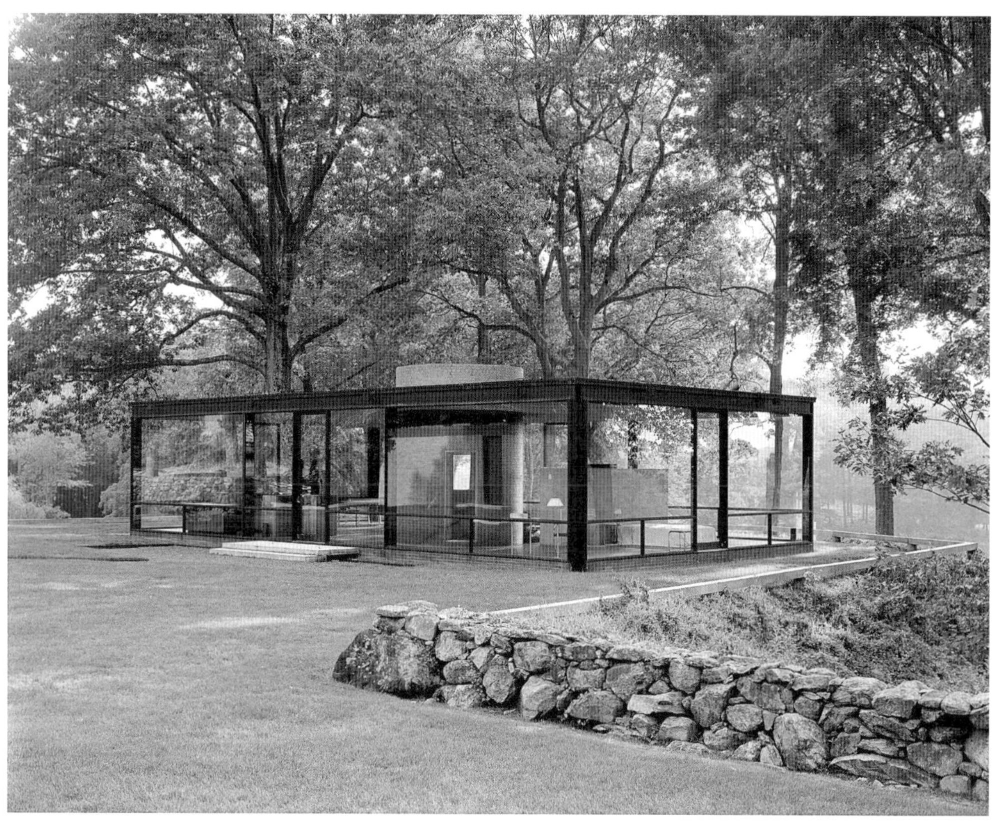

Philip Johnson, Glass House, New Canaan, Connecticut, 1948–9

calling card—as much as life-changing mentorship and establishing networks and dialogues which transformed thought. We built the mission statement around those truly extraordinary aspects of his life.

One might ask—why does that matter, to be so focused on revealing characteristics of one's legacy? The answer lies in making sure that what any organization does, in support of a legacy, be considered with the lens of what defined that person best. In practice, at the Glass House this choice of focus on mentorship, networks, and dialogues resulted in programmes which brought leaders together across industries to have conversations on topics of cross-disciplinary interest. We developed an online network of global design leaders to create engagement and forums for new ideas. We established the Glass House as a centre for Modernism, research, and thought to advance networks in preservation. All of these programmes sprang from that legacy-defined lens versus more generic programmes which would not have had the same impact.

For the Robert Rauschenberg Foundation we took time to gather those people who knew Bob best and capture the terms which defined his essence. Those legacy-based terms included "collaborative", "global", "creative problem-solving", "generous", and "risk-taking", among others. For all artist estates it is easy to imagine that only those who knew the artist well can guide decision-making. That is a very limiting approach and centralizes control with only those who knew the artist versus creating a model which enables future generations. Thus the challenge is how to involve those who knew the artist best and set a series of values which provide a lens for all future decision-making.

Given this lens the early Rauschenberg programmes were reflective of these values. Our early grants supported collaboration, risk-taking, or creative problem-

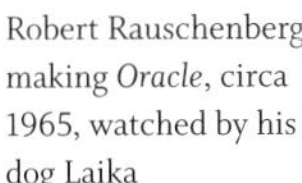

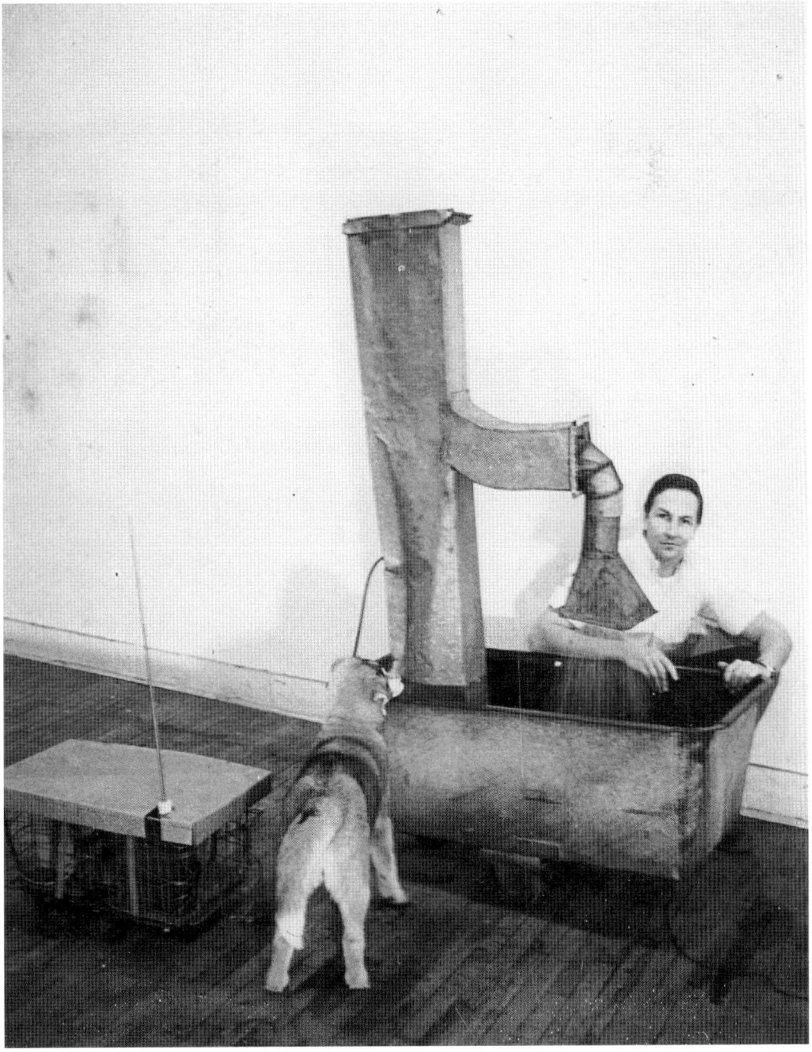

Robert Rauschenberg making *Oracle*, circa 1965, watched by his dog Laika

solving. The MoMA retrospective was centred around his collaborations, as was the Residency in Captiva, Florida. Even his son Christopher Rauschenberg used to say, "If Bob were to have a museum—it wouldn't be in a closed building, the work would be hung from the sides of elephants in a parade so all could see." As a leader and manager of the foundation, these values—the view of what defined Rauschenberg's legacy—helped challenge our team to check our ideas against them. Was the idea global? If not, could we find a way to push it more in that direction? Did the idea provide evidence for creative problem-solving—was it a unique way to approach a solution? If not, we would go back to the drawing board.

From the Philip Johnson Glass House to the Robert Rauschenberg Foundation, both legacies were defined by those who knew them best and helped us ensure that all efforts had a direct and material impact on legacy. Every step counts in supporting and translating those efforts.

LEGACY ASSETS: ARTWORK

The second aspect of legacy is one's physical assets, which might include art, archives, and real estate. The artwork is the most important physical asset to be considered, while the archive and real estate are supportive players. Artwork is the central reason most families pay long-standing attention to the artist's oeuvre through scholarship, exhibition, sales, and authentication. An artist's legacy can be singularly defined by the nature of their work but does not have to be—more often the human characteristics help provide evidence for their legacy and the art speaks to that. An example is that Robert Rauschenberg was an artist who had global concerns—and his work in the Rauschenberg Overseas Culture Interchange (ROCI) series speaks to that aspect of his legacy.

Working with the artwork, and furthering the understanding of the artist's legacy, requires research, scholarship, and time. At the most basic level there must be an inventory of the work. This should be organized by date and can be additionally arranged by subject/theme, methodology, or materiality, among other principles. Having this organized sweep of one's career helps map the artist's work to the artist's life, ideas, or greater historical context. Upon having the artwork organized, one can begin to consider research, scholarship and exhibitions which illustrate the importance of the work. One might say that one's legacy is incumbent upon these stories.

I would like to illustrate an example of legacy relating to the storytelling behind one work of art, and another concerning a whole movement within an artist's career. The first—relating to a single work—is the example of Robert Rauschenberg's *Erased de Kooning Drawing* (1953). It is unique among the entire body of Rauschenberg's career, but is central to so many aspects of his legacy. It captures elements of collaboration, alternative approaches in his thinking, and a capacity to redefine a genre. The simple version of the story is that Rauschenberg went to de

Kooning's studio and requested a drawing with the announced intention of erasing it. De Kooning brought back a drawing dense with markings of graphite and charcoal, and gave it to the young Rauschenberg who spent a devoted amount of time erasing every line until the page was clean. It was, after that, a new artwork—a collaboration between a master and youth. One sees elements of this piece throughout Rauschenberg's career—but the piece stands alone as a story illustrating aspects of his legacy. It provides a clear view of his interest in working with others, thinking beyond the boundaries of methodology, and only now redefines what a drawing is or can be.

A second story about how a body of artwork can provide illustration for a legacy would be to look at Rauschenberg's *Jammer* series (1975–6). These series illustrate Rauschenberg's legacy as a global artist and his experimental use of materials. The pieces were inspired by a trip to India, where the fabrics and colours inspired him in new ways. This work had little examination and, with our gallery, the foundation put forth an exhibition of the works to reintroduce them to the market and museums. These works helped show how Rauschenberg was continually innovating, being inspired by a global context, using uncommon materials in a traditional practice, and interested in what others might discount as common, which Rauschenberg elevates to the position of exquisite. The exhibition, publication, and placement of the works in this series helped provide depth and diversity for Rauschenberg's legacy.

LEGACY ASSETS: ARCHIVES

The archives are not typically the primary driver of legacy, but rather play a supportive role in the examination of legacy. One might say the archives are where the stories reside, which makes them of seminal importance. Fundamentally, an archive is the recorded matter of a person's life and work. Information about the work, documents relating to exhibitions, photographs of the artist's life and community, receipts and notes surrounding the studio practice, video of the artist in all contexts, samples of materials or equipment used in the practice, personal letters and artefacts are a short list of examples of what might reside in an archive. Like the artwork, the archive needs to be organized so that scholars and curators can examine linkages between the work and the surrounding documentation.

There are other chapters in this book about how to organize and resource an artist's archive. The experiences I would like to share relate to the consideration of ongoing management and use. I will begin by squashing the consideration that archives are of immeasurable financial value and will be purchased by a museum or scholarly institution for great sums. Archives are, in fact, an expense centre for those who accept them. Starting with this viewpoint, one will be best prepared to consider the options for management and use in perpetuity.

For the children of Eliot Noyes, their father's archive consisted of all business correspondence between the designer and his CEO clients (which represents a central shift for the role of design in business), models and drawings of his innovations for IBM typewriters and Mobil gas stations to name a few, and plans and documents for his role as MoMA's first Design Curator as well as a founder of the famed Design Conference in Aspen, Colorado. This archive not only supported the work he did as a designer, architect, and leader—it represented the foundation of design in some core institutions in the United States and the emerging role of design in corporate strategy. The archive could not reside responsibly with the family nor in the home, which was intended as a CEO/design leader conference centre: conservation capability was limited and there were little to no points of access, either physical or digital. The most powerful thing to do with the archive was to donate it to a responsible institution which had the programmatic power to leverage its contents.

Prior to approaching any partners we considered all of the institutions with *associations*: MoMA, the Aspen Institute, and Harvard (Noyes's alma mater). Then we discussed the institutions of *volume* such as the Archives of American Art, which provide value in single-stop research. Finally we discussed institutions whose *programmes matched the contents*—Stanford, Massachusetts Institute of Technology, Rhode Island School of Design, Yale, etc.—all of which had programmes that might relate to the legacy of business and design leadership, and the power of architecture and design in cultural history.

What we were looking for was a partner who would accept the archive, conserve it and make it accessible in perpetuity, but moreover instigate programmes which would activate the use of the materials. This last goal was what would activate the legacy into the ongoing historical dialogue versus the archive having only a home awaiting use. Ultimately the Noyes archive resides at Harvard, where Noyes graduated, and they have developed a programme across the business school and design school to extend his legacy in this vein.

For Eric Fischl and April Gornik, they plan to keep their archives along with key works for their foundation. The historic church, which they own and lead through a new non-profit, may someday steward those papers and works for scholars and curators.

ASSETS OF ONE'S LEGACY: REAL ESTATE

Real estate is an asset which has surprising value to legacy and thus should be considered with high priority during planning by an artist, estate, or foundation.

Most older artists, if they purchased versus rented, bought real estate when prices were low, and the renewed value may since have seen a remarkable rise. Artists who purchased in the SoHo neighbourhood of Manhattan in the 1970s or even 1980s; artists who bought land on the east end of Long Island; artists who have

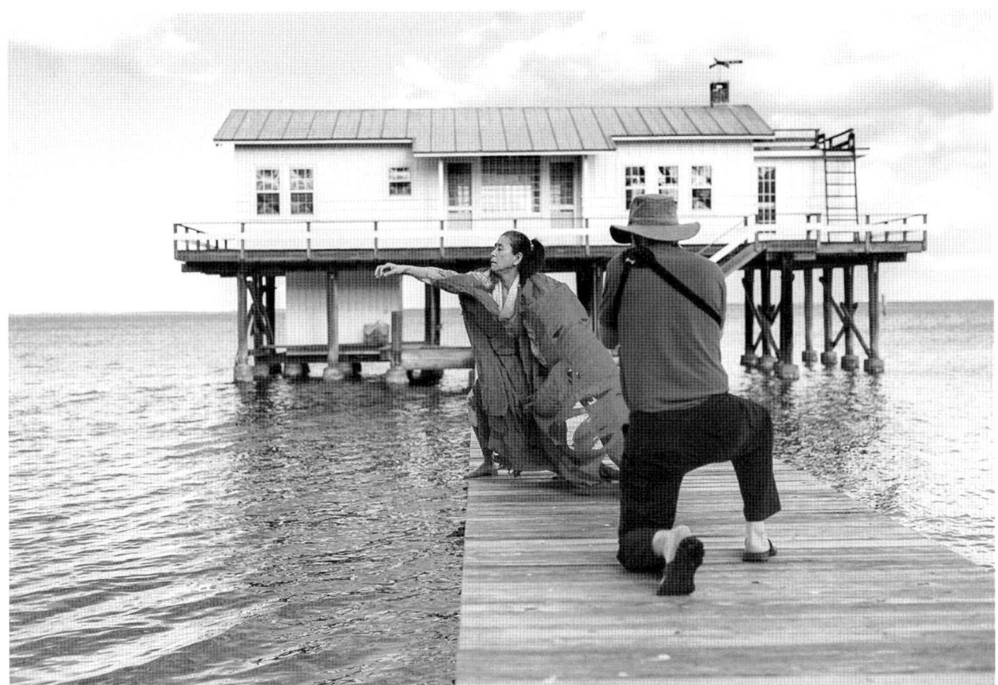

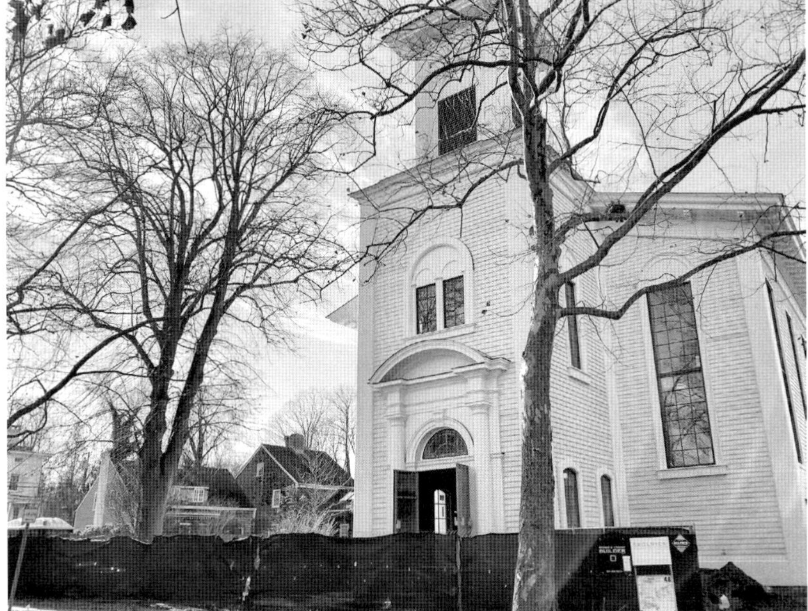

Artist in Residence Eiko Otake performs while her collaborator William Johnston photographs at the Fish House, Captiva, Florida, during Rauschenberg Residency 28, November to December 2017

The Church, Sag Harbor, Long Island, New York, during restoration under the auspices of Eric Fischl and April Gornik for use as an arts incubator, 2019 studios in former industrial locations in Los Angeles, Chicago, or Williamsburg; and artists who bought farms in Maine or Hudson Valley New York will now have a surprising nest egg. Most artists and estates may be surprised that real estate, versus art, is their most liquid asset and one which might sustain their visions most easily.

The question for all artists and stewards is: What is the *use* versus *value* of the real estate toward the legacy? The examination of "use" is both singular to the real estate and comparative to the other assets to be used toward one's legacy (i.e. "It could be a residency" compared to "Could we support or underwrite a residency in the artist's name through a large-scale grant and then not have ongoing operations?"). The examination of "value" is made more straightforward by assessing the financial value of the real estate. Then consider other means to generate that same amount of financial reserve. For example: "This real estate is worth $2 million if sold and costs us XX to maintain—between them they could sustain our operation" in contrast to "We need to sell more artwork, which is our core focus, to sustain our operation."

Here I will offer two examples of an examination of use and then value: the first is the Rauschenberg Foundation's evaluation of the possible uses of the artist's Captiva properties; the second is Eric Fischl's and April Gornik's evaluation of their lofts in SoHo relative to their vision, which resided in Sag Harbor. For the former, the foundation was responsible for over 20 acres (8 hectares) across an island off the coast of Florida. The acreage was assembled by Robert Rauschenberg, who wished to preserve the land and original structures as density and development encroached on his original home. Over decades he bought over half a dozen homes and structures, and land stretching from bay to ocean. The land felt like the last of the original jungle and the homes were historic "cracker" architecture which had survived generations of hurricanes. This patchwork compound contained his own home and studio, where he lived and developed much of his work after the 1980s. Given the foundation had a headquarters in New York and a facility to house the artwork, keeping the land and homes on Captiva required real examination of "use" in ways which would enhance the legacy.

The foundation looked at options for the land's use in whole or in part. Should it move its headquarters to Florida? Should there be a museum in this place in his name? Could this be an inspiring place for other artists in residence? What if we sold it in part—would it have the same legacy narrative? What if we sold it in whole—how useful would that financial reserve be? The most sobering question for all foundations is that for tax purposes, the Internal Revenue Service requires that there be a highest and best use of assets—so what is the highest and best use for a fraction of an island which served as a home and studio? The board reviewed all of the options and decided that there was considerable usefulness in the Captiva property toward Rauschenberg's legacy. It was a unique space that unlocked many of the ways in which one understands his love of nature, the materials of his later works,

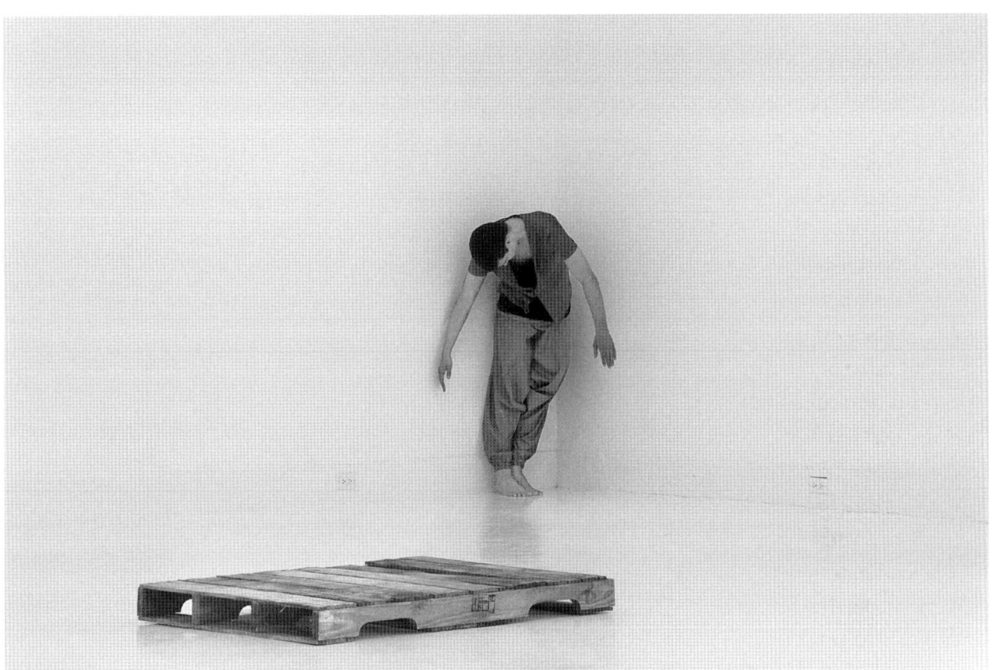

Jonah Bokaer during his residency at the Robert Rauschenberg Foundation in Captiva, Florida, 2019

how he developed community through this generous assembly of properties (which allowed others to reside there) and worked with collaborators and ultimately could inspire generations of artists through giving them access. It was not useful as a location for the foundation, archives, or art. It was useful for residencies for artists who could develop their own work in the inspired environment.

It is important, and a lesson I learned from my time at the Glass House, that piloting the use of a site helps ensure big decisions are made thoughtfully and those decisions can adjust over time. For the Rauschenberg Foundation's land in Captiva we committed to piloting an artist residency on the property and listening to the artists' feedback. After one year the feedback was positive from the artists' experience, but moreover seminal to their understanding of and new interest in Rauschenberg as an artist, environmentalist, humanist. We specifically asked the artists if they would prefer a commensurate amount of money, as a grant, versus the residency and they universally said the experience far eclipsed their value for financial support.

This was an examination of the value to those the foundation hoped to serve—the legacy and the community of artists. We also examined the value of our portfolio of options: If this were sold and a grantmaking pool, would we have greater impact? If this were sold and we kept the funds in reserve, would we be able to sustain the foundation longer and have to sell less art, keeping it for very specific purposes? Which of these actions would have the greater value to the legacy, both short and long term? What is practical as well as valuable? These are all of the questions one should be asking when considering "use" versus "value" for real estate.

Eric's and April's story is one where the living artists are making the decisions. They bought the side-by-side SoHo lofts—one to live in, one for work. As they were purchased in the 1980s you can imagine the value increase. Since we had centred the mission for their foundation and personal efforts on the historic nature of Sag Harbor and expanding creative community, the SoHo lofts looked like a valuable, yet non-mission-aligned, investment. The lofts' use for the foundation required a re-examination of the mission (focused on Sag Harbor) to include New York City. Questions of use arose such as: Shouldn't we be in both locations? Or is it better to focus? Where is the place which will mark our history most and how can we have greater impact? Wouldn't it be easier not to have to change? (The Fischl studio manager and archive worked out of the former studio loft.) All of these questions are harder as a living artist as you put your own comfort aside and consider decisions for the very long term.

The estimates from a real-estate appraiser, however, ended up swaying the dialogue, as both lofts were of equal value to the historic church which Eric and April hoped to purchase and restore in Sag Harbor. The vision of the future was stronger than the challenge of change and the resonance of the past. So, we have sold the two lofts, moved the studio office and archive, and purchased the church. Use and value were weighted toward their vision in the town, toward the preservation of its historic core and enlivening it with creative uses centred on the church. This was a great example of living artists making changes to their existing conditions toward a vision for their foundation's mission.

LEGACY AND MISSION STATEMENT

I want to conclude by returning to the subject of the statement which makes the legacy portable—the mission statement. Going back to our original discussion on values, I challenge you to make sure that the mission statement incorporates the specific values of the artist's legacy to provide that lens on all things, rather than being a generic, uninformative statement that could apply to anyone. Choose words which illuminate the legacy of that particular artist, by the artist him- or herself or those who knew him or her best, and give the power of decision-making to the future generations of stewards. Use bold words to describe the legacy which curators and foundation staff call upon to inspire choices. The mission statement is not a strategy, it is an anthem for time.

9

ARTISTS' ESTATES AND FOUNDATIONS

Art Image Licensing, Publishing, and their Impact on Artists' Legacies

Christine Kuan

For an artist's estate or foundation, owning the copyrights to works of art is a great responsibility and a source of tremendous power. Copyright holders have the power to determine who, how, and when images of artworks may be reproduced. They may also strategically enable images of the artworks to be accessible online, for education, in publications, via merchandising, and other ways of fostering access and visibility for the artist's works.[1] In some sense, controlling the dissemination of images of artworks is one of the most effective ways to advance and preserve the artist's legacy and reception for future generations.

As artists and artists' estates and foundations are increasingly challenged to navigate our modern world of new technologies—high-resolution digital copies proliferate with a click of a button, publishing is a dying industry with fewer and fewer scholarly art publications, and brand consumption drives the global art market—the issue of image licensing has become of greater relevance and opportunity than ever before.

In the past few decades, the conversation around image licensing and artists' copyrights has revolved around the language of "protection". Indeed artists' rights agencies, such as the Artists Rights Society (ARS), have helped to protect many artists' works from being misused and misappropriated, and these agencies have provided valuable services, including helping to collect millions of dollars in licensing fees for publications, merchandise, online catalogues, Web use, advertising, TV and media use, and other licensing products. However, the mechanisms set up to "protect" the use of images, and also the very notion of images *needing protection*, have limited the accessibility of art images in publishing, education, scholarship, and public awareness of artists' oeuvres and their legacies.

Through the policy-making of artists' estates and foundations, image licensing can also be one of the more efficient and impactful ways of increasing awareness, access, knowledge, and research about an artist's works. With websites, digital publications, art databases, and new initiatives to make art more discoverable to educational users, collectors, and the public, image licensing policy can be incredibly valuable to the long-term understanding, brand recognition, and market value of the artist.

A BRIEF HISTORY OF ART IMAGE LICENSING

Since the 1970s and 1980s, artists and artists' rights agencies have set up agencies to manage the growth in requests to license images for various uses, including educational use, publication, commercial use, and non-commercial uses. Today, the largest artists' rights agency in the United States is the Artists Rights Society (ARS, founded in 1987), which now manages the rights of more than 80,000 artists, including the thousands of artists formerly managed by the Visual Artists and Galleries Association (VAGA).[2] Prior to this time, images of artworks were reproduced with or without permission and without established agencies for clearing rights.

With the explosion of social media, major shifts in thinking have begun to occur in the last ten years as artists and arts organizations compete for audiences and visibility in an increasingly image-hungry world. At first, art museums, galleries, artists, and artists' estates feared that access to art images online would spell the decline of visitorship. In actuality, the greater visibility an artist, artwork, or art exhibition has online and in media, the more audiences flock to see the real thing (e.g. the *Mona Lisa*—the Louvre has 10 million visitors annually; or the "Heavenly Bodies" exhibition at the Metropolitan Museum of Art Costume Institute in 2018, which had 1.66 million visitors).

Many of the biggest players in the art world have moved from a "gatekeeping" approach to image licensing, to one of fostering access to high-quality images and accurate information. Additionally, many major artists' foundations now have policies of waiving fees for educational use, including publications, and encouraging the sharing of artworks via social media and online platforms, such as Artsy (artsy.net).

One of the most innovative development policies for art image licensing was spearheaded in 2016 by Christy MacLear, then CEO of the Robert Rauschenberg Foundation, who pioneered a Fair Use Policy of Rauschenberg's images in an effort to remove barriers to image use in art scholarship for education and museums.[3] At the same time, the Rauschenberg Foundation continues to license Rauschenberg images for commercial use, such as in its recent partnership in 2017 with West Elm, which produced a series of furniture items imprinted with Rauschenberg images (chairs, sofa, pillows, and more) for the home.

Many of the commercial licensing opportunities exist for popular household-name artists. Recent artist-plus-brand collaborations include: Andy Warhol and Uniqlo T-shirts; Keith Haring and Artestar clothing; Yayoi Kusama and Louis Vuitton handbags; or Jeff Koons and H&M—to name a few. Those commercial opportunities are often negotiated on a case-by-case basis and will not be covered in depth in this brief chapter.

ART PUBLISHING AND IMPACT ON ARTISTS' LEGACIES

Over the years, scholarly art book publishing has largely vanished as a business, and museum and university press exhibition catalogues and monographs are generally only realized with grants or large subsidies.[4] At the same time top galleries, such as Gagosian and Zwirner, have set up their own publishing arms to create the scholarship around the artists they represent and to further document and catalogue the works by their artists.

In the academic arena, image licensing fees are generally borne by the authors, who are responsible for the time-consuming process of conducting the necessary image and permissions research (because one must secure permissions for the artwork, the photograph, clearing rights for art images which often include fees and terms that are a burden to individual authors, obtaining high-resolution image files suitable for publication, and often needing to pay exorbitant image licensing fees).

In fact, many graduate art history programmes discourage PhD candidates from pursuing certain dissertation topics knowing that the image licensing costs and the challenges of working with certain copyright holders will prevent the dissertation from ever being published, which could significantly reduce the chances of achieving employment and tenure. These licensing conditions automatically narrow the range of publications that publishers are willing to invest in given an already small pool of people interested in art books, and limits the subject matter of publications to those artwork images that are more easily obtainable. In most cases these art books are companions to popular exhibitions or fashionable coffee-table books, not often about the artists who most need research and scholarship published about their works.

The result of image licensing as a standard practice for publications has meant that publishers go through a process of picture research and picture licensing to illustrate art publications. Due to the high cost of picture research and image licensing, many artists have not been included in important art publications because the licensing fees and licensing terms were too onerous for the publisher or author to warrant paying those fees or agreeing to those terms.[5]

From 2003 to 20018, I was the Editor-in-Chief of Oxford University Press' Oxford Art Online/Grove Art Online and *The Dictionary of Art* (34 volumes, edited by Jane Turner), the canonical scholarly art encyclopedia consulted by experts, art historians, students, collectors, and dealers worldwide. In addition, I also commissioned numerous art publications in print and electronic media. The limited budget for scholarly art publications meant that editors/authors were often tasked with

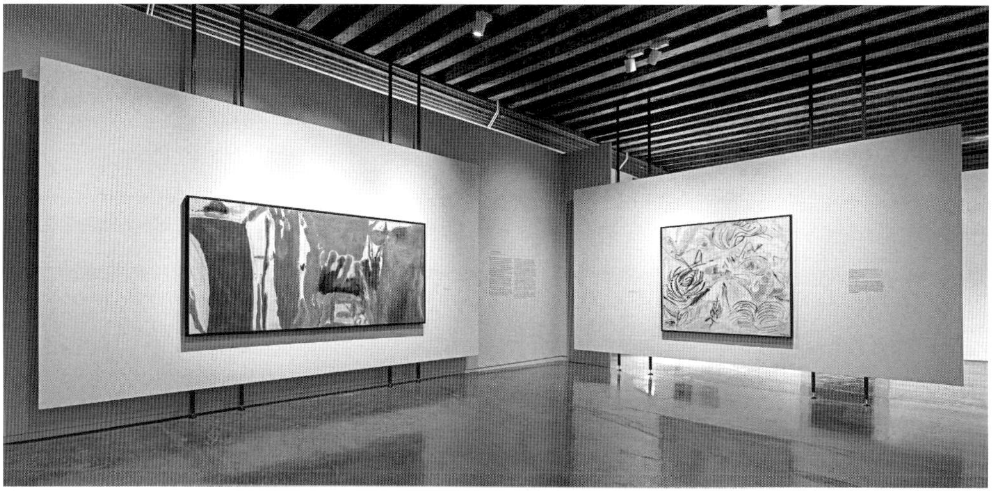

"Pittura/Panorama: Paintings by Helen Frankenthaler, 1952–1992", exhibition at Museo di Palazzo Grimani, Venice, Italy, 7 May to 17 November 2019, showing *Open Wall*, 1953 (left) and *10/29/52*, 1952 (right). © 2019 Helen Frankenthaler Foundation, Inc. / Artists Rights Society (ARS), New York. Photo by Matteo De Fina

the undesirable dilemma of determining which artists would be illustrated. Many lesser-known artists were not illustrated in the publication due to prohibitive costs or unscalable licensing terms, and there was always the expectation that the "more important" artists must have illustrations.

In fact, several living artists who asked for their images of artworks to be included in Grove Art Online/Oxford Art Online were prohibited by their licensing agent from allowing us to publish those images unless the publisher agreed to the terms and conditions of the licensing agency.[6] Not only did these artists' works not appear in the canonical art historical publication, but consequently any gallerist, collector, or dealer interested in researching the artist could not easily find peer-reviewed scholarly documentation with illustrations of his or her works.

One of the greatest problems with the one-size-fits-all image licensing formula is that publishers are often put in the situation of deciding how to use a limited budget for picture rights, and often these decisions simply reinforce the traditional Western canon, e.g. Picasso, Matisse, etc. Artists who may not be in the canon or in the "blue chip" art market should weigh cost of being omitted from websites, publications, educational and commercial publications against the image licensing fees and terms.

When I interviewed Elizabeth Smith, Executive Director, Helen Frankenthaler Foundation and Jack Flam, President/CEO, Dedalus Foundation, in spring 2019, both stressed that their foundations are working with ARS to facilitate image licensing requests. Both foundations review the image request for publication for accuracy, frequently waive fees for non-profit, scholarly, educational uses, try to respond in a timely manner to publishing requests, knowing that time is of the essence, and help to provide high-quality information and accurate information about the artworks.

Both Smith and Flam explained that their foundations have not adopted a similar fair-use image policy for education and museums to the Rauschenberg Foundation mainly because they want to be able to provide a degree of quality control as the artist's foundation: to have the opportunity to become aware of the image request, to review the accuracy of the data for the artwork, to verify that the artwork is indeed by the artist, and to be notified once the new publication or project is available.[7]

While grantmaking activities are core to the mission of artists' foundations, these bodies are also working to ensure that the legacy of the artist lives on in the contemporary art world through publications and the regular visibility of the artist's works. For instance, the Helen Frankenthaler Foundation lends extensively to exhibitions of Frankenthaler's work in contexts ranging, most recently, from at the Museo di Palazzo Grimani in Venice during the 58th Venice Biennale, to Princeton University Art Museum in New Jersey and the Parrish Art Museum in Water Mill, New York, to enhance public exhibition access to and raise the profile of Frankenthaler in the art world and for the general public.

In short, while images of artworks abound online, the in-depth scholarship around art and artists, particularly modern and contemporary art, would benefit greatly from artists' estates and foundations viewing image licensing as an opportunity to enable greater educational and scholarly access to their artists' works in order to foster new research and broader engagement with the artworks and the artist's life and legacy.

SOCIAL MEDIA, DIGITAL PHOTOGRAPHY, AND OPEN ACCESS

The art world is one of the last sectors to embrace social media and the sharing of art images—initially requiring clearance for any photography of artworks and galleries to be used in social media. However, in the last few years, many of these photography restrictions in museums and galleries have been relaxed. On the one hand, it is nearly impossible to police image licensing violations on social media, and on the other, it can greatly benefit the promotion and awareness of the artist (or art organization, art exhibition, art fair) to have art be widely shared on social media and the Internet.[8] Consequently, we have witnessed a sea change in how artists, artists' estates and foundations, the art market, and cultural institutions have utilized social media and the Internet to further serve their own missions and business priorities.

The art world has become extremely active on social media, with collectors, curators, critics, artists, galleries, and art fairs all regularly posting to social media and accumulating large followings. For example, as of July 2019, on Instagram, the Metropolitan Museum of Art has 3.2M followers, the Louvre 3.1M followers, the Gagosian Gallery 1.1M followers, Jeff Koons 342K followers, and Cindy Sherman 264K followers. On Facebook, MoMA has 2M followers, Art Basel 466K followers, and Marina Abramović has 513K followers. While these may seem like large numbers of art lovers, for context, pop culture music icons like Nicki Minaj have 40M followers on Facebook and Kanye West has 29.2M followers on Twitter.

Today, 45% of the world's population (3.5 billion people) are social media users.[9] In addition, as of January 2019 there were 5.11 billion unique mobile users in the world, up 100 million (2%) since January 2018; and there were 4.39 billion Internet users, an increase of 366 million (9%) in the same period.[10] The exponential growth of information access through online technologies versus print media is staggering, and artists whose works are not discoverable online may contend with negative consequences down the road, such as lack of public awareness of or scholarly interest in them, and potentially diminished future market value of their work.

On the museum front, many major art museums have adopted open-access image policies, allowing unrestricted commercial and non-commercial uses of millions of high-resolution digital images of artworks which have no known copyright restrictions or are in the public domain. Museums with open-access image policies include the Art Institute of Chicago, the Getty Museum, the National Gallery of Art in Washington D.C., the Metropolitan Museum of Art, and others. Open-access image policies have made a significant impact on public access, scholarly research, and academic publishing and they have advanced the museums' core mission to educate and to make accessible their art collections to the public. International museums and cultural institutions have also partnered with Google Art Project (now Google Arts & Culture) since 2011 to make gigapixel images and virtual tours of their collections accessible to the public.

Artists' estates, such as the Robert Rauschenberg Foundation, have also worked with museums to make copyrighted images available on museum websites for educational purposes. While some still require their copyrighted images to be

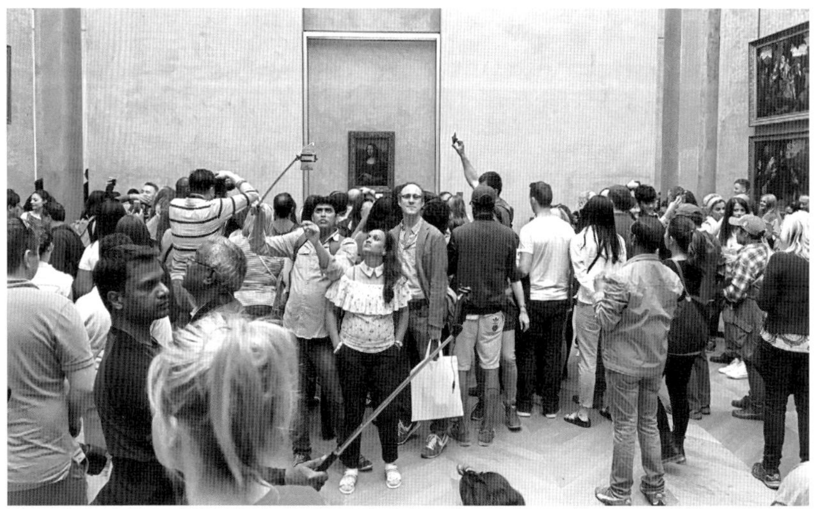

Selfies being taken in front of the *Mona Lisa* in the Musée du Louvre, Paris, in 2017.

Opposite: Robert Motherwell in his Greenwich studio in 1990. Courtesy of the Dedalus Foundation, Inc.

licensed for social media use, artists' estates and foundations can themselves harness social media and online technologies to further enhance the accessibility of the public and of scholars to their artists' works.

CATALOGUES RAISONNÉS

One of the most mission-critical endeavours of artists' estates and foundations is to produce catalogues raisonnés, which provide the definitive source of information about the artists' works and lasting comprehensive documentation about artists for future generations. In recent years, more and more catalogues raisonnés are being published as online databases. Two of the more prominently known digital catalogue raisonné platforms are Artifex Press, founded in partnership with Pace Gallery in 2012, and panOpticon, founded by Roger Shepherd in 2006 and expanded to Web-based services in 2010.

Today, one may find dozens of digital catalogues raisonnés for artists such as Mary Cassatt, Paul Cézanne, Arshile Gorky, On Kawara, Amedeo Modigliani, Sol LeWitt (Wall Drawings), Agnes Martin (paintings), Egon Schiele, and Salvador Dalí. Yet, despite the proliferation of online databases and publications, many artists' estates and foundations still grapple with whether catalogues raisonnés should be produced in print or online.

Some of the value of having the catalogue in print is that is it fixed in time, a permanent record, tangible, and available for future consultation no matter what technology brings or how digital formats may change. There is also the beauty and prestige that printed books still hold in the academic community and in the international art world, which is an important factor in planning the publication of catalogues raisonnés. With the immense cost of such an undertaking, artists' estates and foundations that can afford to do both print and online should opt for both because the print version is an important permanent record and the searchability, convenience, and accessibility of online is invaluable for museums, curators, archivists, students, and scholars.

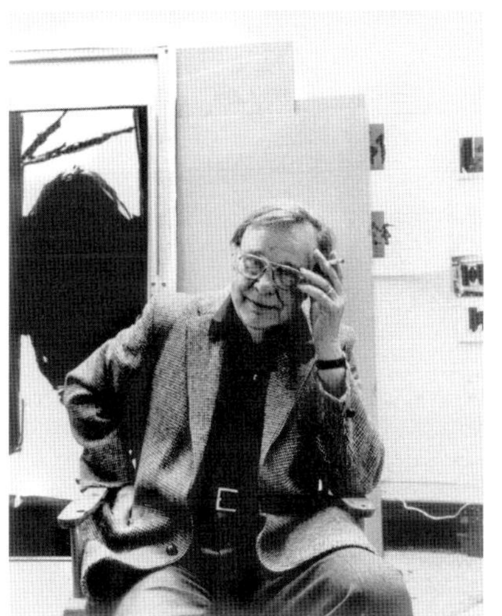

One of the most expensive aspects of producing the catalogue raisonné, aside from the research costs, is the artwork photography—both commissioning new photography wherever those works may be and/or licensing photographs for print and online. In the case of the Robert Motherwell catalogue raisonné, Jack Flam said they were fortunate that Motherwell had everything photographed before the works left the studio. But most artists have not had the resources or forethought to photograph every-

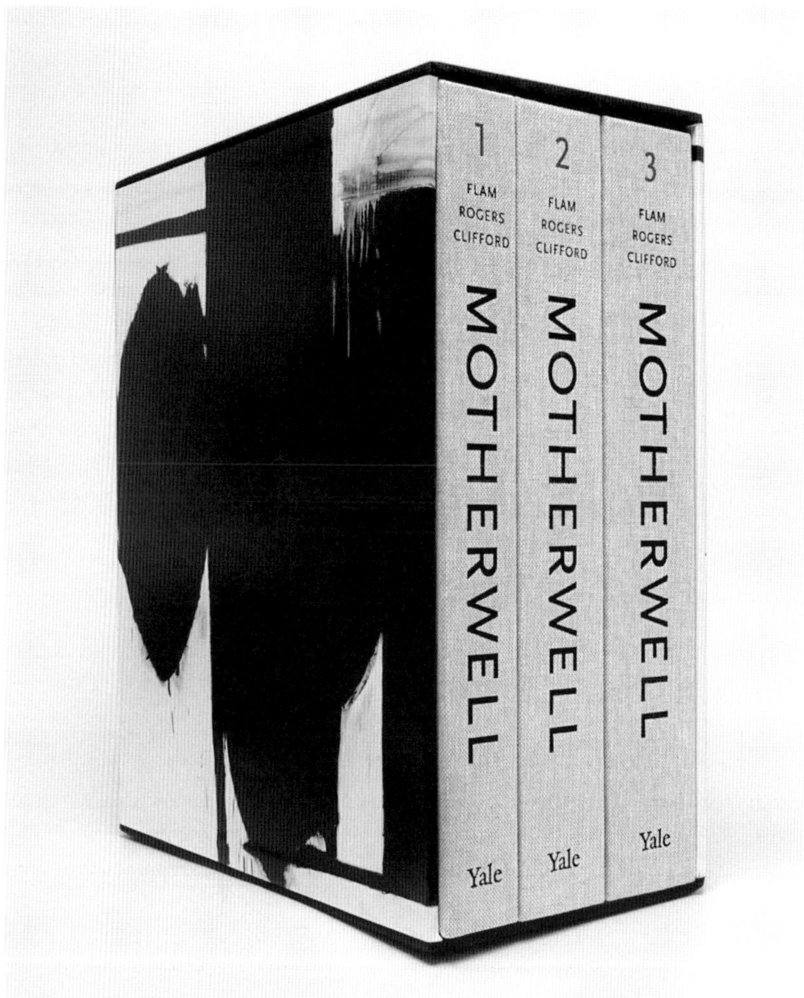

Cover of *Robert Motherwell Paintings and Collages: A Catalogue Raisonné*, 1941–1991 (Yale University Press 2012). Courtesy of the Dedalus Foundation, Inc.

thing, and arranging for new photography for works that may be in public and private collections around the world can represent a staggering cost.

In addition, museums have been generous on the whole, and have worked with the Dedalus Foundation in the creation of the Motherwell catalogue raisonné. Where it might be possible to collaborate with museums on new photography, it would be ideal. Flam mentioned that in one instance, the Dedalus Foundation had to track down the heirs of an Italian photographer to license an important archival photo for the catalogue.

Both image licensing fees and new photography fees can amount to a significant sum by the time the catalogue is completed. If hiring a photographer, it would be best to conduct the new photography as work for hire so that future uses of the images do not require repeat copyright clearance with the photographer. Ensure that any licensed images from museums, private collections, photographers, etc. allow for the photos to be used worldwide, all languages, all formats, in perpetuity (whenever possible) for the long-term sustainability of the catalogue and for the estate/foundation's ability to disseminate the contents of the catalogue in future formats and languages.

It is also worth noting that artists' estates and foundations, once they have high-quality, digital assets which they can share with other platforms, are also able to strategically place artworks to enable broader public discovery. The Richard Diebenkorn Foundation, which released the Diebenkorn catalogue raisonné in 2016, selected 100 artworks for inclusion in Artsy so that the broader public and art experts would be able to access authoritative information for free about the artist. Additionally, artists' estates and foundations had informed me, when I was Chief Curator and Director of Strategic Partnerships at Artsy, that Artsy was consulted daily in the process of assembling catalogues raisonnés because it was the only place where the artists' works and images both in the marketplace at large and in institutional collections were aggregated in a searchable online platform.

WHAT THE FUTURE HOLDS

In conclusion, there have been major strides made in the way in which the art world approaches image licensing, and the increase in information about artists and art has never been greater. Artists' estates and foundations now have a myriad of options for how they wish to approach image licensing, publishing, social media, and catalogues raisonnés in order to advance greater access, appreciation, and understanding of artists.

What if through image licensing policy, artists and artists' estates left behind a legacy of sharing, fostering creativity by enabling their works to be reproduced, reused, and mixed? What if authoritative information on thousands of artists was available online for the public to explore and for scholars to research? As the world moves to a more image-based culture, the widespread circulation of an artist's work in print and online will have a long-term impact on perpetuating the legacy of the artist.

KEY MOMENTS IN ART IMAGE LICENSING HISTORY

Ancient Rome to 18th century: evolution of the public domain as a concept—in Ancient Rome the distinction was made between *res communes* (things that could be commonly enjoyed by mankind, such as air, sunlight, oceans), *res publicae* (things shared by all citizens), and *res universitatis* (things owned by the municipalities of the Roman government); as a legal term, "public domain" first appeared in the 18th century in England

1915: SPADEM: Société de la Propriété Artistique et des Dessins et Modèles, often S.P.A.D.E.M. or SPADEM, is a copyright protection and collection society formed by visual artists and their heirs in France.

1953: ADAGP created, the French royalty collecting and distribution society in the field of graphic and visual arts.

1976: VAGA (Visual Artists and Galleries Association) founded in the United States; merged with ARS in 2018: 6,000-10,000 artists and estates

1987: Artists Rights Society (ARS) founded, later to become the United States' largest rights agency

1990s: Artstor, a digital image library, created by the Andrew W. Mellon Foundation, to make high-resolution art images available for teaching and education

1998: Google founded on 4 September

1998: The United States' Digital Millennium Copyright Act (DMCA)

1999: Bridgeman Art Library v. Corel Corp.—case opinion from the US District Court for the Southern District of New York which found that slavish copies of two-dimensional artworks lack originality and therefore are not copyrightable

2001: Creative Commons (CC) founded

2004: Facebook founded

2006: Twitter founded

2007: Apple iPhone launched

2010: Instagram founded

2011: Google Art Project founded, giving access to gigapixel images

2012: Artsy launched—first curated online platform to combine art images from both galleries and museums, and sales and educational activities

2018: VAGA artists added to ARS membership, now representing some 80,000 visual artists and estates

Notes

1 For the purposes of this chapter, we will focus on artists' estates controlling copyright to artworks. In some cases, photographers also hold copyright in the photograph of the artwork. Many artists' estates today pay photographers to photograph works of art as work-for-hire so that the image rights reside with the artist or artist's estate.

2 In July 2018, VAGA and ARS announced that the VAGA members will now all be represented and managed by ARS, making ARS the largest artists' rights agency in the United States managing the licences of nearly all of the major

artists still under copyright: https://www.cisac.org/Newsroom/Society-News/ARS-and-VAGA-welcome-VAGA-artists-to-common-ARS-repertoire (accessed 25 February 2020).

3 https://www.rauschenbergfoundation.org/foundation/fair-use (accessed 25 February 2020).

4 Oxford University Press, the largest university press worldwide, discontinued publishing art monographs and the majority of scholarly art publications (as had Abrams and other notable art publishers) by 2001.

5 For example, a copyright holder may require that an image licence be renewed periodically and subject to new fee negotiations. For a digital publication, it would be administratively impossible to manage individual image licences which expire at various times throughout the year each year. Additionally, some licensing fees differ depending on whether one is seeking English-language-only rights or all languages, US only or worldwide, etc.

6 While I was serving as Editor in Chief of Grove Art Online/*The Dictionary of Art*, several contemporary living artists represented by artists' rights agencies asked for images of their works to be included in the aforementioned scholarly art encyclopaedias for two editorial updates I commissioned—Women Artists and Asian Contemporary Art—only to be denied permission to be included in the publication without a licensing fee agreement with Oxford University Press. The agreement stipulated thousands of dollars per image for a contract that would expire after a few years. It was not feasible for an online encyclopedia of more than 30,000 articles to enter into an agreement for those few artists when other artists and their galleries granted permissions free of charge.

7 Fair Use doctrine does not require the copyright holder to grant permission. See College Art Association, "Code of Best Practices in Fair Use for Visual Arts", February 2015: https://www.collegeart.org/pdf/fair-use/best-practices-fair-use-visual-arts.pdf (accessed 25 February 2020).

8 See also the Digital Millennium Copyright Act (DMCA) October 28, 1998 United States copyright law that criminalizes production and dissemination of technology, devices, or services intended to circumvent measures that control access to copyrighted works and criminalizes the act of circumventing an access control, whether or not there is actual infringement of copyright itself. Its principal innovation in the field of copyright is the exemption from direct and indirectly liability of Internet service providers.

9 We Are Social global digital report 2019, https://wearesocial.com/global-digital-report-2019 (accessed 25 February 2020).

10 Simon Kemp, "Digital 2019 Global Internet use Accelerates", 30 January 2019, https://wearesocial.com/blog/2019/01/digital-2019-global-internet-use-accelerates (accessed 25 February 2020).

10

TO BUILD A FOUNDATION, YOU DO NOT START WITH THE ROOF

The Battle Over the Estate of Franz West, and Afterthoughts on Planning Ahead

*Judith B. Prowda**

When the celebrated Austrian artist Franz West died on 25 July 2012 at age 65, he left behind his wife, Tbilisi-born artist Tamuna Sirbiladze, and their two young children (born in 2008 and 2009). In his will, West had bequeathed his estate to the three of them. Tragically, Sirbiladze died in March 2016 at age 45, leaving the estate to the couple's children. West's legacy was to become embroiled in a dispute that led to a number of lawsuits.[1] This chapter will focus on the case between the Franz West Estate and the Franz West Foundation.[2]

Born in 1947 to Communist parents, West spent his childhood in post-war Vienna, where his family lived in a housing project "full of old Nazis".[3] His Jewish mother practised dentistry in an office next door to their apartment, using antiquated equipment, and his father sold coal.[4] During his late teens and young adulthood, West studied art and frequented cafés in Vienna. In the 1960s he witnessed avant-garde performances by the Viennese Actionists, and eventually developed his own aesthetic, combining high and low cultural references.[5] He completed his studies at the Academy of Fine Arts Vienna in 1982.[6]

West, whose work has been the subject of comprehensive posthumous retrospectives at the Centre Pompidou in Paris (12 September to 10 December 2018) and the Tate Modern in London (20 February to 2 June 2019), is perhaps most

* The author gratefully acknowledges Michael Isak, Freshfields Bruckhaus Deringer LLP (on sabbatical), her student at Sotheby's Institute of Art, MA Art Business programme, for providing a detailed summary in English of all phases of the Franz West case and commenting on this chapter. She thanks Christoph Kerres, Kerres Partners, Vienna, attorney for the Franz West Estate, for his insight into the case, and Dr Richard Lehun, Stropheus Art Law, for his valuable feedback.

well-known for his *Passstücke* (Adaptives), begun in 1973, papier-mâché works from the 1980s, and *Lemurenköpfe* (Lemur Heads), made in the 1990s, as well as his collages, furniture works, and collaborations with other artists. West represented Austria at the 1990 Venice Biennale. His work has been exhibited in New York's Central Park and Lincoln Center Plaza, as well as in international exhibitions and prominent galleries throughout the world.[7] An important retrospective "showcas[ing] West's dynamic range of work"[8] over four decades, titled "To Build a House You Start with the Roof: Work 1972–2008" (the inspiration for the title of this chapter), was organized by the Baltimore Museum of Art (BMA), Baltimore, Maryland and was held there from 12 October 2008 to 4 January 2009, and afterwards at the Los Angeles County Museum of Art, from 15 March to 7 June 2009.

This essay will discuss the litigation resulting from a "deathbed" decision by Franz West to create a foundation which was ultimately decided by the Austrian Supreme Court in favour of the artist's family.[9] The court's decision was based on a highly technical point in Austrian foundation law, not on the artist's state of mind when he created the foundation days before he died.[10] Nevertheless, as observers have noted, deathbed decisions, such as this one, are "inevitably problematic . . . and always hold the negative connotation of exertion of influence from the outside."[11]

Following this discussion, I will propose a non-exhaustive checklist of issues that every artist should consider in planning their estate and legacy.

THE FRANZ WEST CASE

Background

In 1999, West created the Franz West Archive (Verein Archiv Franz West), which was entrusted with the recording of all of his works, the right to photos and the licence to produce furniture. West entered into licensing agreements with the Franz West Archive to produce certain pieces of furniture[12] as well as reproduction rights to photographs of all his artworks.[13]

In July 2012, just days before West's death, he created the Franz West Private Foundation (Franz West Privatstiftung) (the "Foundation"), a move that effectively gifted the entirety of his works (as well as reproduction rights in relation to his furniture designs) to this entity rather than to his family and the Franz West Archive. His estate was left with €400,000 in cash, five cars, five apartments in Vienna, and a house in Baden, a small town near Vienna.[14] Noteworthy events with respect to the creation of the Foundation, described below, occurred on 19–20 July 2012, while West was hospitalized in Vienna after the severe worsening of his condition in Naples, Italy.

The Signing of Documents by Franz West

On 19 July 2012, West signed three key documents: (i) a foundation deed (*Stiftungsurkunde*); (ii) a supplementary foundation deed (*Stiftungszusatzurkunde*); and (iii) a testament (together, the "Documents"). Importantly, the signing of the Documents occurred in the presence of Dr Ploil (West's lawyer), Mag Ines Turian (West's long-term secretary and business partner), Wolfgang Hienert (West's long-term conservator) (together, the "Board" of the Foundation), and Dr Rupert Brix, a notary (the "Notary").[15] Due to the extended length of time spent at this meeting (delays caused in part by notary requirements under Austrian law and the ad-hoc amending of the Documents), the parties agreed to continue on the following day.[16]

On 20 July 2012, the Board and the Notary met again with West in his hospital room in Vienna where West signed amended versions of the Documents.[17] In addition to the Documents, a binder containing descriptions of 272 artworks was produced so that they could be referenced in the deed of transfer (*Widmungserklärung*).[18] The deed of transfer had not been prepared in advance, but was drafted on site following instructions of the Notary. On the same day (and shortly after the meeting), West was transferred to the hospital's intensive care unit where he died a few days later.

The Franz West Estate's Claims

The Franz West Estate asserted the following claims:

1 West did not sign the Documents himself;
2 West lacked the mental capacity to sign legal documents due to his illness and medicated state;
3 It was unethical and unconscionable to demand from a dying man to enter into legal agreements that would result in the divestment of most of his assets that would otherwise benefit him and his family;
4 Formal requirements with respect to the Code on Notaries (*Notariatsordnung*) had not been complied with;
5 The gifting of the artworks was ineffective due to compulsory portion requirements under Austrian inheritance laws.[19] (Here, the Franz West Estate asserted that the value of the gifted artworks was €48,014,000 and that the Franz West Estate had claims of at least €23,000,000 under such compulsory portion requirements);[20]
6 West mistakenly believed he was incorporating a company for the purposes of tax optimization to benefit his estate, and never intended to establish a foundation;
7 West was under coercion/duress at the time of signing the Documents; and
8 The transfer was ineffective for failure to comply with formal requirements under Austrian foundation law—i.e. due to the specific

sequence of events, the transfer would be categorized as a gift (which required the Foundation's formal acceptance); and the lack of formal acceptance by the Foundation meant that the artworks were never legally transferred to the Foundation.[21]

Legal Issues

Given the evidence and testimony of witnesses, the Court of First Instance did not find the Franz West Estate's assertions (1)–(7) above convincing. The court focused instead on the following three issues:[22]

- whether West had the mental capacity to sign the Documents;
- whether the notary requirements were complied with; and
- whether there was a valid transfer of the artworks to the Foundation.

Court of First Instance Ruling

The court ruled on 26 June 2017 that West had mental capacity and was therefore able to enter into the contracts.[23]

Expert testimony was adduced at the hearing by the court-appointed medical expert, Dr Wolfgang Soukop, who reviewed West's medical history, indicating no signs of mental or neurological decay.[24] Medication that West was taking at the time of signing the Documents would not have interfered with his capacity, nor would his slightly elevated blood ammonia levels in the days before his death have interfered with his mental state.[25] West's concentration span of 20 minutes was estimated to be longer in cases of dealing with important matters (such as the meetings in his hospital room).[26]

Moreover, witness testimony of friends (among them, a neurologist) and acquaintances who visited West in his hospital room, as well as his treating physicians, affirmed that West spoke in a normal manner with no apparent cognitive limitations.[27] Additional detailed testimony by the Notary on the sequence of events on 19 and 20 July 2012, and his perception of West's mental state, suggested that West was alert and aware of his surroundings and asked questions about the technicalities of setting up the Foundation. In the court's opinion, these observations supported a finding that West had the requisite mental capacity to enter into legal agreements.[28]

The court also found that the notary requirements were in compliance. Here, the court referred only to the commentary on the Notary Act (Wagner/Knechtl, Kommentar zur Notariatsordnung, §52 NO Rz 16), which does not require the reading of the appendix by a notary.[29] (The Supreme Court, in its 2018 ruling discussed below, based its judgment instead on the Notary's failure to read aloud the appendix, which contained the list of all artworks.[30])

As to whether there was a valid transfer of the artworks to the Foundation, the court ruled that the transfer was ineffective. By virtue of signing the Documents on 19 July 2012, a valid "pre-" foundation entity (*Vorstiftung*) had been established. The execution of the amended Documents on 20 July 2012 was to be considered a "post-" foundation (*Nachstiftung*), which in itself was a separate legal transaction.[31] By failing to recognize this highly technical aspect of foundation formation (that the Foundation was in fact created on 19 July 2012), the Board did not realize that they needed to follow the formal requirement of accepting the artworks as a gift on 20 July 2012.[32]

So although the parties thought of transfer as a single transaction to the Foundation (not two distinct "pre-"/"post-" foundation transactions), the court interpreted the execution of the amended Documents as a separate transaction.[33] Therefore, the court reasoned that a transfer of the artworks on 20 July 2012 would have required the acceptance of the artworks as a gift through the "pre-" foundation entity established on 19 July 2012 as represented by the Board.

This error also precluded the court from finding implied acceptance (i.e. at the moment that West handed the binder containing descriptions of the artworks back to members of the Board). No one present at the signing of the Documents on 19 and 20 July 2012 was aware that acceptance would be required and thus did not form the will on the part of the Foundation to accept the artworks.

In sum, the Court of First Instance reasoned that the establishment of the "pre-" foundation and "post-" foundation constituted separate transactions. This in turn required the Foundation to accept the transfer as a gift, in accordance with legal formalities under Austrian foundation law. However, since these legal formalities were not followed, the Foundation did not fulfil the requirement for accepting the gift. The transfer of the artworks to the Foundation ultimately failed because of formal defects (i.e. legal acceptance in accordance with Austrian foundation law in relation to gifts).[34] Hence the Court of First Instance held the transfer was invalid *ab initio* and ordered the Foundation to return the artworks to the Franz West Estate.[35]

Court of Appeals Ruling[36]

Affirming the Court of First Instance, the Vienna Court of Appeals agreed that there was a formal error in granting and accepting the artworks.[37] The asserted grounds of appeal put forward by the Foundation were: (i) invalidity of the judgment, (ii) defectiveness of the judgment based on procedural errors, (iii) erroneous fact recording during the procedures following flawed considerations of evidence, and (iv) flawed interpretation of the applicable laws.[38] After addressing each of these points and going into a detailed analysis of the Court of First Instance's reasoning, the Court of Appeals rejected the asserted grounds of appeal and the requested appeal hearing, thus affirming the Court of First Instance decision.[39]

Supreme Court Ruling[40]

In October 2018, the Austrian Supreme Court affirmed the Court of Appeals decision, finding the existence of a technical error in gifting and accepting the gift.[41] However, unlike the Court of First Instance and the Court of Appeals, which gave weight to the establishment of the "pre-" and "post-" foundations (*Vor-/Nachstiftung*), the Supreme Court reasoned that such a question does not matter because in either case (i.e. regardless whether the events on 19 and 20 July 2012 are interpreted as a single legal transaction or as two separate transactions because of the establishment of a "pre-" foundation on 19 July and a "post-" foundation on 20 July), the fact that the artworks (as listed and described in the binder that West skimmed through on the second day) were not read aloud by the Notary was sufficient to result in formal error.[42] The Supreme Court emphasized the importance of the statute's protective effect and the intent of drafters to make transferors aware of the consequences of their actions.[43] Otherwise, parties could easily circumvent notary requirements with respect to gifting property without physical transfer, and statute's protective effect would be nullified.[44]

The Supreme Court also suggested that the parties chose this method of incorporating the list of artworks by reference because of West's poor health and difficulty concentrating for a long period of time (thus intending to circumvent the statute's protective effect, which the Supreme Court could not accept).[45] Moreover, the Notary should have refused the notarial act on this document as he could not ensure that West's "true will" was to transfer the artworks without reading it in its entirety to him before the transfer (following *§ 52 NO*).[46]

In sum, the Supreme Court reached the same conclusion that the transfer of artworks to the Foundation was invalid due to formal error, but approached the problem from a different perspective than that of the Court of First Instance and the Court of Appeals. In order for the binder listing the artworks to form part of the notarized document (the one that was drafted ad-hoc in the hospital room on the second day) by reference, the entire list of artworks needed to be read aloud by the Notary.[47] Thus, after many years of costly litigation, the artwork remaining in possession of the Foundation and proceeds from sold works would be turned over to West's two minor children and their legal guardian.

AFTERTHOUGHTS—PLANNING AHEAD

Below is a discussion of particular issues that artists should consider in planning their estate and legacy. While the list is not exhaustive, it provides a starting point for artists wishing to preserve their creative work for posterity.

Create an Inventory

This is perhaps the most fundamental step an artist can take during their lifetime. Careful documentation of an artist's works throughout their life cycle—from creation to the first sale and beyond—is time well spent. Once a system is in place, it is much easier to plan a strategy for the disposition of works and make critical financial and legal decisions. Also, having a clear record of the artist's complete oeuvre will help in the authentication and the prevention of forgeries circulating in the market in the future. Establishing clear provenance—that is, the chain of ownership or possession of a work from the moment it leaves an artist's studio to the current owner or possessor—can add value to a work and is considered one of the lines of inquiry into authentication (the other two being connoisseurship and scientific analysis). Moreover, the physical examination of works will prompt the artist to categorize their works. For example, an artist may decide which works they would like to be included as part of their oeuvre, and which works they do not regard as their artistic expression and therefore do not want included in a future catalogue raisonné of the artist.[48] Another advantage of creating an inventory is that it can serve as the basis of a catalogue raisonné and inform the artist's archive, furthering the artist's creative legacy and benefiting the public.

What should be included in such an inventory? Ideally, the following information should be collected and updated regularly, using state-of-the-art collection management software:[49]

- title, description, and year of creation
- medium and dimensions, including depths of mounts, frames, and in the case of sculptures, base and weight
- inventory numbers and high-quality photographs (dated, in order to document condition) of each work, as well as the signature and/or casting stamp; name of photographer
- current owner and location of the work
- current condition of the work
- any special requirements for maintenance, storage or display
- information on the process to create the work and materials used (useful for long-term care and preservation)
- invoices
- correspondence (both letters and emails) relating to commissions, loans, sales, or donations of the work, and acquisition by another artist
- exhibition catalogues if available, or reference to exhibition history
- critical essays, reviews, and press reports, including photographs of works
- valuations and insurance documents
- copyright registrations, documentation on transfer of copyright and licences to third parties, if any
- information on the work, such as artist's statements for key pieces in the collection.

Make a Will[50]

Most people do not like to contemplate the end of life, but making sound decisions during one's lifetime and giving clear directions in a will have many advantages. These decisions may include appointing a guardian for minor children, creating trusts and other tax-advantageous vehicles, bequeathing specific works to family members or friends, and supporting a charity. A well-designed will of an artist includes the designation of an executor or co-executors to manage the collection and other assets of the estate. This person or persons should have a high degree of curatorial as well as managerial expertise, and possess art market knowledge, as well as connections with museums and collectors of the artist's work. They should have a good command of tax and other legal questions, ranging from creating a trust to protecting an artist's rights, including artist resale rights in jurisdictions that recognize them (for example, members of the EU, but not the US) and copyrights. These individuals may provide valuable advice during an artist's life as well.

If someone dies without a will, the court will appoint an administrator and the law of intestacy applies. The estate will be distributed to family members according to a strict order of priority (with some exceptions, such as certain life insurance policies, pension policies, and property held in joint tenancy[51]) and may result in unnecessary expenses, delays, and undesirable outcomes.

Decide on a Legal Structure and Select Fiduciaries[52]

The single most important decision an artist must make to sustain their legacy is the choice of legal entity best suited to achieve their goals. All matters relating to the artist's legacy flow from this initial decision, which is guided by the artist's objectives, public recognition, financial resources, and tax considerations.[53]

Many artists' estates are managed privately, which means that heirs are entitled to take ownership of the property and treat it as their own. They may sell or otherwise dispose of the artwork, receive royalties, and publish a catalogue raisonné at their own expense.[54]

Alternatively, an estate may be administered by a separate legal entity, such as a foundation. Here, the estate is transferred to the foundation, which becomes the owner of the assets. A foundation may be for-profit or charitable in purpose. As guardians of an artist's creative work, a foundation plays an essential role as mediator between the art market, museums, and scholarly endeavours, and in some cases controls how the work is exhibited, reproduced, and authenticated.[55] In France, for example, the *droit moral* holder has the right in perpetuity to authenticate that artist's work, which is often bequeathed by the artist to their heirs.

In the Anglo-American sphere, foundations and trusts are commonly used, both for private and charitable intentions. Similar to foundations, trusts receive assets from the estate for dedicated purposes. In the US, trusts may be designed as a mixed-purpose model (charitable remainder *inter vivos*), with both charitable and private benefit aspects (split interest), whereby for a maximum of 20 years, individuals may receive private benefits based on a fixed annual sum (annuity trust), with the remainder paid to a charitable organization.[56] This flexibility enables an artist to support their family with cash payouts or the sale of artworks in order to generate liquidity. Ultimately, the remainder would be destined to a public charity, such as a foundation or a museum. For example, the Robert Rauschenberg Revocable Trust, established by the artist in 1994, became irrevocable in 2008 at his death. The trust inherited Rauschenberg's artistic estate and other assets, and eventually transferred them to the non-profit Robert Rauschenberg Foundation in 2012[57] whose mission is to "foste[r] the legacy of Rauschenberg's life and work".[58] Some foundations advance social causes that an artist cared about during their lifetime. The Robert Mapplethorpe Foundation, for example, which was established a year before the artist's death, supports AIDS and HIV medical research.[59]

Critical to the success of the entity formed to sustain an artist's intentions is the selection of fiduciaries responsible for carrying out their mission. A fiduciary is a person entrusted with authority to act on behalf of another under circumstances that mandate total trust, good faith, and honesty. Conflicts of interest, self-dealing, and breaches of the duty of loyalty to the estate can engulf an estate in years of litigation, as occurred in a notorious case involving the estate of the Abstract Expressionist painter Mark Rothko.[60] In 1975, the New York Surrogate's Court found that the three executors to Rothko's estate had breached their fiduciary duty by entering into contracts to sell 798 Rothko paintings under terms that were not in the best interest of the estate. All three executors were removed and faced severe penalties. The case was affirmed by the New York Court of Appeals.

As illustrated in the Franz West case, the creation of a legal entity is immensely complex and involves complicated trusts and estates laws as well as tax regulations that are unique to each situation. Familiarity with local laws is crucial. Therefore, it is important to assemble a team of competent professionals—attorneys, tax advisors, financial advisors, accountants, estate planners, art advisors, appraisers, and other persons with specialized knowledge—to serve the artist's intentions.[61]

CONCLUSION

Sadly, West's "true will" may never be known. What is certain is that planning early and continuously is an important process for artists to ensure their artistic and cultural legacies and provide financial security for their heirs. It is never too early or too late to start the estate planning process. Delaying or avoiding the process altogether—unwise and not uncommon—may eventually lead to misunderstandings and outcomes that an artist would have not desired.

Notes

1 Other lawsuits have involved production rights for selected furniture designed by Franz West. One such case, Archiv Franz West v. Franz West Privatstiftung, HG Wien 17 April 2015, 39 Cg 26/14p, settled, with the return of all artworks from the Franz West Foundation to the Franz West Estate. Another case, Archiv Franz West v. Gagosian, 1:15-cv-07008-LLS, filed 14 September 2015, was voluntarily dismissed by the plaintiff on 21 April 2016.

2 Verlassenschaft nach Franz West v. Franz West Privatstiftung, LG Wien 26 June 2017, 6 Cg 129/12b—203 (Court of First Instance); OLG Wien 20 November 2017, 11 R 146/17x (Court of Appeals); OGH 30 October 2018, 2 Ob 13/18b (Supreme Court).

3 Peter Schjeldahl, "Postscript: Franz West", *New Yorker*, 27 July 2012, https://www.newyorker.com/culture/culture-desk/postscript-franz-west (accessed 3 March 2020); Tom Eccles, "An interview with Franz West, Vienna, November 13, 2007", in Darcie Alexander (ed.), *Franz West, To Build a House You Start with the Roof: Work 1972–2008*, exh.cat. (Baltimore Museum of Art), Cambridge, MA and Baltimore: MIT Press, 2008, pp.149–50.

4 ibid.

5 David Zwirner Gallery, "Franz West Retrospective", https://www.davidzwirner.com/artists/franz-west (accessed 3 March 2020).

6 Roberta Smith, "Franz West is dead at 65; creator of an art universe", *New York Times*, 27 July 2012, p.18, https://www.nytimes.com/2012/07/27/arts/design/franz-west-influential-sculptor-dies-at-65.html (accessed 3 March 2020).

7 ibid.

8 "Franz West: Guide", David Zwirner, https://www.davidzwirner.com/artists/franz-west (accessed 3 March 2020).

9 Verlassenschaft nach Franz West v. Franz West Privatstiftung, OGH 30 October 2018, 2 Ob 13/18b (Supreme Court).

10 ibid.

11 Loretta Würtenberger and Karl von Trott zu Solz, "Approaches to dealing with artists' estates", in Daniel McClean (ed.), *Author, Authorship & Legacy: A Reader*, London: Ridinghouse, 2018, p.247.

12 Verlassenschaft nach Franz West v. Franz West Privatstiftung, 6 Cg 129/12b—203 (2017) (Court of First Instance), p.17.

13 ibid., p.6.

14 Verlassenschaft nach Franz West (i.e. Franz West's estate; Lazare Otto West and Emily Anouk West [both minors] represented by their legal representative Dr Benedikt Vinzenz von Lebedur-Wicheln) v. Franz West Privatstiftung (i.e. an Austrian foundation entity), LG Wien 26 June 2017, 6 Cg 129/12b—203 (Court of First Instance), p.4.

15 The role of notaries under Austrian law is "to participate in legal processes and to provide legal assistance to the public. The responsibilities of notaries include the execution of public deeds, the safe-keeping of third-party objects,

and the drawing up of private deeds and representation of parties, mainly in the non-contentious area. Notaries are additionally responsible for work as agents of the court in non-contentious procedure. In particular, they are consulted as 'court commissioners' to conduct probate procedures." See Legal Professions, Austria, European Court of Justice, https://e-justice.europa.eu/content_legal_professions-29-at-en.do?member=1 (accessed 9 January 2019).

16 Verlassenschaft nach Franz West v. Franz West Privatstiftung, LG Wien 26 June 2017, 6 Cg 129/12b—203 (Court of First Instance), pp.14–15.

17 ibid., p.15.

18 ibid., pp.15–16.

19 The compulsory portion is a monetary claim to a proportionate share of the estate's value. See European Judicial Network (in civil and commercial matters): Austria, Item 3, "Are there restrictions on the freedom to dispose of property upon death (e.g. reserved share)?", https://e-justice.europa.eu/content_general_information-166-at-maximizeMS_EJN-en.do?member=1#toc_6 (accessed 9 January 2019).

20 Austria (and some other civil-law jurisdictions) have a concept of "compulsory portions" in their inheritance laws. See https://e-justice.europa.eu/content_general_information-166-at-maximizeMS_EJN-en.do?member=1#toc_6 (accessed 22 February 2019)

21 Verlassenschaft nach Franz West v. Franz West Privatstiftung, LG Wien 26 June 2017, 6 Cg 129/12b—203 (Court of First Instance), pp.3–8.

22 ibid., pp.23–7.

23 ibid., p.23.

24 ibid., pp.16–18.

25. ibid.

26 ibid.

27 ibid.

28 ibid.

29 ibid., p.23.

30 Verlassenschaft nach Franz West v. Franz West Privatstiftung, OGH 30 October 2018, 2 Ob 13/18b, (Supreme Court), pp.12–15.

31 "Pre-" foundation refers to the foundation that has not yet been registered with the state. However, the Board would have the authority to act on behalf of such a yet-to-be registered foundation. "Post-" foundation, on the other hand, refers to the act of injecting additional assets into an existing foundation by the founder.

32 Verlassenschaft nach Franz West v. Franz West Privatstiftung, LG Wien 26 June 2017, 6 Cg 129/12b—203 (Court of First Instance), pp.24–6.

33 ibid.

34 Nikolaus Arnold, *Privatstiftungsgesetz-Kommentar 3*, Vienna: LexisNexis, 2013, §4 Rz 7 ff.

35 Verlassenschaft nach Franz West v. Franz West Privatstiftung, LG Wien 26 June 2017, 6 Cg 129/12b—203 (Court of First Instance), p.26.

36 Verlassenschaft nach Franz West v. Franz West Privatstiftung, OLG Wien 20 November 2017, 11 R 146/17x (Court of Appeals).

37 ibid., pp.39–40.

38. ibid., p.18.

39 ibid., pp.18–44.

40 Verlassenschaft nach Franz West v. Franz West Privatstiftung, OGH 30 October 2018, 2 Ob 13/18b (Supreme Court).

41 ibid., pp.12–15.

42 ibid., p.11.

43 Citing § *68 Abs 1 lit e* and *f* and § *66* in conjunction with § *54* of the Code on Notaries (*NO* or *Notariatsordnung*); ibid., pp.11–15. § *54 NO* states that documents that ought to form part of a notarial deed have to be reviewed by the notary in accordance with the requirements of the *NO* and with such document to be affixed to such notarial deed. § *66 NO* states that if the requirements in § *54* are not adhered to, such notarial deed will not be considered a public deed. § *68 NO* requires notarial deeds that are not public deeds to be read aloud by the notary public to the signatories.

44 ibid., p.15.

45 ibid., pp.11–15.

46 ibid., p.14.

47 ibid., pp.11–15.

48 A catalogue raisonné is a comprehensive catalogue of work by one artist, usually presented chronologically, with details such as date, medium, dimensions, references, provenance, and exhibition history. It is viewed by the art market as the gold standard for authenticity.

49 This list is based on recommendations made in Emma Warren-Thomas and Linda Schofield (eds), *The Artist's Legacy: Estate Planning in the Visual Arts*, London: Royal Academy of Arts, 2013, pp.11–12, https://rwa.org.uk/sites/default/files/attachments/The%20Artist%27s%20Legacy.pdf (accessed 3 March 2020). This approach has also been adopted by the Institute for Artists' Estates in Berlin, as discussed in Loretta Würtenberger and Karl von Trott, "On dealing with artists' estates", in Loretta Würtenberger, *The Artist Estate: A Handbook for Artists, Executors, and Heirs*, Berlin: Hatje Cantz Verlag, 2016, pp.22–3.

50 For a more thorough consideration on this topic, see Warren-Thomas and Schofield 2013, op.cit.; Loretta Würtenberger and Karl von Trott, "On dealing with artists' estates", in Würtenberger 2016, op.cit., pp.22–3; and Loretta Würtenberger and Karl von Trott Zu Solz, "Approaches to dealing with artists' estates", in McClean 2018, op.cit., pp.243–57.

51 Angharad Palin, "Where there is a will, there is a way", in Warren-Thomas and Schofield 2013, op.cit., p.20.

52 A wealth of information on this topic is available in Loretta Würtenberger and Karl von Trott, "On dealing with artists' estates", in Würtenberger 2016, op.cit.; Loretta Würtenberger and Karl von Trott Zu Solz, "Approaches to dealing with

artists' estates", in McClean 2018, op.cit.; Christine Vincent et al., *The Artist as Philanthropist: Strengthening the Next Generation of Artist-Endowed Foundations*, Washington D.C.: Aspen Institute, 2 vols, 2010, plus related Supplement, 2013, Reading Guide, 2013, and "Notes on estate planning for artists endowing a private foundation", 2019; and Christine J. Vincent, "What's an Artist to do?—Artist-endowed foundations and legacy stewardship in the United States", in McClean 2018, op.cit., pp.259–82.

53 Loretta Würtenberger and Karl von Trott, "On dealing with artists' estates", in Würtenberger 2016, op.cit., p.30.

54 Advantages and disadvantages are discussed in ibid., pp.32–3.

55 See the chapter by Daniel McClean on pp.45–59 of this volume.

56 ibid.

57 ibid.

58 See Robert Rauschenberg Foundation website, https://www.rauschenbergfoundation.org/foundation (accessed 3 March 2020).

59 ibid.

60 *Matter of the Estate of Rothko*, 84 Misc. 2d 830, 379 N.Y.S.2d 9213 (Surr. Ct. 1975), *modified*, 56 App. Div. 2d 499, 392 N.Y.S.2d 870 (1st Dept), *aff'd* 43 N.Y.2d 305, 372 N.E.2d 291, 401 N.Y.S.2d 449 (1977).

61 For an excellent step-by-step guide on estate planning for artists and a list of resources, see Joan Mitchell Foundation, *CALL—Creating a Lasting Legacy: Estate Planning Workbook for Visual Artists*, undated, http://artsandbusinesscouncil.org/wp-content/uploads/2016/03/call-estate-print-01-20-15.pdf (accessed 3 March 2020).

11

PRESERVING BODILY PRACTICE

Leigh Bowery and Nicola Bateman Bowery

Nathalie Khan

It has been argued that the role of the private collector and the custodian differ greatly.[1] Both can be described as gatekeepers who shape or protect the legacy of an artist. One might also add that they have different motivations, as well as a different understanding and knowledge of the artist or period involved. Such an understanding might link back to personal connections, knowledge or interpretations of artworks, or biographical objects. This chapter aims to unpack some of the issues and motivations behind the role of the custodian in comparison to the collector of fashion in the context of 1980s club culture. The main focus will be on the work of the designer and performer Leigh Bowery. His legacy has played an important role within fashion discourse and to this day his work influences fashion designers and image-makers. His legacy is partly preserved through the custodian Nicola Bateman, his widow and collaborator. In recent years other collections have played a role in shaping the narrative around Bowery's legacy, one example being the private collection of creative director Kim Jones.

Some authors, fashion writers, and journalists have reflected on how Bowery's work can be categorized. He has been described as a performer, fashion designer, or artist. Various exhibitions and publications have placed his work within specific fields or established associations that reflect more on some disciplines rather than others. For example, exhibitions on British club culture and 1980s fashion differ greatly from exhibitions or displays which explore performance art or the process of making. This becomes relevant when legacy is addressed. How should the work of a designer, artist, or performer be placed within a constantly evolving discourse on fashion and the body?

Central to the understanding of fashion and performance is the notion of the body. Lisa Blackman writes: "The body is constructed through symbols, codes, signs signifying activity and discursive practices."[2] Joanne Entwistle argues: "Fashion is about bodies: it is produced, promoted and worn by bodies. It is the body that fashion speaks to, it is the body that must be dressed in almost all social encounters."[3] A performer's legacy can be understood through objects, footage, or documents. The body plays a role in the reconstruction of the natural as well as the cultural body. Objects or garments can hence be understood or experienced as metaphors, which emphasize ideas of social identity such as sexuality or gender. In the case of Leigh Bowery's legacy, clothing is part of bodily experience but more importantly the designer's legacy becomes an embodiment of society.

THREADS AND NARRATIVES

A graduate of Central Saint Martins, Leigh Bowery established himself as a designer in the early 1980s before becoming known for his extreme looks at nightclubs such as Taboo, in central London. His work is linked to his performances with the choreographer Michael Clark and collaborations with Richard Torry and Nicola Bateman in the band Minty. He famously sat for Lucian Freud who painted him and Nicola Bateman towards the latter part of his life. Leigh Bowery died of AIDS-related illnesses on New Year's Eve in 1994 at the age of 33.

Through his participation in London's club scene, Bowery influenced 1980s counterculture, and his body of work exists within various narratives and recollections of this period. A number of people have shaped his legacy since his death—most importantly the artist and close friend Sue Tilley, through her memoir *Leigh Bowery: The Life and Times of an Icon* (1997).[4] In addition the documentary film-maker Charles Atlas has represented Bowery's life and work in *The Legend of Leigh Bowery* (2002). The film makes use of footage and interviews with close friends and collaborators such as Cerith Wyn Evans, Boy George, Rifat Ozbek, Michael Clark, Michael Costiff, and Rachel Auburn, among others.

Various exhibitions on social and design history, with a focus on Bowery's influence on club culture, fashion, and performance, have featured his garments, video footage, and/or photography. In the UK two of the most significant exhibitions took place in the same year: "A Journey Through London Club Culture" at ICA Off-site: The Old Selfridges Hotel (2013), and "From Club to Catwalk" at the Victoria and Albert Museum (2013). Both focused primarily on British club culture as community but took an entirely different approach in the way they explored the link between 1980s art and fashion. As a designer Bowery's work is linked to his self-image through the way he manipulated his body. In this light, various exhibitions outside the UK did not merely focus on club culture but have continued to produce Bowery as a figure of dissent, rebellion, or transgression. There have been numerous exhibitions centred on Bowery's work as an experimental performer, most notably "Leigh Bowery" (2010) at Contemporary Fine Art Mitte, Berlin, "Fashion Drive: Extreme Clothing in the Visual Arts" (2018) at Kunsthaus Zurich, Switzerland, and "The Inner Skin: Art and Shame" (2017) at MARTa Herford, Germany.

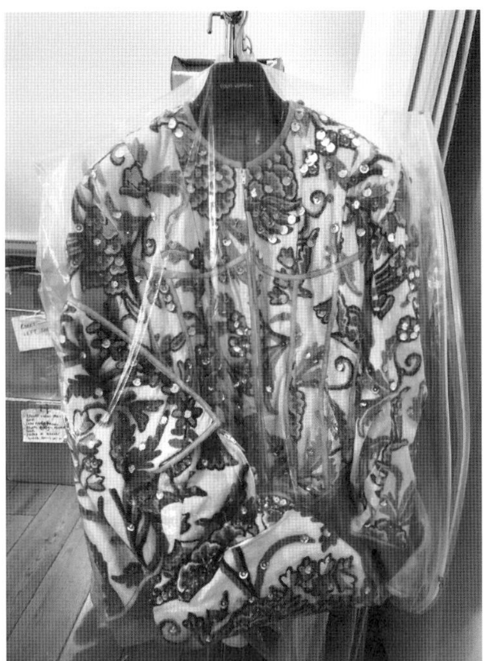

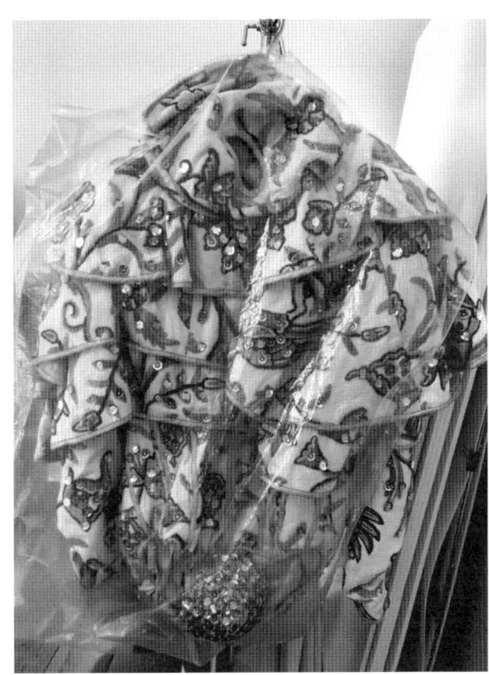

Leigh Bowery designs in Kim Jones' office at Dior headquarters, London, 2018

The Leigh Bowery Estate, managed by Nicola Bateman, has supported two major retrospectives: "XTRAVAGANZA: Staging Leigh Bowery" (2013) at the Kunsthalle Wien in Vienna, and "Take a Bowery" (2004) at the Museum of Contemporary Arts, Sydney.

The collector Kim Jones, who holds a vast archive of Leigh Bowery's garments,[5] has also contributed to some exhibitions. However, recent publications have showcased his private collection within the context of fashion media publishing—most notably the 2019 edition of the annual publication *A Magazine Curated By*, edited by Dan Thawley.[6] This way of presenting archival material is an entirely different approach to the norm. It tells us little about Bowery's work itself but instead promotes the designer Kim Jones as collector. It perpetuates a narrative which presents Jones as a connoisseur of fashion and counterculture. This chapter aims to look more closely at how this way of linking Bowery's artistic legacy to the creative director of a major fashion brand commercializes the legacy of one of the major figures of British fashion and performance art.

CLUB CULTURE AND AUTHORSHIP

Clothing and one-off garments are relevant in the study of fashion and social change. They can be caught in various narratives and interpreted differently depending on the context in which they are viewed. In this way the evaluation of artist legacies differs from the heritage of fashion designers. One-off garments which are associated with designers or specific communities, such as the looks created by Bowery and his peers, are connected to notions of selfhood and image; however, they are also a product of their time and circumstance. Yet there are some parallels between the legacy of fashion designers and artists. In her discussion of "demonstrable legacy", Penelope Curtis argues that sculpture is often a subject of collaborative effort and "pluralistic authorship".[7] This approach can also be applied to the making of one-off garments and creative communities. Consequently authorship can be determined in different ways, on the one hand through direct or biographical knowledge and shared experience and on the other through the connoisseurship of collectors and indirect knowledge and appreciation of social history.

The making of garments is always a collective effort, and this is the case in the production of Bowery's looks as well. Those who have worked on iconic pieces are not always credited in publications or mentioned by curators. In the case of Leigh Bowery, they include Nicola Bateman, Mr Pearl, and Lee Benjamin. Club culture

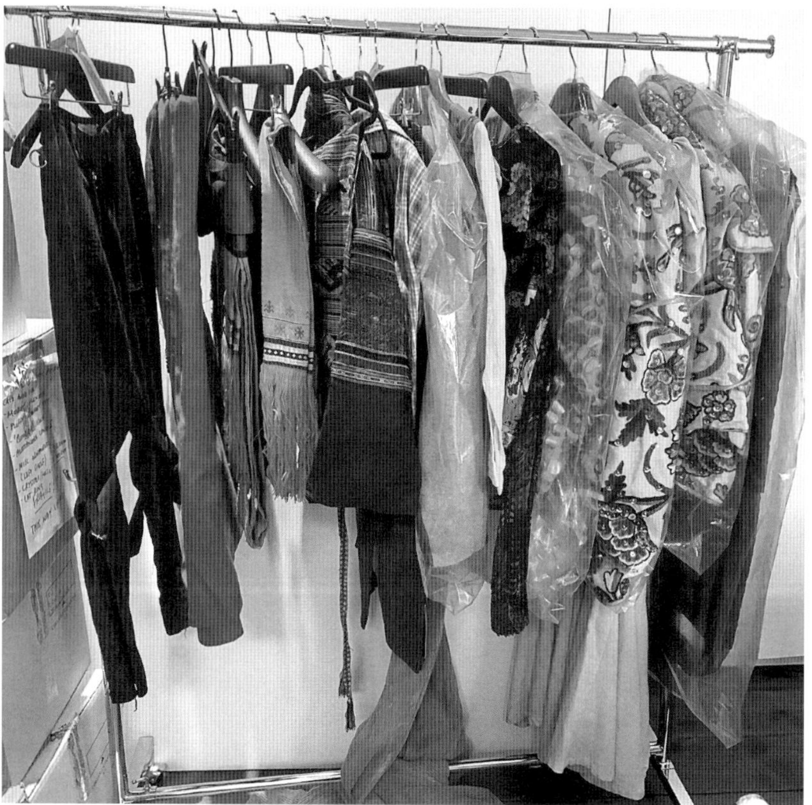

Leigh Bowery designs in Kim Jones' office at Dior head-quarters, London, 2018

is based on collective and shared experience, which has been explored as part of academic discourse on authenticity and subculture.[8]

As Shaun Cole observes, "London's nightclubs, like their clientele, established their own identities through styles of music and presentation that was uniquely integral to each."[9] Clubs as well as the community associated with them established these unique identities at a moment in time. As a cultural movement, club culture as described by Sarah Thornton is based on experience made to come alive at the particular moment but ultimately based on fleeting experience.[10] The concept of club culture in its historical context was based on the notion of performativity, but also as a movement or process as described by Kasia Maciejowska: "The character construction achieved through this process highlights the extent to which the clubs they were going to were performative spaces. This scene was a subculture where camp self-conscious characterization was the subject of respect and reverence."[11]

Individual clubs and club nights serve to support and shape the biography of numerous members of the community, who continue to be invested in its narrative. London club culture of the late 1980s and early 1990s continues to be enormously influential on fashion, style, and art.[12] The issue of who continues to own its legacy has polarized some of those still involved in shaping club culture in London today. Martha Buskirk reflects on the topic of ownership and the significance of the artist's name as a way of preserving legacy. Buskirk states that a signature serves as an act of designation but is also a way to brand the work. However there are other markers which can elevate objects to a higher status as they authenticate an idea as well as 'a singular physical object'.[13] In the case of Bowery's looks, which were manifestations of individual expression and collective experience at the same time, authentication is far more complex. Each outfit was the result of collective effort, hence the making as well as the performance of each look informs the legacy of London club culture. In this sense a specific object or name may overshadow the complex mechanism and numerous recollections which continue to preserve and document this culture.

THE MAKER AS CUSTODIAN: NICOLA BATEMAN

Nicola Bateman, the widow and executer of the late Leigh Bowery's estate, was instrumental in making many garments which shaped British club culture in the 1980s and 1990s. She first met Leigh Bowery at the club Taboo where she approached him before becoming part of his inner circle. Nicola engaged in what can be called the practice of making club culture. This does not only consist of dressing up, getting ready, and going out—although the act of dressing up and getting ready is famously an integral part of club culture. But Nicola was very involved in the process of producing and labouring over carefully designed one-off garments.

The graphic designer Peter Saville argues that pop culture in the UK is about shared experience.[14] He describes it as a kind of crucible of culture, which thrives on mutual engagement. At its core is fashion, which is based on image as well as identity. In the case of London 1980s club culture the practice of making relied on communities. Although the focus is often on the few individuals who performed in the limelight, it was the labour of teams and communities which was at the core of the garments and bodily practice. Nicola Bateman was instrumental in the practice of making, which blurs the boundaries between her role as gatekeeper and author of the garments.

Clothes are and always will be suffused with both physical and social significance. The idea of embodiment, but also the concrete and material production that goes into creating club culture, can be described as an act of transgression. In her discussion of experimental fashion, the fashion historian Francesca Granata links queer culture in the work of Bowery and Nicola Bateman: "Bowery's often hyperbolic artificiality, combined with his questioning the dividing line between life and art, as well as an opposition to a 'common sense' understanding of what constitutes the serious aspect of life, places him squarely within its realm."[15]

Granata based her research on interviews with Bateman, which addressed her level of engagement with both the process of making and her involvement in the performance—in particular the "birth" performance, which was captured in Fergus Greer's iconic image *Leigh and Nicola Bowery, Session VII, Look 37* (1994). Queer theory and discourse may help to unpack the link between the body and performance in this context. One might argue that the garment or objects which embody queer materiality, or what Judith Halberstam refers to as "subjectless desire",[16] would be Bateman herself. In this image and during the iconic performance she is worn like a garment. She embodies what Judith Butler describes in her seminal text *Gender Trouble* (1997) as "fantasized body".[17] Her body becomes costume, aids embodiment, and breaks the binarism between queer and heterosexual identity.

Bateman's own practice was focused on embellishment and the craft of decorating parts of or entire garments with sequins or beading. This intricate process demands skill, precision, and time. I met and spoke to Nicola Bateman in preparation for this chapter and she described the rush, urgency, and intensity which was part of the making of Bowery's costumes. Materials were cheap and a look was determined by what was available or simply around. Production became more managed over time, and this is mirrored in the way sequins or beads were chosen and arranged. Larger sequins characterized her early work. Bateman explained that these took less time to be sewn onto the surface, as the fabric could be covered with them more quickly.[18]

During my interviews with Bateman, she described how the time spent on individual outfits increased and gradually the work became more detailed and elaborate. She also began to collaborate with Mr Pearl, after completing Leigh

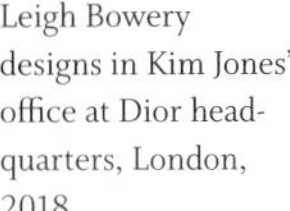

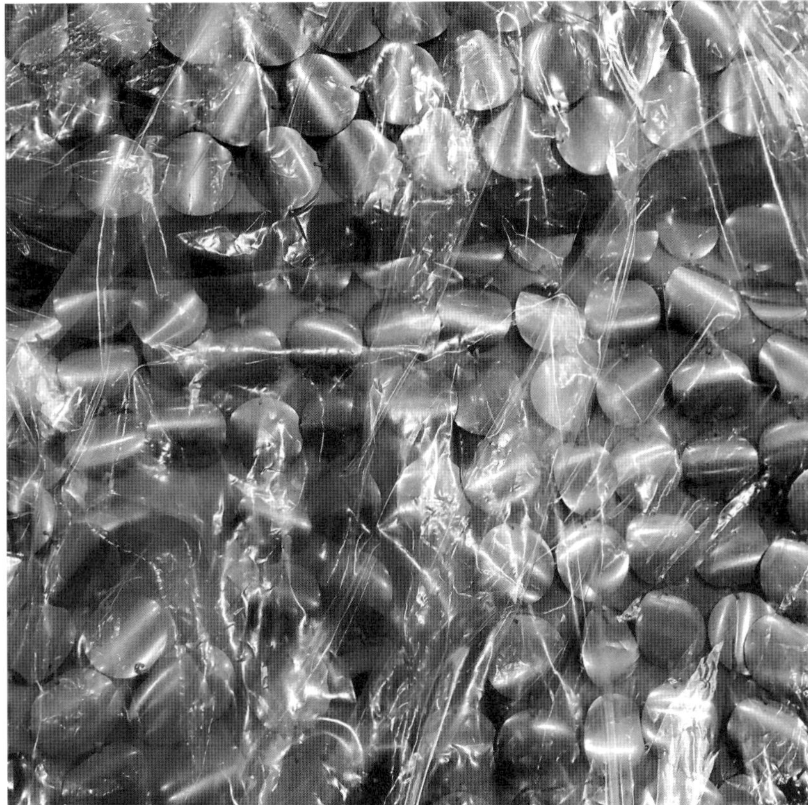

Leigh Bowery designs in Kim Jones' office at Dior headquarters, London, 2018

Bowery's costumes for Michael Clark's *I Am Curious, Orange* (1988) and *Because We Must* (1989).

From the early 1990s onwards Bateman took on more work with Mr Pearl and transferred her skills from looks worn in clubs or on stage to Paris couture. The practice involved was similar as it included stitching of the sequins and beading for designers such as Thierry Mugler, Jean Paul Gaultier, Rifat Ozbek, and Vivienne Westwood. She also worked for British fashion designer Bella Freud whom she met through her work as a life model for Lucian Freud, Bella's father. The level of skill and intricacy involved in Bateman's practice should not be underestimated. She often worked outside the studio or atelier on her own. This was contract work through Mr Pearl. Her labour consisted of long shifts: often 20 hours at a time for five days a week in order to complete the beading or sequins on a particular dress or corset. Each element of her work can be seen as visual and tactile as well as performative, as the sequins shape the look or feel of the surface. Sequins and beading had already become a trademark of Bowery's look at the time Nicola began to transfer her practice to high fashion.

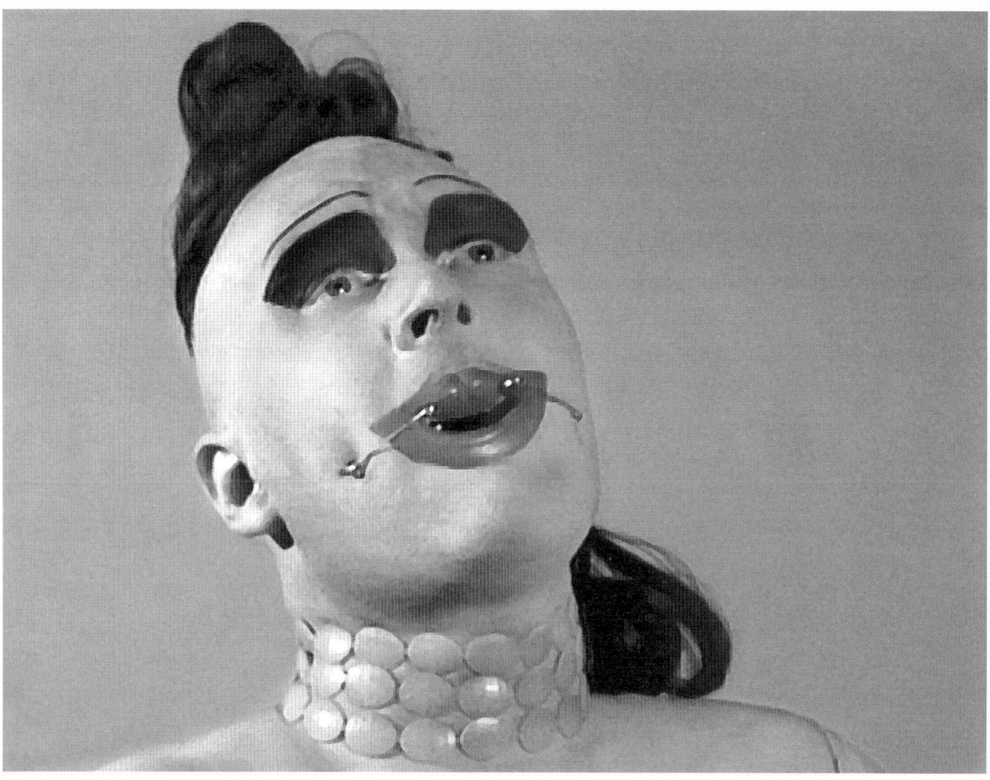

Leigh Bowery still from *Teach*, 1992–8, a video by Charles Atlas

One might argue that her work relied on queer and destabilizing mechanisms which offer a different understanding of gender within club culture as well as Paris couture. A corset embellished by Bateman and commissioned by Mr Pearl took more than 100 hours to complete. The techniques and detail are similar to the embellishment used for Bowery's costume, especially early examples where Bateman worked on ornamenting edges rather than large sections. It could be argued that one practice is transferred to another: what we see here is that club culture borrows from the practice and technique of couture, and its influence is, in turn, fed back into couture. More important however is that Bateman's sequins and beading delimit ideas on transgender identity or even drag.

Bateman's approach is defined through craftsmanship and intricate embellishment, which translated well within the couture context. Equally relevant is the role sequins and beading play within club culture and drag. It is important to note that Bateman sewed the sequins on Bowery's most iconic pieces, now part of Kim Jones' archive. Linking her work back to a queer reading, one might argue that her highly intricate ornamentation becomes a symbolic act. This kind of surface embellishment is something we may traditionally associate with feminine dress and style, and hence becomes part of a gendered performance. If translated into creative context her practice can be seen as a contribution to what Granata, in her discussion of Bowery's style, describes as a destabilizing of gender norms.[19] Hence Bateman's practice can be seen as a performative crossing point between gender binarism.

After Leigh Bowery's death in 1994, Bateman continued to perform in the band Minty, which she started with Bowery, Richard Torry, and the club promoter and musician Matthew Glamorre. The Mint Tea Rooms, a club located in Camden Town, which has been described as an underground art scene, served to channel the anger of those marginalized through reasons of sex, sexuality, or education, toward creative outlets.[20] The venue offered a space where nightlife, popular culture, and art collided. Music, nightclubbing, performance, and visual art have an august tradition of cross-fertilization; films by Cerith Wyn Evans, Alison Leary, and Pulp's Jarvis Cocker were shown. Performances were staged by groups such as Link Leisure's Osmosis and Beauty Clinic, as well as body-piercing routines involving tattoo artist Alex Binney.

It is this shared experience and authorship of the work which has put Bateman into the position of custodian of the Leigh Bowery Estate. Existing research offers only some insight into her extraordinary engagement with this particular chapter of fashion history. In this way her involvement differs greatly from others who have associated themselves with this period.

THE CREATIVE DIRECTOR AS COLLECTOR: KIM JONES

Kim Jones, who is currently creative director at Dior Homme, is an avid collector of 1980s London designers and club culture. Jones has shared his interest in this field and his collection with various journalists over the years, and has stated that he owns around 600 outfits from the period 1970 to 1987.[21] Among the designers mentioned by Jones are Richard Torry, Christopher Nemeth, Vivienne Westwood, Malcolm McLaren, Rachel Auburn, Melissa Caplan, and of course Leigh Bowery.

When I interviewed Jones it was clear that his understanding of this period is grounded in his deep interest in and enthusiasm for design history and the distinction he makes between fashion and culture.[22] As an individual collector his archive has turned into an institution in its own right, as his interest crosses various disciplines, from fashion to music, flyers, magazines, and biographical objects. He recalls, "When I started collecting I didn't know what it would turn into. It is amazing to have them, framing them and to have them in the house."[23]

Jones is interested in accumulating and preserving, and has occasionally lent parts of his collection to museums or curators. In addition he has lent pieces to photographers for fashion editorials. As a creative director of a major couture house, Jones is interested in design, construction, fabrication, and beauty when selecting pieces. He works mainly with the commercial sector and second-hand trade, but also swaps and borrows pieces to add to his collection. He works closely with Steven Phillip, the owner of the independent vintage boutique Rellik, and has acquired pieces from Bowery's close friends, such as Sue Tilley.

The collector plays an important role in the preservation of an artist's legacy. In this case this is due to the fact that Jones shares his knowledge and enthusiasm openly with the public. By placing Bowery's work next to that of other designers in his archive, he establishes connections which might not otherwise exist. Jean Baudrillard discusses the role of the collector as a "system of possession": "We are now in a better position to appreciate the structure of the system of possession: A given collection is made up of a succession of terms, but the final term must always be the person of the collector."[24]

When in 2019 Kim Jones was asked to curate an edition of *A Magazine Curated By*, he focused on sharing his close circle of friends, collaborators, and inspiration as well as his archive.[25] Going through the pages of the magazine, it becomes clear how the designer is caught up in the role and image of the collector. The club culture of the 1980s and the community associated with that period are referred to frequently throughout. Leigh Bowery is mentioned in interviews and editorial features. One specific editorial titled "Punk", photographed by Jackie Nickerson and styled by Ellie Grace Cumming, is particularly relevant in this context. Several pieces are ascribed to Bowery: a hat and top (1983), a jumpsuit for Michael Clark (1987), and a jacket (1985). The editorial also features numerous other designers from the same period such as Vivienne Westwood and Rachel Auburn. It is important to note that it mixes archival material with items from the current season—although the only contemporary pieces shown on the same pages are from Dior Homme. In this way the collector blurs commercial and historical context, promoting both the brand he represents and the archival material he owns. It comes at no surprise that the 1987 jumpsuit by Leigh Bowery for Michael Clark features sequins sewn on by Nicola Bateman.

CONCLUSION

This chapter has aimed to show that an artist's legacy is not rooted in one idea or approach; instead it is based on a dynamic and ongoing conversation with an artist's work. In the case of Leigh Bowery, ideas and concepts relating to the body, performance, and shared authorship are intrinsically linked to the culture he was part of and continues to shape. The role of the custodian, as in the case of Nicola Bateman, can also be caught up in ideas of authorship. These connections should be addressed and acknowledged, as her practice as designer is rarely mentioned. The role of the collector comes with equal responsibility to that of the custodian. Even if the collector may not speak for the artist directly, he or she will continue to be in conversation with the work. Nothing can be presented the way it was, as it only exists in the moment, but legacies continue to live and breathe. Leigh Bowery's designs are a sign of the dynamic of an artist's presence.

Notes

1 See Daniel McLean (ed.), *Artist, Authorship & Legacy: A Reader*, London: Ridinghouse, 2018.
2 Lisa Blackman, *The Body: The Key Concepts*, London: Routledge, 2008, p.67.
3 Joanne Entwistle, *The Fashioned Body*, Cambridge: Polity, 2015, p.35.
4 Sue Tilley, *Leigh Bowery: The Life and Times of an Icon*, London: Sceptre, 1997.
5 See Lou Stoppard, "The obsessive archives of Kim Jones", *AnOther*, 24 July 2015, https://www.anothermag.com/fashion-beauty/7626/the-obsessive-archives-of-kim-jones (accessed 20 May 2019).
6 Dan Thawley, *A Magazine Curated By: Kim Jones* (no.19), 2019.
7 Penelope Curtis, "Demonstrable legacy; or, what sculptures leave behind", in Daniel McClean (ed.), *Artist, Authorship & Legacy: A Reader*, London: Ridinghouse, 2018, p.131.
8 See: Sarah Thornton, *Club Cultures: Music, Media and Subcultural Capital*, London: Bloomsbury, 1995; Ted Polhemus, *Streetstyle: From Sidewalk to Catwalk*, London: Thames & Hudson, 1994; Graham Smith and Chris Sullivan, *We Can Be Heroes: London Clubland 1976–1984*, London: Cornerstone, 2015; Shaun Cole, "New styles new sounds: clubbing, music and fashion in 1980s London", in Sonnet Stanfill (ed.), *From Club to Catwalk: 1980s Fashion*, London: V&A Publishing, 2013, pp.30–47.
9 Cole 2013, op.cit., p.33.
10 Thornton 1995, op.cit.
11 Kasia Maciejowska, *The House of Beauty and Culture*, London: ICA Publishing, 2016, p.77.
12 Cole 2013, op.cit.
13 Martha Buskirk, "Retraction", in Daniel McClean (ed.), *Artist, Authorship & Legacy: A Reader*, London: Ridinghouse, 2018, pp.55–68.
14 "Interview: Peter Saville" (conducted by Lou Stoppard), SHOWstudio, 13 May 2015, https://www.showstudio.com/projects/in_fashion/peter_saville_uncut?autoplay=1 (accessed 18 March 2020).
15 Francesca Granata, *Experimental Fashion, Performance Art, Carnival, and the Grotesque Body*, New York: I.B. Tauris, 2017, p.67.
16 Judith Halberstam, *In a Queer Time and Place*, New York: New York University Press, 2005, pp.1–22.
17 Judith Butler, *Gender Trouble*, London: Routledge, 1997, p.96.
18 Interview between the author and Nicola Bateman, 15 October 2015.
19 Granata 2017, op.cit.
20 Gregor Muir, "The Mint Tea Rooms", *Frieze*, 11 September 1995, https://frieze.com/article/mint-tea-rooms (accessed 18 March 2020).

21 Stoppard 2015, op.cit.; Ben Reardon, "The story of Kim Jones for Dior Homme", *iD Magazine*, 5 November 2018, https://i-d.vice.com/en_uk/article/pa97p7/kim-jones-dior-homme-alasdair-mclellan (accessed 23 May 2019); statistic from: "Interview: Kim Jones—artistic director Kim Jones interviewed by Georgina Evans on 28 May 2019 as part of SHOWstudio's *In Fashion* series", https://www.showstudio.com/projects/in_fashion/interview-kim-jones?autoplay=1 (accessed 30 June 2019).

22 Interview between the author and Kim Jones, 1 November 2018.

23 ibid.

24 Jean Baudrillard, "The system of collecting", in John Elsner and Roger Cardinal (eds), *The Cultures of Collecting*, London: Reaktion Books, 1994, pp.7–24 (p.12).

25 Dan Thawley (ed.), *A Magazine Curated By: Kim Jones* (no.19), 2019.

12
SKETCHY BUSINESS

Architectural Legacies

Mark Morris

In an interview on 25 October 2019, Mark Morris, Head of Teaching at the Architectural Association (AA), discussed the intricacies of architects' bequests with AA Archivist Edward Bottoms.

As the oldest independent architecture school in the UK, not to mention one of the most prestigious in the world, one would imagine the AA has a long-lived archive. Not so. Established in 2010, the AA Archives grew out of the association's library. The alma mater of Archigram, Frei Otto, Will Alsop, Kenneth Frampton, Zaha Hadid, and Rem Koolhaas, the AA has been at the forefront of architectural education and discourse particularly since the administration of Alvin Boyarsky in the 1970s and 1980s. Since then it has grown as a school and an influence, with visiting programmes stretching across the globe.

The diverse output of architects—sketches, measured drawings, blueprints, models, digital drawings, and virtual models, wed to devices and software that upgrades, moves on, or goes defunct—presents challenges to any architectural archive, particularly one nested within a busy school of about a thousand students and staff. Scanning fragile drawings and photographing delicate models on a small budget lends some urgency to our conversation. In my interview with Ed, we look to how a grand institution came to have a late-in-the-day archive, how architects generally archive themselves (and how that can be a blessing and a curse when they donate things), how students and scholars use and abuse the archive in an educational setting, and how things are donated by happenstance and sometimes against stated policies.

We begin by discussing how the AA Archives' acquisition policies work, and a recent large gift, including a model, from Gillian Hopwood of the influential firm Godwin and Hopwood. Ed explains the firm was founded by Hopwood with her partner John Godwin, both of whom studied architecture at the AA and qual-

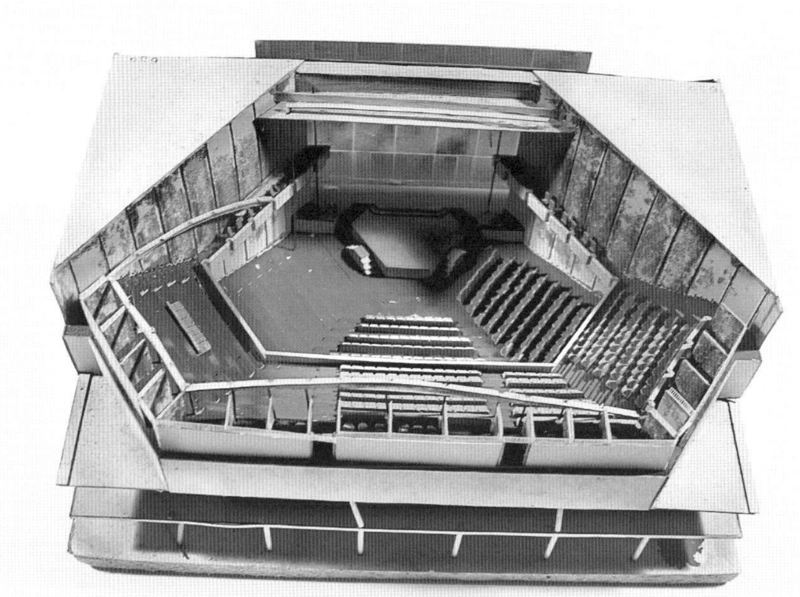

Gillian Hopwood and John Godwin, Design model for a National Theatre School, Architectural Association (AA), London, Year 4, 1948/49

ified in 1950. "They set up their own office in Nigeria in 1954 and they became the biggest architectural practice in Lagos." Regarded as iconic figures in the history of architectural practice in Nigeria after spending about 60 years living and practising there, they were involved in designing many significant projects in the city. John also established an academic career as a Professor of Architecture at the University of Lagos. "They remained there during the civil war and I believe they retired only three or four years ago. . . . The model we've got is one that they did as part of their practice, so we shouldn't really have collected it, because it's not part of our collecting policy, but we wouldn't have got their other material if we hadn't collected that."

When asked what other material was acquired, Ed continues: "The gift includes all of Gillian's AA school work, and a beautiful little theatre model, a project on which they worked together. And we've been promised John's school work; he drew beautifully. The other model is for the university in Lagos, which is still standing. It's quite a big model, of a kind of 1960s postcolonial building that could have come out of the AA's Tropical Department. It looks a bit like work by Maxwell Fry. It's a nice model of its period, which would be by a modelmaker they employed who was also an AA graduate and it's been digitized for the Archives so we've got it in the round."

I ask how the AA Archives come to acquire material like this: *"Did they come back to the AA for a lecture or for an exhibition?"*

"They are part of a network of AA alumni with whom I'm in touch, though I forget how I got in contact with them initially. As I recall we had a Le Corbusier conference back in approximately 2007 at which one of the people we invited was a student who had been in communication with Le Corbusier. He had become a good friend of the Godwins through that event, so he contacted them when he gave us all his material and his archive. We've done an oral history with Gillian, so we've got her story on tape, and we became friendly and just kept in touch. Eventually, when they moved over here permanently in retirement, we got the entire archive from them."

When asked if happenstance really plays such a large role in acquiring material for the AA Archives: *"'A friend told me you might be doing this' and then you strike up the relationship and then 8 years later boxes arrive?"*

Ed says pretty much, yes, although a bit of chasing is involved, and in this specific case it was more complicated. "The model must have come from Africa and survived all that time, which is in itself, at least as regards our archiving in the UK, unusual for a practice, let alone one where a model has got to be transported. You've also got climatic issues in Nigeria, and there was the revolution and the survival of the thing during transport."

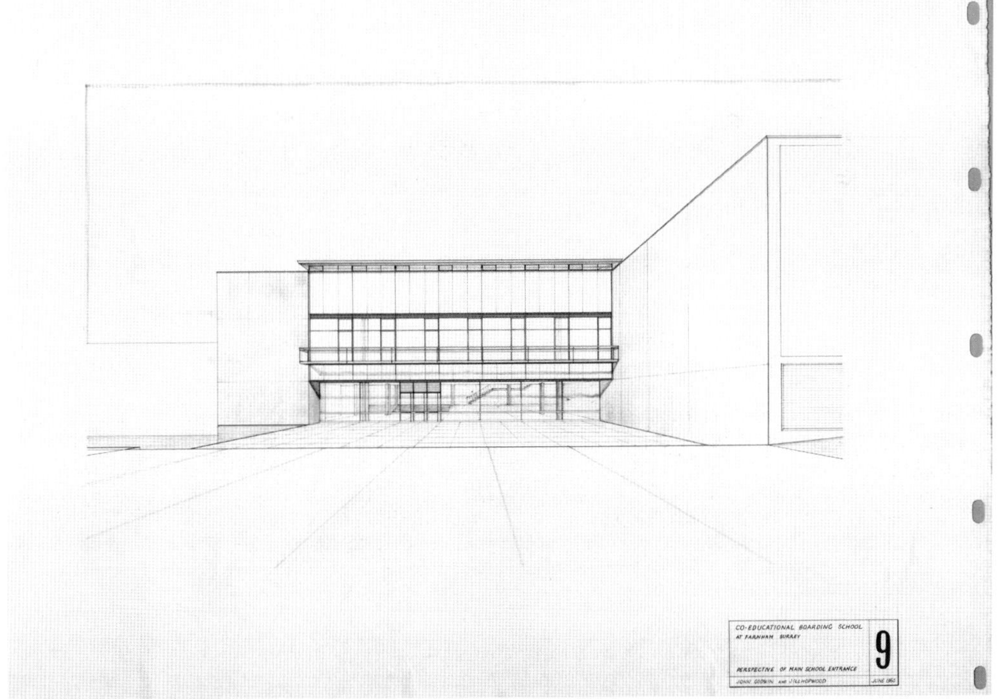

Gillian Hopwood and John Godwin, Perspective of the main entrance for a 'Co-educational boarding school at Farnham', AA, Year 5, 1949/50

Ed explains that the AA's Tropical Department was set up in 1954: "The Godwins began their practice just before that, so they're kind of 'early achievers' of that movement immediately after the war when architects went elsewhere to look for work because of the recession here. And they're the longest survivors of the movement, because they remained in Nigeria. And they're both still with us. They have the nicest house in Cheltenham and a place in Herefordshire, and they're pretty much indivisible; you can't speak to just one of them!"

The discussion moves to the question of where models and similar material are stored off site, and how material there is accessed. "The off-site storage is up at Heyford, near Bicester in Oxfordshire. We don't really tend to check on it often, because basically we have individual items brought here so we can look at the bar codes. At a certain point, during a temporary move, everything, including the photo library, was sent out but nothing was labelled, so we have to try to figure out how to bring everything back into the digital system."

Moving to how the archive works with students and visitors, I ask Ed how he engages with people who walk into the AA Archives with only work by Zaha and Archigram on their minds: *"Do you let them know that the material isn't here or do you have token things from Archigram or Zaha that are segues to the more robust part of the archive?"*

Ed replies that "It really depends on who the person is and what their interest or purpose for coming to the AA archive is. We try to establish that first, and then, if it's a first-year student who wants to see Zaha's work, for example, we would straight up say we don't have any of Zaha's student work, but might show them something visually attractive from the same time as when she studied here and then say something like: 'other people are doing similar things' or 'this is the context in which she was working as a student' and try to help them that way."

I ask if there are any remnants of Archigram's work remaining at the AA.

Ed replies, "We do have a little bit of material, odds and sods really. Obviously we've got *Archigram* magazine, and we've also got some postcards which they published but which they sent to friends. So what we have tend to be things that people have received and that then come to us. There was no AA Archive at the time, and Archigram kept everything themselves. I've got a man coming in soon who says he worked for Archigram and has some of their posters and original artwork. He'll be bringing some of that material in, which will be nice."

"In general, with those big collections it's been tricky. Because we only set up about ten years ago, we missed the boat for a lot; we don't have the Koolhaas kind of graduation project, and Cedric Price's archives went to CCA [the Canadian Centre for Architecture]. And Archigram obviously want money for their collection, so that kind of rules us out as well."

The people who come to the AA Archives vary from serious scholars to those who arrive with only assumptions. I ask Ed how he interacts with the latter: "*Where do you end up leading them if they are here for a day and they're not going to see those things they expect? Where do you pivot them so there's a way to engage with the Archive?"*

"To be honest we don't get many people who come in that manner. We get students who'll just come on the off-chance, and they'll envisage spending half an hour or one hour here, in which case if it's clear to me that they just want to browse, then I can just pull out some kind of sexy stuff, generally from the 70s; that's the kind of thing that they want to see. Quite often students will come and they will want to see recent work, so I find guiding them to Honours projects from the last few years is helpful, to see how they should be presenting their own work."

"We also get quite a few that are lost in their unit's studio work and want to have a breath of fresh air to clear the brain, to actually feel free of the unit and so to free up their creativity a little bit by seeing something totally different, but related, from a different period. Because they're coming to the AA archive, as opposed to a library or archive in another institution, students find something which is connected—if not to the unit, to the school. It can be sometimes very specific, so: 'I'm working on this in my unit as my project, have you got anything that's similar?' So I'll pull up something, say, from the 50s, and dealing with a similar issue."

The ability to anticipate a student's unexpressed need brings up the matter of Ed's intimate familiarity with the whole of the archive, and not just the digitized or indexed components. I suggest that as the first archivist, he is in an interesting place as he knows it so well that he will instantly know what resources might be helpful to users: *"You've seen it all and anyone who'll come after you will not have that intuitive sense of 'where'. And as things go off site, given the constraints of place, even the regular collection—the material that tends to be in specific locations—goes away too."*

"Yes, and that's the worry really, that as things become digitized the archives will become more useful if you are a researcher and you know specifically what you've got the time to research, but less useful for a lot of the people today who just come in and want something, but they're not sure what, and they don't have or won't take the time to go through the catalogue to find it. It's very typical for here. I think people want visual images that are fast, and that work for them."

I ask what percentage of the collection has thus far been digitized.

"For the Archives in terms of drawings we're pretty well done; probably up to 75%. In terms of the manuscripts, which are less used, it's probably about 20%. These are all catalogued rather than digitalized, so someone can find them by looking in the catalogue though they won't be able to see any images. Theses would generally be in the AA Library.

"It's things like teaching records or the administrative archive for the school, such as accounts from 1880, which are really interesting if you're looking at the growth of professional societies and the growth of architectural education. But you don't get many people looking at those except for scholars like PhD students looking at networks of Victorian architects' apprentices and that kind of thing. Those records are a gold mine, but because so few people ask for them they're not as high a priority for digitizing or cataloguing."

With limited resources, Ed must make the call about use and constituency: *"My fantasy is that you've got scholars calling you up, and you've got a scholar a month coming by and doing something serious. Is that so, or is it more sporadic than that? Beyond our own students, what is that other world?"*

"About 50% of the readers are external; mostly postgraduate students and academics; probably again about 50% each. And then aside from that we get a few artists coming in, often looking for 'found stuff'. So that's another interesting question: how do you 'find' something for somebody? It's an artificial kind of process."

"We don't get many historians coming in. We get publishers looking for material but for the most part we get postgraduates, serious academics, really, who come and spend time here. And they're the external users that we are aiming for. We also get quite a few international people who tend to stay for a week or so. And when people stay a bit longer you have the opportunity to engage and develop a good relationship with them, and that creates more networks and more people hear about the archive, which is all to the good."

I ask whether the AA archive is in a consortium or partnership with any others.

Ed answers yes, very much so: "We export our catalogue records to something called AIM25, which consists of archives located within the M25 motorway that wraps London. Somebody can go onto that website and access all those archives in one place. There's another web consortium of archives which covers the whole of the UK, so you can search our records in there. We get quite a few people using that. Obviously, we're in the National Archives too. We're listed in their records as a repository of architectural drawings, and some people come to us that way. Then the records are in both the AA Archives catalogue and in the AA Library catalogue. It's all a bit complicated!"

"The AA Archives also have a very informal relationship with the RIBA (Royal Institutue of British Architects), so a few people a year come here in the hope of finding details about a project for the purpose of Grade 1 or Grade 2 listings, or something about English Heritage. These tend to be architects, wanting to find original drawings or plans. We've got a good many of those because in the 19th century a lot of the students would go out on excursions to draw on site; they'd be doing measured drawings of buildings which are now drastically changed."

The question of scandals comes up since, as with most archives and libraries, inevitably things occasionally go missing. I ask Ed if anything has walked out the door in his time.

"Not that I know of for certain. I remember when I first arrived someone showed me a signatures book in the library's storage area—it was for when you were signing out a book or something like that—which contained signatures from a Who's Who of architects from the 1920s and 30s and 40s, including both Le

Corbusier's and Frank Lloyd Wright's signatures, and I have never been able to find that since. It didn't come to the archive and so that might have walked!"

"And in the 1960s the AA gave a lot of material to the RIBA on permanent loan, including many Pre-Raphaelite paintings. Can you believe it?! Also work by Charles Barry. Legally we can ask for it back and they'll have to return it, but in terms of our relationship to the RIBA that would be it, seeing as they've paid the storage and the conservation for the last 50 years. In fact—last year, I think it was—I was asked if it would be possible to reclassify those items from a permanent loan to an actual gift. I said, 'Well if you want that you'll have to put it in writing and I'll have to raise it with Council, and if that happens who knows what Council will want to do?' There was silence after that."

"There are other things. We've got an inventory of stuff from after the war when everything came back from the old Welsh mines where it had been stored away from the bombs. And that inventory bears no resemblance to what we've got in the building now, so there's a lot that went missing somewhere."

In the unexpectedly social world of acquiring material for the archive, which links exhibitions and personal relationships, professional and school relationships, I wonder whether the AA ever gets caught up in any lawsuits or disputes, or whether material is ever claimed back: *"Extract it from the archive! It was never meant to be there. Granddad didn't know what he was doing . . ."*

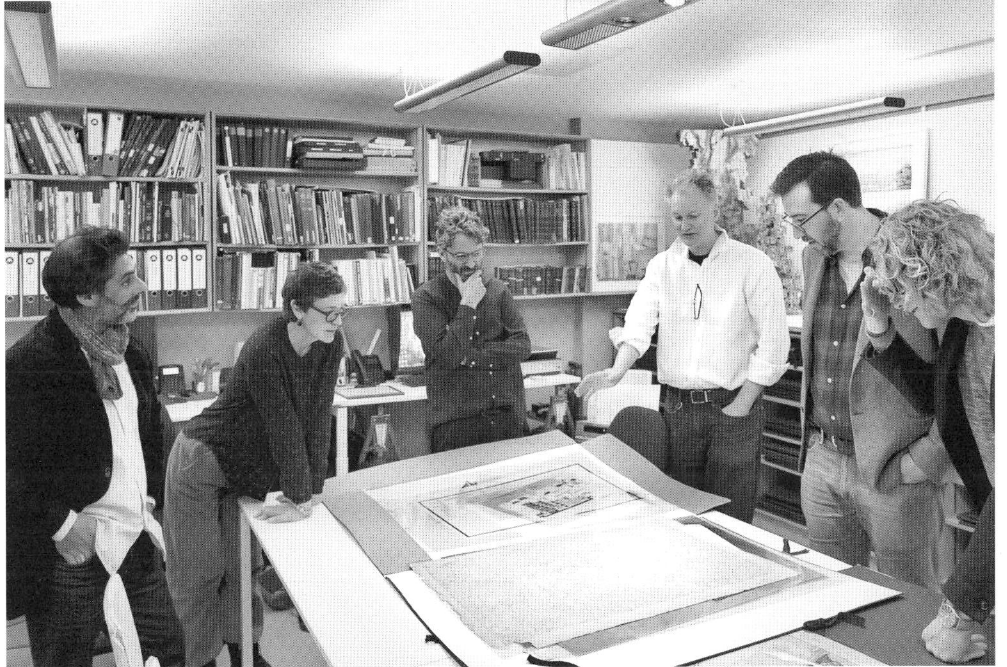

Party of visiting academics in the AA Archives Reading Room, 2019

"Since we've started acquiring stuff for the archive *officially*, we've had an acquisition deed which needs to be signed, it's a legal document. Before that we basically had nothing, and there's a lot of material which came to the AA before the archive was set up, and we have no idea how it got here. So it's possible that in the future someone might show up and there could be claims. For example, there are the [Charles] Barry drawings for the Houses of Parliament. We've no idea how we got them or whether they were lent to the AA for an exhibition and never returned, or whether somebody gave them in their will or what. We've absolutely no idea. There's a lot of material like that."

The inherent messiness of the material the AA Archives deal with, its diversity—ranging from blueprints to ephemera like postcards, and all types of models—coupled with the longevity of architectural careers, throws up challenges for the archivist. During a certain period almost every architect was also a keen photographer, so archives contained boxes and boxes of prepared slides. These are time-consuming to scan, bulky to store, and few people ask to see them. Additional complications are presented by the diversity of approaches each architect has for cataloguing his or her own work during his or her lifetime. Work might include preparatory sketches, real drawings, blueprints, and photomechanical transfers. The archivist has to decide what is important, and how material fits into the AA Archives' educational mission.

"I think architects are generally very good archivists or at least they keep their records much better than other professions—like writers, for example. Part of that is obviously legal, architects have to keep proper records for X number of years. But traditionally architects are organized people, or tend to be, in the way their offices are run and that reflects in the way they store and order things. I don't know how much of a generalization that is, but having seen many other archives and different types, I'm always amazed when material from architects comes here and we're told it's all come from the office and hasn't been touched, and it's all in order. Moreover, the very fact that architects are so meticulous in their self-collecting makes them archive-friendly."

When looking at architects' collections of day books, every spine for decades in the same hand, and pages tabbed for different topics throughout a complete adult life, one becomes aware of the trails behind creative careers. I ask Ed whether any additional external order is applied to an externally well-ordered box of documents that comes in. Presumably it is not disturbed?

"Yes, that's a kind of golden law: the first principle is that you don't disturb it unless there's clearly no visible order. You've got to make the material accessible somehow, but using the lightest touch possible. If you can discern absolutely no order, then the standard archive theory is that you order it by function. But this kind of theory is really developed for large institutions, where it is easy to establish that this is the financial function of the company, this is the production function, and these are the human resources. The theory is harder to transfer to an architecture school archive. But it does mean that here we simply separate out student work, and then we are free to subdivide that in any other way. Here at the AA that would be student work and output of the school, and then you might have a publishing arm, you might have teaching records underneath another branch of school work, Council would be under governance, finances, too. In a sense it's a false structure, because we're imposing an order on the material based on our own critical assumptions."

I ask whether he is describing the AA Archives' in-house order or whether the hierarchy has been borrowed from elsewhere.

"I've got a diagram showing the tree, but it's developing and changing constantly. The good thing is that it's almost irrelevant in a way, because when you've got it all on a catalogue then you can search through that catalogue however you want, by keyword or by topic, or names. The diagram just helps, and acts as the filter."

Making decisions about what material to discard must be difficult. I ask Ed how those decisions are made.

"Generally, because we're a fairly young archive, if anything is dross, I'll make that decision at the point of cataloguing the material. I wouldn't be going back later and looking at the catalogue and saying, 'We don't need this bit and this bit.' But there might be a situation in which we will go back later. Because we have very little from the 1910s, for example, the moment anything comes in from the 1910s, even if it's the worst kind of student, we'd grab it just as an example of what's being taught and an example of the pedagogy and what students were doing at the time. But if suddenly we find in ten years' time that we've got 50 portfolios from 1910, then we can go back and limit the collection to the strongest ones. But on the other hand, sometimes the good material is not always exactly what standard work is for the time. So if it's an archive that's supposed to reveal the pedagogy of the AA, if you had only Diploma Honours material then these are people who are exceptions rather than the general. So sometimes it's good to have mediocre stuff and bad stuff, because it tells you what was the norm."

"In fact there is no right way to decide whether what comes in is dross, or what's not useful. And you don't know what historians in 20 years' time will be looking at. When you look at the list of Diploma Honours, for example, it's fascinating because, although I might be exaggerating, maybe 60% of them you'd never have heard of. And then if you were to make a list of famous architects who didn't get Diploma Honours it's probably much longer. So it's very subjective, that way of collecting."

One of the greatest challenges during the processing of a gift or bequest, and making decisions about what to keep and what to discard, is the matter of physical storage space: the more cubic metres/feet of storage a bequest requires, the more likely it is that other bequests will be limited. At the same time, the archivist making those decisions is aware that what is kept and discarded will determine how historians will write about the subject in the future.

"It does impact on the way historians write. Because I've read so much material—basically everything that has been written on the AA in the last ten years—I've been able to see this. What's been written about the AA is focused exactly on only the things that have survived. It's the material that very much determines what's written. Our choices now are important because they reflect how the history is made, because people are dependent on what survives."

Only a handful of books and essays have been written about the history of the AA, including titles like John Summerson's centennial history of the AA (1947), James Gowan's *Continuing Experiment: Learning and Teaching at the Architectural Association* (1975) and *Drawing Ambience: Alvin Boyarsky and the Architectural Association* (2015) by Igor Marjanovic and Jan Howard. I ask Ed what to his mind are the best resources if someone were interested in learning about the AA.

"Irene Sunwoo's *Pedagogy's Progress: Alvin Boyarsky's International Institute of Design*, published by Grey Room in 2009, is probably the most rounded on the Boyarsky period. Another scholar is working on a book on the AA of the 1950s that's very good, but they're both extended studies so they're not using just drawings. In fact they use very few of the drawings; they're using the documentary archives. More recently we had the 'AA XX' series of events and a fascinating discussion about when women were first enrolled at the AA 100 years ago. Those projects take a lot of archival research, but the material is there. It's fascinating to me. That's the really interesting part of the archive—it's hard to get to and it takes time to dig out, but you do find gold."

"In Boyarsky's case that's work within his office as Chair, or the policy-making documents and Council Minutes; the written evidence, in a way, to supplement the drawings. You get other kinds of essays in which most of the writing is obviously about the 70s and the 80s, and most of that is done by people wanting to sell a mythology or a sexier story. And although that's a kind of valid story, it's also a very partial story, and it's usually done by people who were either participants in it or who have got access to participants who are then recalling events wearing rather rose-tinted spectacles. And I don't want to sound cynical, but there are articles—where I know from having seen manuscripts and papers here—in which what they describe is just wrong, didn't happen or is out of sequence."

"And once something has been written, it's used as a source and quoted in other books and essays."

"Yes it's a continuing cycle, especially as there's not all that much material been written about the AA. There's obviously no correct kind of version though."

I wonder whether the paucity of written material about the AA leads to greater inaccuracies when people research secondary sources: *"In the case of the history of Harvard's architecture programme, you'd have three hundred titles that you could go to, and if you cross-indexed them all would you arrive at a fuller version of the truth?*

"You'd arrive at a more internally consistent version, yes. But there's always a middle ground and when a student comes in here I'm as guilty of mythologizing as anybody by showing them the finest drawings and of getting them enthusiastic about that kind of thing—but that's what history is in a way, isn't it?"

"You're making a pedagogical judgment that in order to trigger a longer sustained interest in these things, you want the first impression to be a compelling one?"

"Yes, that's right."

By way of conclusion, a student knocks on the door to the archive and, true to our respective roles, Ed and I jump to help. She is researching the history of parties and celebrations in the long life of the AA. Ed has lots of photographs, almost all digitized, of the legendary AA pantomimes of the 1920s and 1930s to show her, including plays and original sheet music handwritten in haste by students. The architectural allusions and in-house puns from that era are hard to grasp, but the young people striking poses in wild costumes in old photos speak clearly to us. As does documentation of carnivals and concerts of the 1960s, when Pink Floyd played in the old lecture hall or the goth Bauhaus band played in the 1980s. There's even a rough recording or two to listen through. Ed comments that he wants graduates from those years to get in touch and donate more odds and sods related to such happenings. The archive works its magic and we all tumble into its folds. Youthful and imperfect though they are, the AA Archives do their best work on this impromptu basis, where the past meets pedagogy and the door remains open.

13

ENGLISH ARISTOCRATIC COLLECTIONS AND THEIR LEGACIES

Alexandra Bowes-Lyon

The aristocratic owners of some of Britain's most well-known country estates and art collections have, in the last century, had to re-evaluate how best to keep their centuries-old art collections and/or estates together. Why is it so important that we keep these collections and estates together? Is it simply for historical value, or something more profound, and what are the contemporary solutions for age-old issues? Should the government be incentivizing and assisting keeping together valuable and historical collections and preserving British history and the legacies of historically important family collections, or are we just delaying the inevitable? Are all collections merely guarded for future generations to disperse and reconfigure?

As a case study, I will examine a particularly significant collection owned by the Duke of Bridgewater, known as the Bridgewater Collection.

ARISTOCRATIC COLLECTIONS, THE WORLD WARS, AND TAXATION

For much of the last 400 years, members of the British aristocracy have concerned themselves with the collection of artefacts. As the agricultural depression began to decrease their wealth in the 1870s and 1880s, they were forced to sell some of their prize possessions. Art such as portraits, furniture, and iconography were a testament to a family's status, wealth, and taste. As the 4th Baron Somerleyton stated, "I think the hereditary peerage worth preserving and its principle creates a sense of innate commitment to the welfare of the nation."[1]

In actual fact, this system went much further back, to the Agricultural Revolution in the 18th century when the extent of owned land decided your station in society. Subsequently, this dispersed to much more than just land. The aristocracy had initially used religion as an excuse to appropriate land in the Early Middle Ages: they seized land freely when they conquered it, and they used every aspect of their hierarchical positions to take any land and estate they thought worthy. Their wealth was further strengthened by ostentatious exhibitions of affluence (feasts, jewels, decorative clothing). This abundance of wealth and ownership was ultimately what the fundamentals of society were fabricated upon. Lands were taken from the poor and added to the already vast estates of the rich to manage and ultimately wield as a statement of power, influence, and position in society.[2]

In a nutshell, collecting land, estates, and the riches of art that came with them identified a family with wealth, nobility, and education. Take for example the "Grand Tour" that young aristocrats were sent on to explore the riches and culture of Europe. This was designed to give them an education and for them to return as refined and tasteful young ladies or gentleman with great knowledge of the arts as well as having added to the family collection.[3]

The author Evelyn Waugh was perhaps most famously known for his portrayals of English country life in all its opulence. *Brideshead Revisited* (1945)—much like its American counterpart, F. Scott Fitzgerald's *The Great Gatsby* (1925)—offered an insight into an exclusive and opulent society and all the privilege, wealth, and splendour that it entailed. Towards the end of the book, however, Waugh accurately captures a shifting mood of a declining world, where the country estate which was seen to resemble power and wealth was fast disappearing. A new world and a new order were approaching.[4]

During the Second World War many large houses were commandeered for military use, hospitals, and government operations—for example, Bletchley Park in Buckinghamshire, which was used for code-breaking operations. By the end of the war when the houses were returned to their owning families, many of them were in a state of dilapidation and in much need of repair. Precedence was given to rebuilding what had been destroyed during the war, rather than the immediate repair of large elite homes. The British public was still suffering from food rationing, and the need for ancestral estates to be restored was of little priority. To add to this, increased taxation to pay for the cost of war resulted in many seeing abandoning their estates as the only option. It seemed all too clear that the old order had passed.

Prior to the 19th century, the British aristocracy enjoyed a life relatively free from taxation. Staff were abundant and incredibly inexpensive, and every estate would have had them—indeed they were dependent on their staff to run them. Estates not only provided a generous income from tenanted land but also political power. This all changed after the world wars. Staff were either killed during one of the wars, were no longer needed, or looked for better wages elsewhere. Thus began the disposal of material assets such as art to effectively be able to keep the estate running. This, coupled with a lack of legislation or interest to protect what is now considered to be the nation's heritage, saw the beginning of the end of an era for the aristocracy of Britain.

The desire or need to keep collections together, and the issues getting in the way of these legacies, began long before the 20th century with the gradual introduction and increase of taxes on income and further tax on inherited wealth. The taxation after the world wars was what really changed the landscape, and would alter Britain's past and its future. The burden of tax forced many estates and famous collections to be sold in whole or in part, and it is estimated that some of the most prominent families sold around seven million acres (three million hectares), or a quarter of England itself. As Charles Spencer wrote in *Vanity Fair* in 2009, "What is left of the British aristocracy today is, with a handful of exceptions, a mere echo of what many successive generations saw as the fabulously wealthy, intensely powerful, outrageously glamorous class that rose with the British Empire but hit the rocks a generation before."[5]

Most importantly, the incoming Labour Government raised death duties to astronomical heights in 1945. The need to finance the cost of war forced the Government to raise revenue through increased taxation. This was the killer. Death duties, or inheritance tax as it is known, slowly increased and became a silent assassin for country estates throughout the first half of the 20th century. In 1940 death duties were raised from 50% to 65%, and they were subsequently raised twice more between 1946 and 1949. In 1948 estate tax was charged at 75% on estates worth more than £1 million. This was crippling to any estate and family. Politicians and the public were unsympathetic to the situation.[6]

The Bridgewater Collection is an example of the detrimental effects of the world wars on family collections. Death duties meant that millions of pounds had to be spent on inheritance tax, and in the following decades the Duke of Bridgewater was forced to sell parts of his prestigious collection to fund this. There was little spent on unnecessary superfluities after the war, and this was reflected in the sale of October 1946 when Christie's auctioned 180 of the gallery's paintings, 32 of which came from the Orléans collection from the Palais Royal in Paris, for a measly £13,038—a true sign of the times (they would be worth £13 million or more today).[7] Later in the 1970s the duke sold at auction a group of Old Master drawings which had once formed part of the celebrated collection gathered by the portrait painter Sir Thomas Lawrence. The collection, mostly of drawings by the Carracci family, but including works by Guercino, fetched nearly £500,000.[8] Subsequently, the duke sold works by Turner, Van Dyck, and Reynolds. News of this sale provoked a row in parliament over the impact of high capital taxes on private art collections and a campaign to keep two of the most important works—a seascape by Turner and a *Virgin and Child* by Van Dyck—from being exported. In the event, the Turner was sold to a British collector for £340,000 while the Van Dyck was saved for the nation when the Fitzwilliam Museum in Cambridge raised more than £200,000 to buy it.[9] In 1984, four paintings from the Bridgewater Collection that had been on loan to Edinburgh since 1945—respectively by Gerard Dou, Lorenzo Lotto, Jan Steen, and Tintoretto—were sold to the National Gallery for £2 million, exempt of tax, with the proceeds going into a maintenance fund for the family estate.[10]

21ST-CENTURY ISSUES AROUND FAMILY ESTATES: DEBT, DIVORCE, TAXATION

Thus far I have discussed how struggles to keep a collection together arose and the context behind British aristocratic family estates and collections. In the second section of this essay I discuss what the current issues facing aristocratic family collections are, and whether these are a mere continuation of what has been happening up until now or different.

The ethical dilemmas of selling a collection that has been in the family for years, if not centuries, are complex and plentiful and weigh on many an heir today. To be the heir that split up the family collection that holds so much family history, pride, and wealth is what some might feel to be unconscionable. More to the point, the ethical nuances surrounding whether or not it is appropriate to split up a historically valuable collection that only holds meaning as a collection rather than individual works of art is often contentious.

Some may argue that these collections are records of moments in time, and are thus of historical significance. This was exemplified in Titian's *Diana and Actaeon* (1556–9) from the Duke of Bridgewater's collection, which was deemed to be a national treasure and therefore necessary to keep in the UK. Its retention was seen to be in the interest of safeguarding Britain's artistic heritage and preserving its historical legacies. The work was painted for Philip II of Spain, and was owned by a series of European monarchs and noblemen before coming into the hands of a group of English aristocrats—men who forged taste in British art at the time. This group founded what was to become one of the greatest art collections of paintings and drawings in 19th-century London in private hands.

Following the sub-prime mortgage crash in 2008, due to estate cost pressures the Duke of Bridgewater was forced to put two works up for sale, one of which was Titian's *Diana and Actaeon* and the other Titian's *Diana and Callisto* (also 1556–9). The British Government deemed these paintings of such cultural and historical significance that it wanted to raise the money to keep the works in the country; failing that, an outside buyer would be able to purchase them, and they would inevitably disappear from the UK and from its history. The headline in the *Telegraph* newspaper on 14 February 2009, the day of the sale, was: "The national art treasures Britain cannot afford to lose".[11] Titian's *Diana and Actaeon* was saved for the nation following a highly publicised campaign to raise £50 million (with a tax offset) to buy the work from the Bridgewater Collection. The picture is now split between the National Gallery of Scotland and the National Gallery in London, which take turns in displaying it.

David Barrie, the director of The Art Fund, which donated £1 million to the *Diana and Actaeon* campaign, said, "The public should be given the opportunity to enjoy great works of art at every opportunity. Many of these works have formed part of the furniture of British cultural life, they have informed creative imagination and

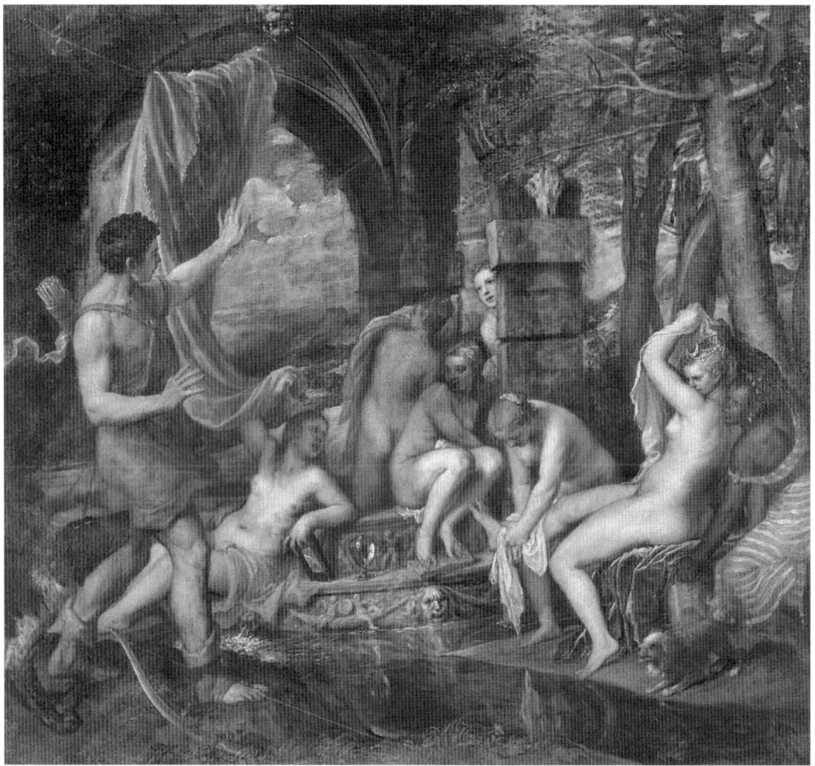

Titian, *Diana and Actaeon*, 1556–9

literature, so it is right that we attach great importance to keeping them in this country."[12] Nicholas Penny, the Director of the National Gallery, said, "To lose these paintings would be terrible because people have had them as such an important part of their visual experience in this country for so long . . . they are hugely significant historical documents which tell us so much about the era in which they were created."[13]

Estates in Britain have survived (or not survived in some cases) wars, taxes, and economic depressions, among other things. A more recent issue to add today is divorce. The UK courts are among the most "pro-wife" divorce courts in the world. As most people are aware, the British aristocracy today is often what is referred to as "asset rich and cash poor". Prenuptial agreements are not always accepted as legally binding, and in order to finance expensive divorce settlements, assets often need to be sold off. There goes the art collection and furniture—and sometimes even the estate itself is broken up. How can this be prevented?

Many estates are now put into trusts to protect them—this may protect from divorce and outside pressures such as family disputes, but it does not protect from increasing taxation, economic downturns, and the costs of an estate's upkeep. In addition every ten years there is an additional charge on the Trust.

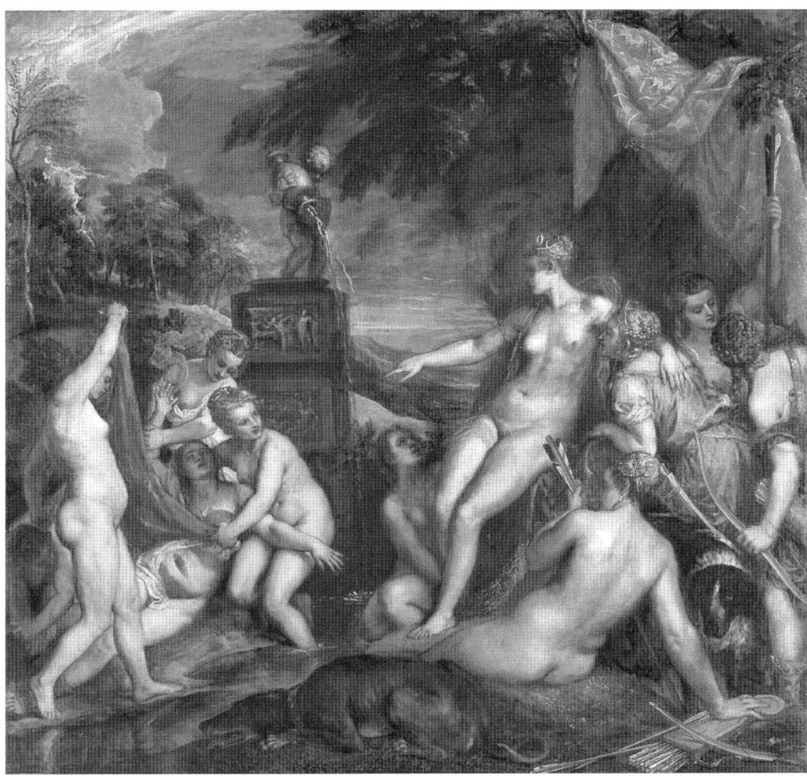

Titian, *Diana and Callisto*, 1556–9

The struggle to maintain ancestral estates, stately homes, and their contents has led to the gradual erosion of most of Britain's old collections. In some cases the selling off of one's assets to pay for those costs is the only realistic solution. The Duke of Bridgewater, who owns numerous estates, shares these problems and so far has managed to keep his family's collection reasonably intact. "I would hate to fail after previous generations had managed to hang on to them . . . I will try hard not to be the one who breaks the chain," he says.[14] He maintains that tax changes are the chief threat; they risk bringing to an end the philanthropic tradition of putting paintings from the collection on show in public galleries, which has endured for two centuries.

According to a 2010 investigation by the *Art Newspaper*,

> the owners of some of Britain's most famous country estates have sold treasures worth £100 million since the start of the recession. Much of the cash has been needed for the renovation and upkeep of stately homes. Cuts in government spending have raised concerns that treasure with heritage value will increasingly be sold abroad as museums and galleries

> are unable to afford them. All these artworks come from stately homes, most of which are open to the public. Around £80m worth of major works have been sold in this way, while additional, smaller works are being marketed discreetly.[15]

Art, after all, is a disposable asset and no matter how important the collection is, ultimately in the face of increasing taxation, budget cuts, and recessions, there is little else to do but sell hard assets. Across the nation, as was seen during the post-war climate, the collections of aristocracy are of little importance to the majority of the nation during a recession.

It is thought that the value of historically important works that have *not* been put up for sale amounts to something in excess of £1 billion.[16] In 1922, the Government drew up a "Paramount List" of the most important works of art that it vowed to contribute to keeping for the nation should they ever come up for sale. In that original list were two Titians from the Duke of Bridgewater's collection: the aforementioned *Diana and Actaeon*, and *Portrait of a Man* (1556–9). However, this list was then discarded in the 1950s after the costs of war meant that the Government could not afford to keep its promise of assisting in providing funds for these works of art.[17]

Many families have ceded their homes to the National Trust or to a charitable trust of their own devising, with all the associated tax advantages. The Government has provided structures which are advantageous, whether that be selling in lieu of inheritance tax or the National Heritage Memorial Fund which was set up in 1980 to save the most outstanding parts of the British national heritage. Tax incentives for important heritage items such as the Duke of Bridgewater's *Diana and Actaeon* have allowed for relief of death duties. Ultimately, a work that has been passed down generations may be increasing in value, but it is not earning money whilst sitting in a private collection, and every time it is passed down due to a death in a family the taxation can be crippling. Deals are made with the Government when the works are deemed to be of historical significance, but what about those that do not make the cut?

It is arguable that in no other country have aristocratic art collections survived the way that they have in Great Britain. Carefully devised tax incentives (such as inheritance tax planning) introduced by successive governments mean that most art is on public view, directly augmenting public life. However, as mentioned previously, a change of government can bring a change of tax structures which can doom an estate. The present Government, for example, is said to be considering whether to abolish the acceptance of works of art in lieu of tax, a system which helps keep valuable artworks in this country. The story of the Bridgewater Collection demonstrates better than any other what is at risk if the owners of historic art collections are penalized by tax changes of that kind.

Public funding for the arts has been cut and no doubt will be again. The fact that the Government was raising money to save the Titians in a time of economic recession rather than securing its economy caused outrage among many, and with an increasingly polarized world these questions are asked: Are historical artefacts and estates of as much importance as welfare for a nation? What is the measurement of the importance of British history in these artefacts? Is it up to governments or the individuals to secure their collections, or both?

SOLUTIONS FOR THE FUTURE: ENTREPRENEURIAL INITIATIVES AND PRIVATE/PUBLIC PARTNERSHIPS

The story of the picture collection formed in the last years of the 18th century by the 3rd Duke of Bridgewater is one case study. Its paintings have been passed down through generations and, rather than being sold for personal enrichment, they are available for public viewing as a result of the tax deal that was created. The current Duke of Sutherland has 27 pictures (worth over £250 million) on loan to the National Gallery of Scotland. The National Gallery of Scotland has had three Raphaels, five Titians, three Rembrandts, a Hobbema, eight Poussins, a Tintoretto, a Van Dyck, and a Rubens on long-term loan from the Duke of Bridgewater since the agreement negotiated in 1945. Prior to this the works had all been exhibited to the public in Bridgewater House, one of the family's ancestral homes in London. The collection was moved to Scotland so as to preserve it from the Luftwaffe's raids. The house was then badly bombed and the collection never returned.

Are there alternative solutions? If the Government starts to fail on its supporting structures, or inheritance tax is simply too much for the newer generations, is there another option? James Reginato, in his book *Great Houses, Modern Aristocrats*, examines what both past and present generations who have inherited these estates and collections have done. This ranges from opening their homes to endless tour groups through to advantageous marriages, such as that of the 9th Duke of Marlborough who owned Blenheim Palace and in 1895 married the massively wealthy American heiress Consuelo Vanderbilt. The National Trust becomes the proprietor of many of Britain's ancestral homes, such as Waddesdon Manor, bequeathed to it in the 1950s by James de Rothschild (even though the Rothschild dynasty, who had built the house, were remarkably untouched by the UK's changing economy). Reginato writes in the book's introduction, "I came to see how modern they were, in fact, as they came to adapt themselves to changing times and changing concepts of country-house ownership."[18]

An example of these changing times is evident in Chatsworth House. Like any building of its era, Chatsworth House is fragile and requires constant care and attention. Its £32.7 million renovation master plan began in 2005 and is one of the largest projects undertaken at Chatsworth since 1828. In order to finance the maintenance costs of the house and its vast grounds, the Duke and Duchess of Devonshire brought in Sotheby's to help make one of England's greatest stately homes into a key venue for the art world—modernizing, while keeping the old still present. The garden showcases some of the world's most famous artists, some of whom create site-specific pieces. Sotheby's curates a yearly exhibition and auction of dynamic and influential artists, making Chatsworth not only an art world destination but also an intriguing public spectacle. The revenue made from the sales of the works in a highly anticipated Sotheby's auction and from the visitors helps fund the estate, as well as enticing more people to the house. From 2018 Chatsworth is also hosting artist residencies. In addition, Sotheby's has produced a 13-episode *Treasures from Chatsworth* video series with insight into the Chatsworth collection.[19]

Private owners have started to showcase their collections in privately funded museums open to the public. Private patronage of the arts is nothing new. Solomon R. Guggenheim established a foundation for his art collection in 1937, and two years later opened a museum to house it—the precursor of the great museums in New York and elsewhere that today bear his name. Philanthropic investment of this kind produces many fruits, such as regeneration and investment in surrounding environments and new architecture projects, as well as employment opportunities and artistic initiatives. The Getty Museum in Los Angeles did the same. Previously inaccessible works of art that belonged to private collections will be made available to the public, and with the opportunity to take a tax incentive this becomes more and more appealing.

To conclude, whatever the personal choices and reasons for the sales and demolitions of estates and their legacies, the underlying and unifying factor was always financial. Historical collections are an insight into British history and its past traditions. The creative legacies of this period of time, the family, the estate, and the events around the creation of it will undoubtedly be lost as these collections are slowly disbanded. The transaction of splitting up an estate will be the death of it. Whether or not the responsibility lies with government or with ourselves, to come up with new and innovative ways to preserve these precious memories of history, solutions must be found.

Notes

1 Chris Bryant, *A Critical History of the British Aristocracy*, London: Doubleday, 2017.

2 See: Peter H. Reid, "The decline and fall of the British country house library", *Libraries and Culture*, no.36 (2001), pp.345–66; Giles Worsley, *England's Lost Houses: From the Archives of Country Life*, London: Aurum Press, 2002; James

Lees-Milne, *Some Country Houses and Their Owners*, London: Penguin Books, 2009; Giles Worsley, "Country houses: the lost legacy", *Daily Telegraph*, 15 June 2002, https://www.telegraph.co.uk/culture/art/3578853/Country-houses-the-lost-legacy.html (accessed 4 March 2020); and Mark Girouard, *Life In The English Country House*, New Haven, CT: Yale University Press, 1979.

3 See: Deborah, the Dowager Duchess of Devonshire, *Chatsworth: The House*, London: Frances Lincoln, 2002.

4 Evelyn Waugh, *Brideshead Revisited*, Boston, MA: Little, Brown and Company, 1945.

5 Charles Spencer, "Enemies of the State", *Vanity Fair*, 14 December 2009, https://www.vanityfair.com/news/2010/01/english-aristocracy-201001 (accessed 4 March 2020).

6 For further information, see: ibid.; Alan Cole, "Estate and inheritance taxes around the world", The Tax Foundation, 17 March 2015, https://taxfoundation.org/estate-and-inheritance-taxes-around-world/ (accessed 4 March 2020); Antony Seely, "Inheritance Tax (Research Paper 93 & 95–107)", 1995, House of Commons Library; James, Austen-Cartmell, *The Finance Act, 1894, So Far As It Relates to the New Estate Duty and Other Death Duties in England*, London: Wildy and Sons, 1894; and Robert Dymond, *The Death Duties*, London: The Solicitors' Law Stationery Society, 1920 (3rd edition).

7 Geraldine Norman, "The masters that may vanish from view", *Independent*, 2 April 1995, https://www.independent.co.uk/arts-entertainment/the-masters-that-may-vanish-from-view-art-market-1613985.html' (accessed 4 March 2020).

8 ibid.

9 ibid.

10 ibid.

11 Roya Nikkhah, "The national art treasures Britain cannot afford to lose", *The Telegraph*, 14 February 2009, https://www.telegraph.co.uk/culture/art/4624021/The-national-art-treasures-Britain-cannot-afford-to-lose.html (accessed 4 March 2020).

12 Barrie quoted in ibid.

13 Penny quoted in ibid.

14 Duke of Bridgewater quoted in Norman 1995, op.cit.

15 At the time of going to press the shut-downs necessitated by the COVID-19 pandemic prevented the author from establishing the exact, title, date and author of the article.

16 Nikkhah 2009, op.cit.

17 ibid.

18 James Reginato, "Introduction", in *Great Houses, Modern Aristocrats*, New York: Rizzoli, 2016.

19 https://www.sothebys.com/en/series/treasures-from-chatsworth (accessed 4 March 2020).

14
JEWELLERY

A Different Kind of Estate

Robin Wright

Estates containing jewellery can be very different from those containing fine arts. Although jewellery is a wearable art form, it conjures an entirely different set of priorities and responses. Jewellery means different things to different people; some see it as an invoker of romance, an artefact representing an occasion or a moment in time, and others look at it simply as an investment vehicle. In this essay I explore the many facets of this art form and the complex emotional role that jewellery plays in estate planning and resolution.

JEWELLERY VERSUS FINE ART ESTATES

Many times as an auction house specialist I find myself listening to countless stories, some very interesting and some of which I'm sceptical, but all of which are important to the teller. As with estates of any kind, individuals can have completely different motivations for collecting. If executors or heirs are not in unison, it can cause a great deal of angst and result in resentment and legal turmoil. This is why I often encourage ageing clients to settle things before they can no longer make sound decisions. I advise them not to leave things until after their deaths, leaving their respective heirs to tangle with the disposition of the collection. The loss of a loved one is a time in which emotions are generally intensified, whether good or bad. This is usually a moment of heightened nostalgia or malice, and heirs forced to navigate and engage deep-seated memories or conflicts during the grieving process can facilitate poor decision-making and hurt feelings.

Family dynamics play significantly into estate disposition. I have seen attorneys who typically just wish to complete their fiduciary duty in the most efficient manner break down in tears when speaking about their lifelong client with whom they formed a personal bond. On the other hand, I have spoken with long-term spouses or children who just want to get as much money as possible from their loved one's pockets. It is not necessarily the largest estates that are the most contentious.

Once I watched a family splinter over a single US$26,000 Buccellati bracelet, a relatively insignificant item in comparison to the exponentially more valuable jewellery pieces within the collection. To my knowledge, the recipient has yet to wear the bracelet; this person's only desire was to wrest it from his sibling's possession.

Since it is the only wearable art form, jewellery is perhaps the most personal of possessions and nearly always brings a connotation of love, romance, status, or reward. I could not tell you where I bought my last car or piece of furniture, but I *can* tell you the occasion surrounding every piece of jewellery that I own, whether it was a gift or self-bought. Many people similarly identify with their jewellery as highly emotive objects, which is why handling jewellery within estates can be significantly more challenging than dealing with other assets or belongings.

Jewellery not only differs from other art forms in how it elicits emotions but it also has an enormous inherent monetary value, unlike, for example, the inexpensive canvas and paint used in a painting. The materials used in the making of fine jewellery are rare and expensive metals and gemstones, which therefore hold a tremendous value. These materials always play a factor into the pricing of a piece of jewellery.

A gemstone's rarity can also be a significant variable in determining value, as is an artist's oeuvre or a work's provenance. There will not be a new Picasso made after 1973, but there will likewise be no Kashmir sapphires released into the world as these mines are now depleted.[1] So the value of jewellery is based on two primary considerations: the value of the underlying materials, and the artistry of the design and its crafting.

Jewellery further differs from fine art in that many people are essential in the creation of a piece of jewellery from the conception of its design to its completion as an object. A piece of jewellery will most often pass through many different hands before it makes its way to the consumer. The people involved in the creation of jewellery have specific, technical skills in addition to having an eye and talent for being creative. In that vein, jewellers and the professionals who work with jewellery are very similar to artists. Without the careful extraction of a stone from a mine one will get a broken crystal that will have lost significant value. Without the expert and steady hand of a tremendously skilled cutter one will get a very dull, visually boring stone. And without a tasteful and skilled designer one is left with a potentially ugly bit of precious metal. All of these steps go into making a beautiful piece of jewellery whereas a single painter or sculptor may toil over their art in solitude before handing a work over to a dealer or client directly.

Despite there being so many talented designers and craftsmen and women, only a small percentage of jewellery in the world is signed. Many of the greatest designers and fabricators of jewellery never signed their work. One of the most significant designers was Suzanne Belperron who in the 1930s famously declared, "My style is my signature."[2] One of the greatest talents of the era, Belperron had an unbelievable eye for colour, style, and workmanship. She was a trailblazer, and one of the very few women to have achieved commercial success and a loyal following in the early part of the 20th century.

Ironically, few manufacturing jewellers ever reach the recognition of a lauded artist. Most bench jewellers historically have worked for several firms and are never able to sign what they create as their own. Their expertise and exceptional talent are recognizable to some in the jewellery industry, but they often go unrecognized personally.

David Webb and Van Cleef & Arpels both serve as examples of companies that have workshops in New York and employ exceptionally talented jewellers, carvers, and cutters who are prohibited from including their personal signature on the pieces destined for sale through these venerable retailers. Oscar Heyman and Brothers, a third-generation jeweller based in New York, manufacture beautiful jewels under their own prestigious Oscar Heyman & Brothers brand, yet they also have historically designed and manufactured for other exceptional brands such as Van Cleef & Arpels, Marcus & Co., and Tiffany & Co.[3] There is a blurred identity for who created each specific work given the fact that many people create pieces for many different brands.

MARKETING OF JEWELLERY ESTATES

Marketing is another way in which a jewellery estate differs greatly from those composed predominantly of fine art. Art *can* be emotional in how people react and process the experience of viewing it, but jewellery is almost entirely based in emotion in the way it is marketed to buyers. The significance of owning, acquiring, and living with a jewel is almost solely based upon how one viscerally identifies with the object. The emotional allure of jewellery is how specialists entice consignors and cajole purchasers to bid, differing from a painting or sculpture.

As an auction house is essentially the liaison between a consignor and a buyer, there is nothing more satisfying for me as a specialist than meeting with a family to view its collection. The relationship of a jewellery specialist with both consignors and buyers is personal and intimate. After meeting with a family, a specialist will spend months preparing a jewellery estate for auction and will also be equally committed to the end purchaser for the same lot.

One of my most memorable estates included three siblings who brought in a blue diamond to consign. I worked closely with the family for months to travel it around the world and bring the gem to auction. The romance of the narrative surrounding the stone was integral to how we marketed the piece. The story of the blue diamond ring was nearly as important as the value of the stone itself. The heirs told the story of their mother wearing it for decades, only to drop the ring down the garbage disposal, which took a large chunk out of the diamond. Just sharing that story with potential purchasers lent even more desire to own the ring. The diamond, estimated at US$2,000,000, sold for a world-record $6.6 million in the light of our marketing strategy, which was based on the emotional association of the diamond, not only on the market for blue diamonds.

A large part of marketing a jewellery estate or gaining a consignment lies in tapping into an individual's values, which is accomplished almost solely by listening. If you allow someone to talk without interruption, they will tell you everything you need to know, and then some, which allows for the creation of a sales proposal engendering what matters most to the consignor. It is enticing for some consignors to know that their collection will be presented in a respectful way, whether by including the use of names, photographs, and/or biographies of their loved ones. In other situations, consignors would rather their property be shown in a completely anonymous way with little fanfare. It all depends on the values of the individual. Like paintings or sculptures, jewellery is given an equal amount of care and research, but its story is enhanced in an auction catalogue in an entirely different manner focused on an emotional narrative and relative to the consignor's own personal wishes.

Marketing to *buyers* requires a different type of strategy. We market the jewels that we have taken into auction in many different ways. A printed catalogue is the favourite norm for many who like the tactile sensation of something printed, but we also market and advertise extensively through the newer forms of online digital catalogue format and social media. Again, we listen to what our purchasing clients want to see and hear. There is a seduction in combing through every page of a printed catalogue—the heft of the paper, the professional photography, and the visceral smell of the pages. However, I have also witnessed people around me scrolling feverishly through our online catalogues, taking notes, checking condition reports, and viewing additional photos of each lot. No matter how one prefers to receive information, it is important that we reach as many potential customers as possible, which is why our aim to capture an individual's imagination through marketing is executed across different media. A large percentage of buyers will never see the jewellery first hand before they purchase it, so it is imperative that we give accurate and thoughtful descriptions on every single piece, no matter how insignificant.

Speaking further to the marketing and advertising of jewellery estates, many of the major jewellery firms' marketing campaigns have helped significantly in the impression that jewellery is worth the price paid by appealing to buyers' emotions. The De Beers marketing slogan, "A Diamond is Forever" is largely responsible for imbuing the belief that our society expresses love with diamonds, further strengthening the romantic association buyers have with jewellery. Jewellery marketing implies a sense of happiness, love, or joy that the buyer will experience through the purchase of a piece, and the durability of the materials further allows the buyer to believe these emotions will last forever.

Other great firms have presented their brands to the status-conscious or aspirational buyer. Branded jewellery is perceived to be better than unsigned jewellery because a name is familiar. Even though the value of diamonds and precious metals is quantifiable, the perception of status associated with big names allows us greater latitude when selling. There are some jewellers who, throughout history, have differentiated themselves with extraordinarily beautiful design and artistry. Pieces from these jewellers or of this quality further play on buyers' desire to purchase certain pieces. Many jewellers can manufacture diamond solitaire rings, but a diamond ring stamped Graff or Harry Winston is deemed to be superior. The diamonds could be the exact same carat, weight, colour, and clarity—but once a famous maker's mark is stamped inside of the shank, the item's price increases significantly. Signed pieces from well-respected brands do tend to hold their value *better* since collectors have been bombarded with testimonials that particular designers craft superior jewellery. For example, a Van Cleef & Arpels' Alhambra necklace will sometimes sell for more than full retail price at auction, not necessarily because this vintage necklace has been discontinued but because of the popularity of a style or maker.

REASONS PEOPLE BUY AND SELL JEWELLERY

As discussed earlier, jewellery is arguably the most *personal* of the arts in that it is literally worn on one's person. There is no necessity for jewellery except for the purpose of timekeeping or to show that an individual is partnered, which is traditionally a Western construct that has taken on mainstream appeal during the last century. Most jewellery is simply made for accessorizing fashion or one's body, yet it elicits feelings of beauty, love, and wealth.

One may wonder why anyone would want to sell that feeling. There are as many reasons to sell as there are people who are selling. Some people inherit jewellery that is not to their taste or style, some are in the midst of a divorce and just want to be rid of any unpleasant memories, and some have the money earmarked for medical expenses, taxes, or a child's education. No matter what the reason for selling, consignors frequently feel either trepidation or nostalgia when navigating the process of deaccessioning a particularly meaningful piece.

Thousands of people contact us each year wishing to sell their jewellery. I see approximately 10,000 pieces of jewellery each year, of which only about 10% is deemed appropriate for auction. Therefore, we have to say "no" most of the time, which is met with a host of different reactions. I have had people lash out in disbelief or cry, and once I had a lady put a hex on my cat. But more than once I have had someone tell me that it made them happy that I said "no" because it gave them an excuse to keep the piece that they really didn't want to part with.

As for the reasons for buying, there are equally as many. We have buyers that are true collectors who purchase to assemble a cohesive collection of jewellery that

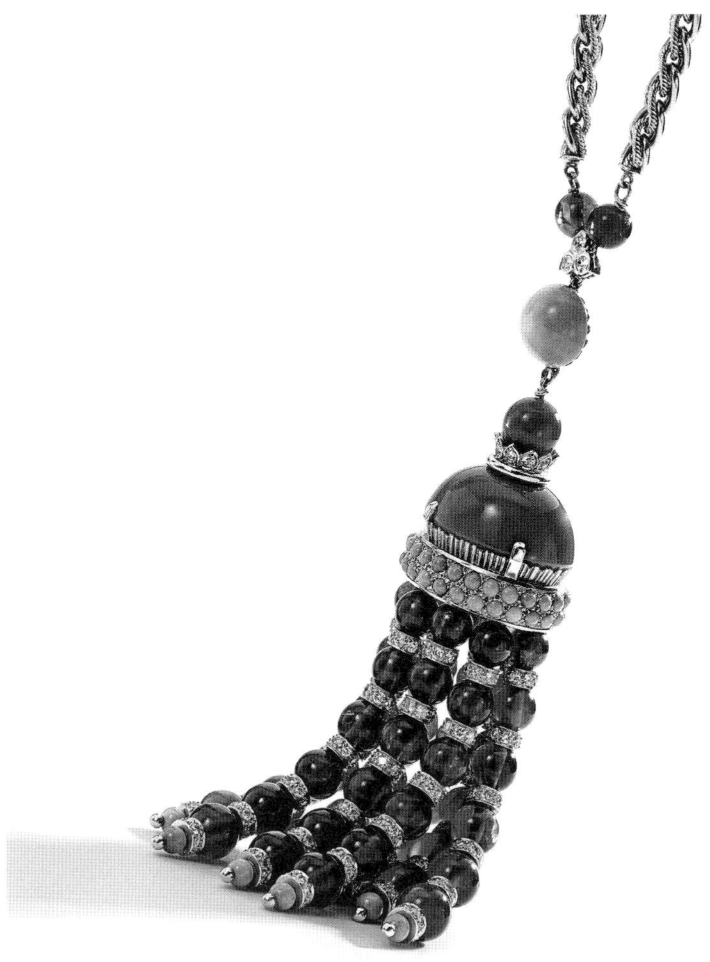

Van Cleef & Arpels coral and amethyst tassel necklace, Sotheby's New York sale N09594, 8 December 2016, Lot 401

reflects their taste and aesthetic. There are also buyers who are looking for a good price or something they may have seen elsewhere at one time, or they may be looking for a rare piece that they have never seen before. There are also lovebirds who buy presents for each other, and there are many women who buy jewellery as a reward for a specific achievement or just to display their individual style and status to the world. Working with purchasers is every bit as rewarding as working with consignors. Winning that bid is success to most. Seeing a client get exactly what they want is fulfilling. We have many clients who bought their engagement rings at auction and have continued to hone their eyes to become true collectors. Now I see some of these collections becoming estates, working with the next generation.

I once worked with an esteemed American family whose name everyone would recognize: grandchildren of an US president and children of a titan of industry and his socialite wife. One would think this family had every privilege and propensity for haughtiness, but it was just the opposite. I have rarely worked with such a gracious clan. Their mother's fabulous collection of jewellery was a bastion of the style, taste, and wealth of the era. There were stories behind most of the pieces of jewellery, which the family shared with me. The occasions for which they were given, which outfit they matched, and the personalities or events that would have seen the pieces were jaw-dropping.

Once we had selected the jewels that would go to auction, five adult siblings convened in my office to distribute the remainder of the less valuable property. I spent a couple of hours with them and listened to them recall the seemingly every-

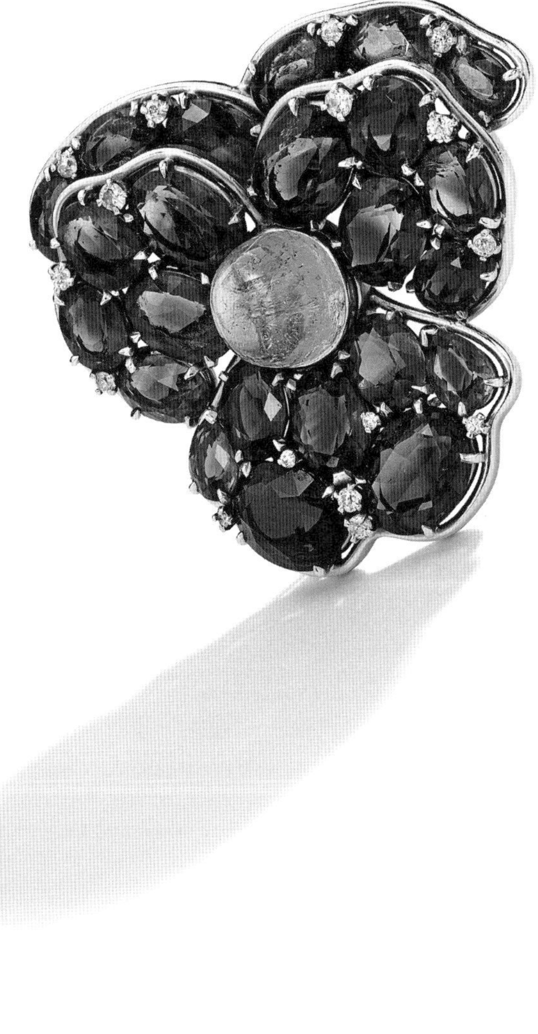

Verdura amethyst and emerald pansy brooch, Sotheby's New York sale N09594, 8 December 2016, Lot 364

day events in which they remembered each item. There was no fighting or selfishness. If one sibling had a particularly nostalgic draw to one of the pieces because their mother wore that to their school play, that sibling would put that piece in his or her pile. They all wanted to be fair and equitable. Wonderful memories were shared, some with tears and some with laughter, but all with respect and genuinely warm sentiment. It was a rare and wonderful testament to a loving, well-reared family.

The images included in this chapter show two items of great importance from the sale of this prominent family's estate, and each item illustrates a separate point in this discussion. The tassel necklace was made by Van Cleef & Arpels. The house also has had, at different moments in its history, jewels manufactured by Oscar Heyman and Brothers, for example. The pansy brooch was made by Verdura, and was reacquired by Verdura for the jewellery house's archival collection. The brooch's provenance has come full circle; it was manufactured by Verdura, purchased by a private client, and sold from the family estate back into Verdura's possession. Both jewels were from the same prominent family collection and highlight key nuanced aspects of working with jewellery estates that significantly differentiate jewellery from painting, sculpture, fashion, or architectural legacies.

DETERMINING THE VALUE OF ESTATES

Few people know the actual fair market value of their jewellery. Most people have an insured or retail replacement-value appraisal for valuable items. But an auction estimate or fair market value is very different. An insurance value is what it would cost to replace a piece at today's full retail price. A fair market value is what a piece of similar kind and quality has sold for on the secondary market in recent history. There is significant mark-up in retail. In my two decades of retail experience prior to Sotheby's we would routinely mark up the stock at 200–400%. It takes a lot of money to keep the lights on, pay salaries, advertise, and keep inventory in stock. A piece that is purchased at full retail price will therefore take many years before its fair market value reaches the retail value, if ever.

Grand collections tend to sell better when the collection is marketed as a whole. If the pieces are part of a grand single-owner collection of a famous or glamorous person, that provenance drives prices up astronomically, as in the case of Jacqueline Kennedy Onassis. One great example is the oft-photographed triple strand of faux pearls that sold at auction in the 1998 sale of her jewellery. The winning bidder paid $220,000 for those pearls, which were fake! This is an example of the *celebrity* factor. The power of that whole collection being sold at once made the sale even more impactful. Individual pieces from her collection have been re-offered several times throughout the years; however, they frequently fail to garner prices higher than when they were offered in the original collection.

Much goes into the valuation of a jewel. There is no school to teach one how to price jewellery. It takes years and years of research and examination. The clues are there if one looks hard enough for them. The back of the jewel is just as important as the front. The value of materials, history, provenance, fame of the designer, workmanship, wearability, and overall beauty all play a part in the assessment.

We also rely heavily on research as well as the experience of our esteemed colleagues. *Understanding Jewellery*, by David Bennett and Daniela Mascetti, who have nearly 80 years of experience combined, is one of the most useful and beautifully illustrated resources.[4] This tome covers basic jewellery materials and techniques, and is probably the best reflection of the eras, helping us to identify and date jewellery.

At the auction house I have been fortunate to work with some of the smartest people in the industry. But it is just as important to be curious and to seek answers. Read the books and articles, and pick up every piece of jewellery you can. Look at the front (through a loupe) and the back for construction methods, signatures, assay marks, maker's marks, and serial numbers. All of these things play a role in the jewel's creative legacy.

Notes

1 See "Magnificent Jewels" catalogue, Sotheby's New York sale N09594, 8 December 2016, http://www.sothebys.com/en/auctions/2016/magnificent-jewels-n09594.html?locale=en (accessed 22 March 2020).

2 See Patricia Corbett, *Suzanne Belperron: My Style is My Signature*, London: Thames & Hudson, 2016.

3 See Yvonne Markowitz and Elizabeth Hamilton, *Oscar Heyman, The Jewellers' Jeweller*, Boston, MA: MFA Publications, 2017.

4 See David Bennett and Daniela Mascetti, *Understanding Jewellery*, Woodbridge, Suffolk: Antique Collectors' Club, 2007 (1st edition).

CONTRIBUTOR BIOGRAPHIES

Kathy Battista is Program Director Emerita, MA Contemporary Art, Sotheby's Institute of Art, New York, and a curator of exhibitions in museums and galleries.

Alexandra Bowes-Lyon is Director of Philanthropy at Space for Giants and a graduate of Sotheby's Institute of Art, London, whose thesis research investigated aristocratic British houses and their legal and cultural implications.

Bryan Faller is a third-generation financial advisor and adjunct faculty of Sotheby's Institute of Art, New York. He is a consultant to several private artist estates.

Nathalie Khan is a cultural historian, based in London, specializing in fashion history, theory, and the impact of fashion on digital film and television.

Christine Kuan is Director/CEO of Sotheby's Institute of Art, New York.

Lisa Le Feuvre is a curator, writer, editor, and public speaker. She is the inaugural Executive Director of the Holt/Smithson Foundation, an artist-endowed foundation dedicated to furthering the creative legacies of Nancy Holt and Robert Smithson.

Christy MacLear was the first Executive Director of the Philip Johnson Glass House and the Inaugural Director of the Robert Rauschenberg Foundation. She has also assisted artists Eric Fischl and April Gornik in planning their Foundation and establishing a cultural hub in their hometown Sag Harbor, Long Island, called "The Church".

Daniel McClean is a partner at the law firm Cypress LLP, based in Los Angeles, and heads the firm's Art Law Group. He is also a consultant at the London law firm Howard Kennedy LLP. He is a leading international art and cultural property lawyer, advising a global network of art market clients.

Tom McNulty was Fine Arts Librarian at Bobst Library, New York University, and faculty at Sotheby's Institute of Art, New York. He was an author, focusing on art market research and issues relating to artists' estates and the preservation of archives in the 21st century.

Mark Morris is Head of Teaching and Learning at the Architectural Association School of Architecture, London.

Judith B. Prowda is faculty member at Sotheby's Institute of Art programme in New York. She is an attorney, mediator, and arbitrator, and a founding member of Stropheus Art Law. Recently, she participated in the creation of the Court of Arbitration for Art (CAfA) in The Hague, a tribunal dedicated to the resolution of art law disputes worldwide.

Ann-Marie Richard is Program Director, MA Fine and Decorative Art and Design at Sotheby's Institute of Art, New York.

Christine J. Vincent is Project Director, Artist-Endowed Foundations Initiative/AEFI, the Aspen Institute, headquartered in Aspen, Colorado.

Eric M. Wolf is Head Librarian and faculty member at Sotheby's Institute of Art, New York, and a lecturer, scholar, and writer on art, architecture, and museums.

Robin Wright is Senior Vice President and Senior Specialist of Jewelry at Sotheby's New York.

Loretta Würtenberger is founder of the Institute for Artists' Estates, based in Berlin, Germany.

ACKNOWLEDGEMENTS

The editors would like to thank Lucy Meyers and Jos Hackforth-Jones for trusting in our vision by commissioning this book. We are also grateful to Rochelle Roberts and Sarah Thorowgood at Lund Humphries, for reading the manuscript and taking it through production. Abigail Grater's careful copy editing was much appreciated.

We are also immensely grateful to the 14 authors who contributed their time and expertise; we are inspired by your generosity, intelligence and patience. It is heartbreaking for us that one of the authors, Tom McNulty, passed before the book came to fruition. His friendship and essential counsel on this project helped us formulate the final shape of the book; he selflessly gave his time, was the first author commissioned and also helped flesh out the conceptual framework for this scholarly discussion.

We are so grateful to the archives, foundations, gallerists and artists who provided images to illustrate the essays found within: Lisa Le Feuvre and Tom Martinelli at Holt/Smithson Foundation who provided the stunning image for the book's cover; Gianfranco Gorgoni, Charles Atlas for kindly and generously allowing use of a film still of Leigh Bowery; Douglas Baxter and his assistants, John Mason, Vincent Wilcke and Andrea Kustenkow at The Pace Gallery and the Maya Lin Studio for their help with securing images and permissions for Maya Lin's Vietnam War Memorial; April Gornik and Erik Fischl; Marian Goodman Gallery and Fondazione Prada for help approving and clearing installation images of John Baldessari's, *The Giacometti Variations*; Eirik Johnson; Mitra Khorasheh and Jonah Bokhaer of Signs and Symbols; The Ellsworth Kelly Foundation, Allie Heath, the Blanton Museum of Art, the University of Texas at Austin, Lexi Campbell and Matthew Marks Gallery for helping approve images of Ellsworth Kelly's monumental work, *Austin*; Julie Martin of E.A.T.; Mark Morris and Edward Bottoms at the Architectural Association School of Architecture; Sotheby's New York and their jewelry department; Francine Snyder at the Robert Rauschenberg Foundation; Verdura for permission to reproduce an image of the brooch reacquired into the company's corporate archive, Van Cleef & Arpels, The Glass House Foundation, Eiko Otake, Jack Flam and The Dedalus Foundation, Kim Jones and Dior Homme, Dan Trujillo at ARS and Stephan Pascher for his guidance and the extraordinary effort, time and research he gave in support of this scholarly conversation, Aaron

Berlow and Wildenstein & Co., Monica Heslington and Goldman Sachs, David Nolan and David Nolan Gallery.

Finally, we thank our colleagues and friends for support in myriad forms, some of whom may not be aware of their impact on our work: Mary Dinaburg, Saul Ostrow; Roger Shepherd, Yayoi Shionori, The Faller Company, Phyllis Hawkins for her help with compliance and Lincoln Investment.

IMAGE CREDITS

AA Archives: 150, 151, 155; © Charles Atlas: 144; © John Baldessari, courtesy of the artists and Marian Goodman Gallery: 51; © Ellsworth Kelly Foundation, Courtesy Matthew Marks Gallery. Blanton Museum of Art, The University of Texas at Austin, Gift of the artist and Jack Shear, with funding generously provided by Jeanne and Michael Klein, Judy and Charles Tate, the Scurlock Foundation, Suzanne Deal Booth and David G. Booth, and the Longhorn Network. Additional funding provided by The Brown Foundation, Inc. of Houston, Leslie and Jack S. Blanton, Jr., Elizabeth and Peter Wareing, Sally and Tom Dunning, the Lowe Foundation, The Eugene McDermott Foundation, Stedman West Foundation, and the Walton Family Foundation, with further support provided by Sarah and Ernest Butler, Buena Vista Foundation, The Ronald and Jo Carole Lauder Foundation, Emily Rauh Pulitzer, Janet and Wilson Allen, Judy and David Beck, Kelli and Eddy S. Blanton, Charles Butt, Mrs. Donald G. Fisher, Amanda and Glenn Fuhrman, Glenstone/Emily and Mitch Rales, Stephanie and David Goodman, Agnes Gund, Stacy and Joel Hock, Lora Reynolds and Quincy Lee, Helen and Chuck Schwab, Ellen and Steve Susman, and other donors. Photograph by Kate Russell: 82; Courtesy of the Dedalus Foundation, Inc.: 119, 120; Courtesy of E.A.T. Archive, photograph by Billy Kluver: 105; Bryan Faller: 19, 20; © 2019 Helen Frankenthaler Foundation, Inc. / Artists Rights Society (ARS), New York. Photo by Matteo De Fina: 116; Photo: April Gornik: 109; Courtesy of April Gornik and Eric Fischl: 102; © Holt/Smithson Foundation/Licensed by VAGA at ARS, New York. Photograph by Gianfranco Gorgoni: 89; Photo: Erik Johnson: 104; photograph © Nathalie Khan, 2018: 139 (both), 140, 143; photo © Christine Kuan: 118; © Maya Lin, courtesy Pace Gallery: 81 (both); Photo: Leilah Mesdaghi: 111; Photo: Mark Poucher: 109; Photograph courtesy of Sotheby's Inc, December 8th 2016: 175, 176; Stiftung Arp e.V., Berlin/Rolandswerth: 37, 38.

INDEX